TRADITIONAL NEIGHBORHOOD
HOME PLANS

170 Designs for Living in Villages & Towns

Edited by Looney Ricks Kiss Architects

With a Foreword by Andres Duany

HOME PLANNERS, LLC
Wholly owned by Hanley-Wood, LLC

Published by Home Planners, LLC
Wholly owned by Hanley-Wood, LLC
Editorial and Corporate Offices:
3275 West Ina Road, Suite 110
Tucson, Arizona 85741

Distribution Center:
29333 Lorie Lane
Wixom, Michigan 48393

Rickard D. Bailey, *CEO and Publisher*
Cindy Coatsworth Lewis, *Director of Publishing*
Jan Prideaux, *Executive Editor*

Edited by Looney Ricks Kiss Architects:
J. Carson Looney, *Architectural Editor*
Jim Constantine, *Senior Editor*
A. Dawn Kenley, *Assistant Editor*

Home Planners Editorial and Design:
John Shaheen, AIA, *Architectural Editor*
Laura Hurst Brown, *Editor*
Matthew S. Kauffman, *Designer*
Morenci Wodraska, *Text Writer (plans)*

Front cover   Photo by ©Jeffrey Jacobs/Mims Studios
Design by ©Looney Ricks Kiss Architects, Inc.

Back cover   (top) Photo by ©Northlight Photography
Design by ©Northwest Home Designing, Inc.

(below) Photo by ©Jeffrey Jacobs/Mims
Studios, Design by ©Looney Ricks Kiss
Architects, Inc.

Frontispiece   Courtesy of Looney Ricks Kiss Architects, Inc.

This page   Photo by ©Jeffrey Jacobs/Mims Studios

Opposite   Photo trio by ©Jeffrey Jacobs/Mims Studios
and ©Jeffrey Jacobs/Architectural Photography

Pages 33 and 192
Photo by ©Jeffrey Jacobs/Mims Studios
Designs by ©Looney Ricks Kiss Architects, Inc.

Page 61   Photo by ©Riley & Riley Photography, Inc.
Design by ©Donald A. Gardner Architects, Inc.

Page 119   Photo by ©Jeffrey Jacobs/Architectural
Photography, Designs by ©Looney Ricks Kiss
Architects, Inc.

Page 171   Photo and design by ©Living Concepts

First printing, February 2000

10 9 8 7 6 5 4 3 2 1

Printed in the United States of America
Library of Congress Catalog Card Number 99 075388
ISBN (softcover): 1-881955-66-4

CONTENTS

Foreword *iv*

FOREWORD
By Andres Duany

The houses in this selection have been designed to be built in traditional neighborhoods. It would be appropriate then to explain the neighborhood pattern which is to be their setting and to describe some of the positive consequences of living in one such neighborhood.

The history of urbanism in North America is not a complicated one. There have been only two patterns of settlement: the neighborhood, which was prevalent until World War II, and suburbia, which is 50 years old. They are similar in their initial capacity to accommodate people and their activities. The difference between them is that suburbia causes environmental, social and economic problems that ultimately degrade the quality of life of its residents.

Neighborhoods everywhere have certain features in common:

◆ The neighborhood is a comprehensive community. When it is clustered with others, neighborhoods make up a town; when standing free in the landscape, a neighborhood is known as a village. The neighborhood can vary in population and density to accommodate local conditions.

◆ The neighborhood is always limited in extent so that most of its residents are within a 5-minute walking distance to its center. The ordinary shopping and social needs of daily life should be available within this area.

◆ The buildings vary in function, but they are compatible in size, architectural language and siting. There is usually a mixture of townhouses and houses (like the ones in this catalog), ancillary apartments and small apartment buildings, shops, restaurants and offices.

◆ The neighborhood streets are laid out in a network, so that there are alternate routes to every destination. This permits most streets to be smaller and, with slower traffic, they are walkable.

Photo by ©Mike Watkins
Illustration courtesy of Duany Plater-Zyberk & Company

- The streets are spatially defined by buildings which line the sidewalks with storefronts, porches and stoops. Parking lots are not visible and garage doors are pulled back, away from the streets.

- Open space is provided in the specific form of squares, playgrounds and parks.

Conventional suburbia has quite different attributes:

- Suburbia has no size limit. It is laid out as separate pods, which are dedicated to single uses such as shopping centers, office parks and housing subdivisions. All of these are inaccessible from one another, except by car. The housing is strictly segregated into large clusters containing units of equal cost.

- Suburban traffic is allowed to control the scale and form of the public space, with parking lots everywhere and streets usually dedicated primarily to the automobile.

- In suburbia, there is a high proportion of cul-de-sacs and looping streets. Through traffic uses only a few connecting streets, which consequently become easily congested.

- Suburban buildings are set back deeply from streets. They are unable to create spatial definition or the security of "windows on the street." Street frontages are dominated by garage doors.

Living in conventional suburbia has negative consequences:

- By assuming that most people will drive to and from all activities, the need for large streets and parking lots increases. By paving extensively, the natural landscape is destroyed.

- By consigning the available public budget for roads, the human infrastructure of educational and cultural buildings is starved.

- In suburbia, the young are dependent on adults for their social needs. They attend schools to which they cannot walk, and they wait isolated at home until their working parents arrive.

To live in a traditional neighborhood has several positive consequences:

- By bringing most of the activities of daily living into walking distance, everyone, especially the elderly and the young, gains independence.

- By reducing the number and length of automobile trips, traffic congestion is minimized, the expenses of road construction are limited and air pollution is reduced.

- By providing walkable streets of comfortable scale, neighbors can gather, come to know each other and watch over their collective security.

- By providing buildings at easy walking distances from a stop at the neighborhood center, public transit becomes a viable alternative to the automobile.

- By providing a full range of housing types and work places, age and economic classes are integrated and an authentic community is formed.

Those who do not already live in a traditional neighborhood would do well to go out and find one. Then they should select the design in this catalog that would best fit their family needs and the character of the neighborhood. The end result will be most gratifying, I can assure you.

TRADITIONAL NEIGHBORHOOD

SUBURBAN SPRAWL

INTRODUCTION
Building Better Places to Live in Traditional Neighborhoods

Photo by ©Jeffrey Jacobs/Mims Studios

By Jim Constantine and J. Carson Looney

Americans have long held a fascination with small-town living—celebrated throughout our culture from the works of Norman Rockwell to Disney's Main Street, to the idealized television neighborhoods of Beaver Cleaver and Mayberry. These revered images of home and community, however, stand in stark contrast to the pattern of suburban sprawl that has dominated the latter half of the 20th Century. For many people, reality consists of an isolated subdivision dressed up in trendy architecture that fades quickly out of style. Monotonous streetscapes with more garage doors and pavement than front doors and landscaping provide no real sense of place. And often, there is no center of town to walk to—just strip malls and shopping centers scattered along traffic-clogged roads.

In recent years, a growing number of developers, architects and planners have sought a more lasting vision, a better way to build future homes and communities. In Traditional Neighborhood Developments, as they are called, builders and designers have discovered lessons and inspiration in the older towns, villages and neighborhoods that Americans cherish, such as Williamsburg. There is a timeless quality to the architecture—an authentic aspect to homes that never really goes out

of style. Narrow, tree-lined streets that are more comfortable for pedestrians and safer for children create a special sense of community and provide a friendly place to sit on a porch and enjoy being part of a neighborhood.

Traditional neighborhoods are the perfect setting for homes reminiscent of Grandma's house, with updated floor plans and amenities that cater to the way people live today. Diverse styles coexist easily when a few timeless architectural principles are followed. Classically-derived vertical proportions are used for entrances, windows and columns, and dignity is achieved with balance and restraint, with no single element overpowering the facade. Parking is discreetly tucked away from the front of the home or placed along back alleys. The goal is to create a harmonious streetscape that's the main attraction, not a cluster of individual houses screaming for attention.

This portfolio of plans provides a collection of truly high-quality homes that will fit comfortably within a classic town, village or neighborhood. The plans are arranged in the way a traditional community is structured, with a center, a midtown and an edge. Smaller homes that belong near Main Street are in the *Town Center* section, single-family homes ideal for Elm Street are in *Midtown Village*, and

spacious residences that relate to the surrounding countryside are found at the *Edge of Town*.

Town Center
A home near the center of a town or village is ideal for people who want the convenience of living within walking distance of community gathering places, shopping, services and other activities. This desire to be close to the action can appeal to both young and old, and is especially attractive for singles, working couples, one-parent families and retirees.

Living in the center of a community may mean trading square footage and yard space for the many advantages of being close to town. With less time spent driving around on errands and doing house and yard work, the homeowner has more time to spend with family and friends or to walk around town and meet neighbors. For many people, actively participating in the public realm is what community life is all about.

Midtown Village
Towns and villages, and even many cities, include a diverse mix of homes in residential neighborhoods that surround the center of the community. These areas range in scale and character from small-lot bungalows on a narrow lane to tree-lined streets

Photo by ©Looney Ricks Kiss Architects, Inc.

Life in a traditional neighborhood, town or village is different from one's experience in sprawling cookie-cutter subdivisions and strip shopping centers. Whether one lives in the center of town, the midtown area or at the edge of town, one shares a sense of belonging with other residents in *all* parts of the community. Contributing to this stronger sense of place is the way in which the homes, shops and civic buildings fit together collectively. Houses harmonize with neighboring homes, appear inviting to passersby, and relate to public squares, parks and other places that serve as the gathering places for the community.

The homes in this collection respond to modern needs and recapture a timeless way of life. A wide range of square footages—from grand manors to cozy cottages—provides a diverse mix ranging from vintage styles to visionary ideas. The look is formal and friendly, sophisticated and livable, with breezy front porches and well-drawn interiors. These designs are different because they reinforce the public realm at the front while ensuring private spaces to the side or rear of a property. This balance of public and private creates a house and a neighborhood that one can forever call *home*. Some will continue these traditions in older towns, villages and neighborhoods while others will forge the bonds anew in the growing number of Traditional Neighborhood Developments being built from coast to coast.

that showcase a mix of architectural styles, and stately homes sitting atop elevated front lawns. Regardless of size or cost, the architecture displays a shared vocabulary of simple building forms, properly proportioned windows and doors, human-scale elements such as columns and porches, and time-honored details derived from centuries of building.

Close to the center of town and punctuated by schools, parks and places of worship, these midtown neighborhoods are ideal areas to raise a family. The mix of different sizes and types of homes on nearby streets, or even next door to each other, also means that elderly relatives can live a block away from their children and grandchildren rather than being removed to a remote retirement community.

Edge of Town

The perimeter of a community is a place of transition from urban to rural, from community to countryside. Reflecting this transition, homes at the edge of town are situated on larger lots, often in relationship to an open space such as a park, greenbelt, nature preserve, golf course, woodlands, agricultural fields, or a stream or lake.

People who prefer to live in these locations have a need for more space and may want to live close to nature. But living at the edge of a community is not the same as living in the middle of nowhere. Those who live at the edge of a town or village still relate to the center of the community as a focal point for everyday needs and social activities.

Guest Houses and Garages

Traditional neighborhoods are often distinguished by the discreet placement of garages and auxiliary buildings. While most of the homes in this collection thoughtfully place attached garages to the side or rear, another option is a detached garage, possibly connected by a breezeway or porte cochere. The enclosed yard space between the home and outbuilding can frame luxurious patios and gardens with much greater privacy than an open yard. A detached garage is the perfect complement to a comfortable home, serving to keep vehicles nearby, providing storage space for tools and lawn equipment and creating a workspace apart from the bustle of household activities. An outbuilding can also be used as a guesthouse, home office or studio.

Photo by ©Looney Ricks Kiss Architects, Inc.

Neighborhood Gallery

A Collection of Fine Designs

Formal rooms provide an atmosphere that's both subdued and sophisticated.

A courtyard and covered porch invite enjoyment of the outdoors.

Photos by ©Jeffrey Jacobs/Mims Studios

This home, as shown in the photographs, may differ from the actual blueprints.

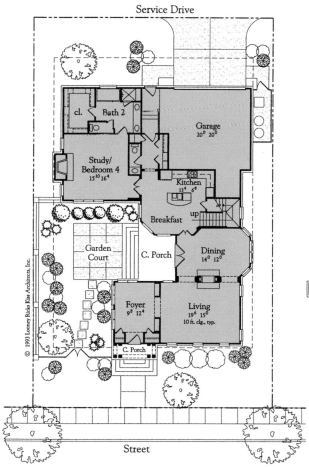

Lindsay Circle

A finely crafted porch and covered balcony complement classical elements, such as a portico and triple symmetrical dormers, on this stately yet charming Town home. The entry leads to a foyer that's brightened by three sets of windows. A through-fireplace connects a crowd-size living room and a formal dining room that leads to a side porch and courtyard. The first-floor bedroom has a fireplace and easily converts to a study. A rear-loading garage keeps the car out of public view but handy for out-of-town errands.

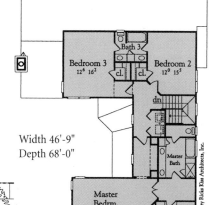

Width 46'-9"
Depth 68'-0"

PLAN W500

First Floor: 1,681 square feet
Second Floor: 1,342 square feet
Total: 3,023 square feet

Bedrooms: 4
Bathrooms: 3½

DESIGN BY
©*Looney Ricks Kiss Architects, Inc.*

TOWN

Thomas Square

Photos by ©Jeffrey Jacobs/Mims Studios

This home, as shown in the photographs, may differ from the actual blueprints.

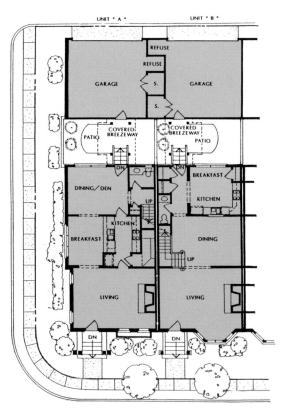

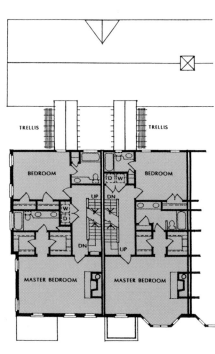

Width 23'-0"/22'-0"
Depth 42'-0" (without garage)

PLAN W501

First Floor: 970/940 square feet
Second Floor: 970/940 square feet
Third Floor: 351/229 square feet
Total: 2,291/2,179 square feet

Bedrooms: 2
Bathrooms: 3½

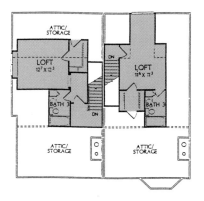

TOWN

A refined row house, this design is a perfect fit for the Town Center area of the neighborhood. With tidy covered entries, a stately facade provides plenty of curb appeal and a warm welcome to family and friends. Each floor plan offers spacious formal rooms, a massive hearth, a casual dining area and a private breezeway and patio. The second-floor plan includes a lavish master suite with a private fireplace, two walk-in closets and access to an upper-level loft with its own bath. The dining room or den of Unit A leads outdoors to a private patio and covered breezeway, a comfortable place for friends to gather or the homeowner to find repose. Unit B provides a service entrance and a rear staircase that leads to pleasing outdoor areas. The garage for each unit is thoughtfully placed to the rear of the property.

DESIGN BY
*©Looney Ricks Kiss
Architects, Inc.*

Linear elements add quiet definition to the open arrangement of the living and breakfast areas.

Traditional meets comfortable in the living room.

Friendship Plaza

This home, as shown in the photographs, may differ from the actual blueprints.

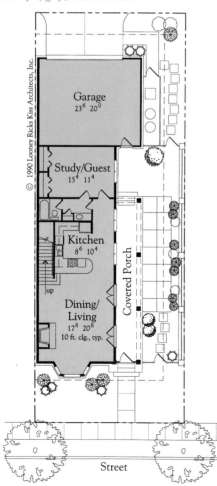

© 1990 Looney Ricks Kiss Architects, Inc.

Garage
23⁶ 20⁰

Study/Guest
15⁴ 11⁴

Kitchen
8⁶ 10⁴

Covered Porch

up

Dining/
Living
17⁸ 20⁶
10 ft. clg., typ.

Street

Width 24'-2"
Depth 74'-2"

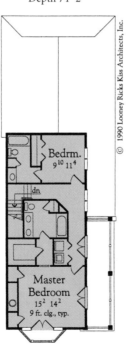

© 1990 Looney Ricks Kiss Architects, Inc.

Bedrm.
9¹⁰ 11⁴

dn

Master
Bedroom
15² 14²
9 ft. clg., typ.

DESIGN BY
©Looney Ricks Kiss
Architects, Inc.

These stunning Town houses have a breezy disposition yet, inside, provide the perfect blend of formality and comfort. Plan W534 includes an open dining/living area with a hearth and a bay window. A flex room serves as a study or guest bedroom with private access to a hall bath. The U-shaped kitchen surrounds casual dining space, which overlooks the covered porch. The second floor offers a vaulted master bedroom that leads to both a private and a shared balcony through two sets of lovely French doors.

PLAN W534

First Floor: 952 square feet
Second Floor: 766 square feet
Total: 1,718 square feet

Bedrooms: 2 or 3
Bathrooms: 3

TOWN

This Town house variation has a comfortable interior, tailored for couples and families. The front porch leads to a spacious family room with a fireplace and a three-window view. A galley-style kitchen opens to casual dining space, which has access to a side porch with steps down to a courtyard. The first-floor master suite provides a walk-in closet and additional linen storage in the bath. Upstairs, each of two family bedrooms provides a set of French doors to the upper porch as well as private access to the shared bath. Both plans W502 and W534 provide a rear-loading garage with a pedestrian entrance.

PLAN W502

First Floor: 1,075 square feet
Second Floor: 604 square feet
Total: 1,679 square feet

Bedrooms: 3
Bathrooms: 2½

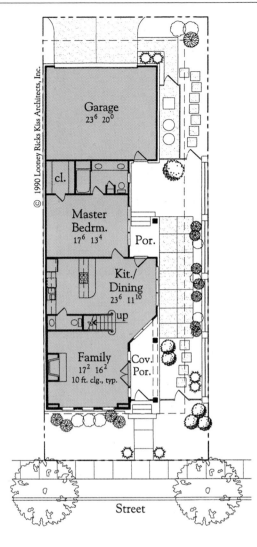

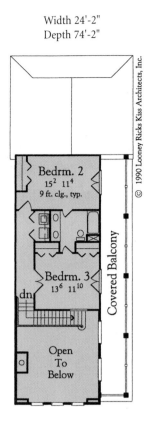

Width 24'-2"
Depth 74'-2"

DESIGN BY
©*Looney Ricks Kiss Architects, Inc.*

Exquisite French doors extend the living space outdoors to a private courtyard.

Trinity Place

Even the formal rooms have a kick-your-shoes-off attitude in this charming Town home.

This home, as shown in the photographs, may differ from the actual blueprints.

Photos by ©Jeffrey Jacobs/Mims Studios

ere's a Town home that's both beautiful and compact. This fortunate homeowner will never feel crowded, with a well-drawn interior of spacious rooms and plenty of indoor/outdoor flow. A double portico presents a charming welcome and invites enjoyment of the outdoors. The entry leads to an open arrangement of the living and dining rooms, warmed by a fireplace. A center hall provides access to a garden court and path, where family members can linger or begin their stroll to the Main Street shops. Upstairs, the sleeping quarters include two secondary bedrooms and a master suite that opens to a covered balcony.

PLAN W503

First Floor: 781 square feet
Second Floor: 1,034 square feet
Total: 1,815 square feet

Bedrooms: 3
Bathrooms: 2½

Width 19'-9"
Depth 69'-0"

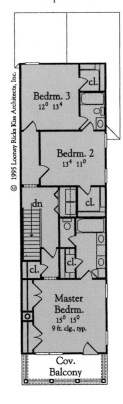

© 1995 Looney Ricks Kiss Architects, Inc.

Bedrm. 3
12⁰ 13⁴

cl.

Bedrm. 2
13⁴ 11⁰

dn

cl.

cl.

cl.

Master Bedrm.
15⁰ 15⁰
9 ft. clg., typ.

Cov. Balcony

DESIGN BY
©*Looney Ricks Kiss Architects, Inc.*

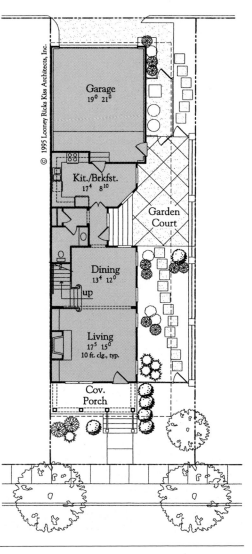

© 1995 Looney Ricks Kiss Architects, Inc.

Garage
19⁰ 21⁰

Kit./Brkfst.
17⁴ 8¹⁰

Garden Court

Dining
13⁴ 12⁰

up

Living
17⁵ 15⁰
10 ft. clg., typ.

Cov. Porch

Moncks Corner

Photos by ©Jeffrey Jacobs/Mims Studios

This home, as shown in the photographs, may differ from the actual blueprints.

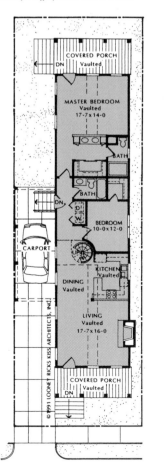

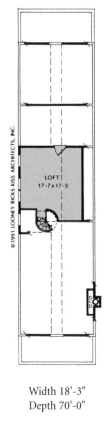

Width 18'-3"
Depth 70'-0"

The gently rustic facade of this Town design bears a mild resemblance to a seaside cottage. But a carefree interior provides amenities for both traditional entertaining and casual gatherings. A vaulted open living and dining space includes a fireplace and a stunning interior vista of the winding, wrought-iron staircase. The center of the plan provides a flex room, which can serve as a family bedroom, guest room or home office. A privacy door leads to the master bedroom, bath and dressing area. The homeowner's bedroom leads out to the rear porch.

PLAN W504

First Floor: 1,278 square feet
Second Floor: 256 square feet
Total: 1,534 square feet

Bedrooms: 2
Bathrooms: 2

DESIGN BY
©Looney Ricks Kiss
Architects, Inc.

TOWN

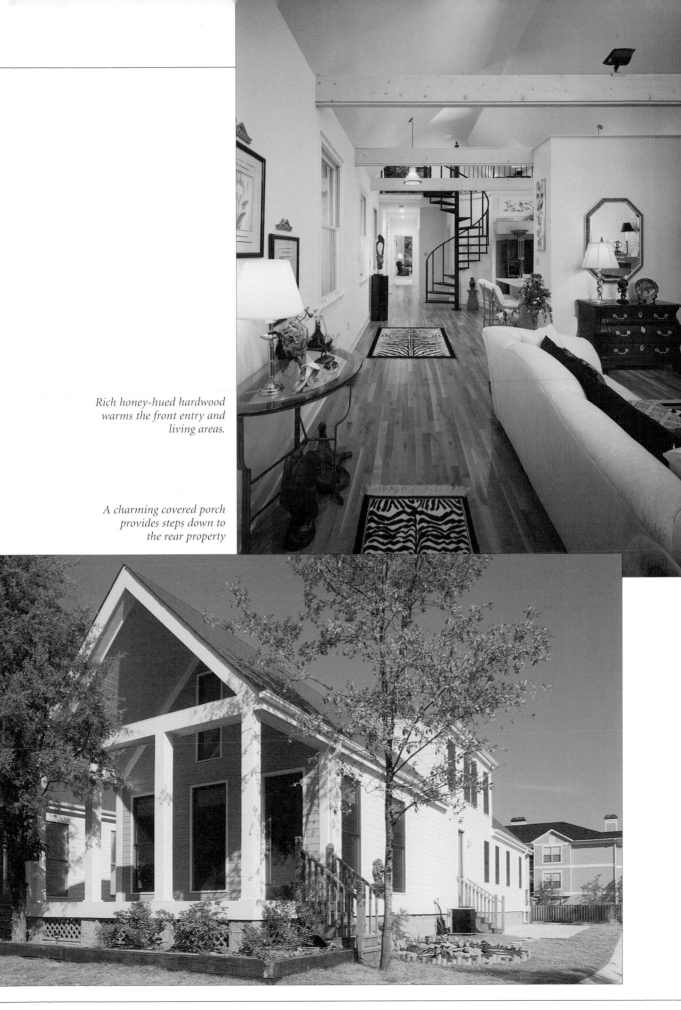

Rich honey-hued hardwood warms the front entry and living areas.

A charming covered porch provides steps down to the rear property

Wentworth Place

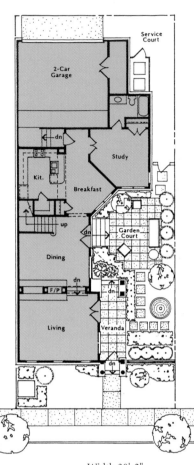

Width 30'-2"
Depth 74'-2"

A through-fireplace lends warmth and a touch of class to the heart of the home.

DESIGN BY
©*Looney Ricks Kiss*
Architects, Inc.

There won't be any chilly mornings for the homeowner within this lovely Town home. The second-floor master suite boasts a massive hearth, flanked by built-in shelves. French doors open from the bedroom to a private balcony, where gentle breezes may invigorate the senses. A gallery hall leads to a secondary bedroom, which has its own bath and a walk-in closet. On the first floor, formal rooms share a through-fireplace and offer doors to the veranda and garden court. A secluded study easily converts to a guest suite or home office, and convenient storage space is available in the rear-loading garage.

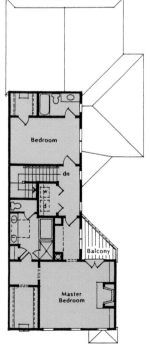

PLAN W505

First Floor: 1,282 square feet
Second Floor: 956 square feet
Total: 2,238 square feet

Bedrooms: 2 or 3
Bathrooms: 3

TOWN

Cambridge Circle

This home, as shown in the photograph, may differ from the actual blueprints.
For more detailed information, please check the floor plans carefully.

Photo by Bob Greenspan

lassic columns and balusters decorate a charming wraparound porch on this comfortable Village or Edge plan. Inside, a secluded den on the first floor offers a through-fireplace to the family room, which opens to the outdoors. The morning nook and L-shaped kitchen, with a cooktop island counter and built-in writing desk, open through columns to an elegant formal dining room. The second-floor master suite opens through French doors and offers a spacious bath. Two family bedrooms share a full bath.

DESIGN BY
©*Alan Mascord Design Associates, Inc.*

Width 43'-0"
Depth 69'-0"

PLAN 9557

First Floor: 1,371 square feet
Second Floor: 916 square feet
Total: 2,287 square feet

Bedrooms: 3
Bathrooms: 2½

QUOTE ONE®

Cost to build? See page 182
to order complete cost estimate
to build this house in your area!

VILLAGE   EDGE

Brennan Field Square

Photo by Riley & Riley Photography, Inc.

This home, as shown in the photograph, may differ from the actual blueprints. For more detailed information, please check the floor plans carefully.

Inviting porches are just the beginning of this lovely Edge home. Inside, a columned entry provides a classic touch to the spacious great room, which has a cathedral ceiling, built-in bookshelves and a fireplace. An octagonal dining room with a tray ceiling provides the perfect setting for formal occasions. Nearby, the gourmet kitchen includes an island cooktop and a built-in pantry, with the sunny breakfast area just a step away. The master bedroom, separated from two family bedrooms by the walk-in closet and utility room, offers privacy and comfort.

PLAN 9748

Square Footage: 1,737

Bedrooms: 3
Bathrooms: 2

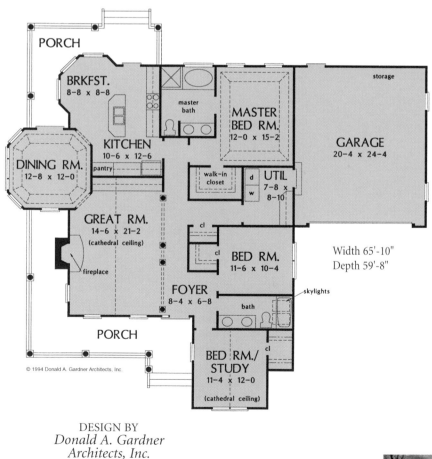

PORCH

BRKFST.
8-8 x 8-8

master
bath

MASTER
BED RM.
12-0 x 15-2

storage

GARAGE
20-4 x 24-4

KITCHEN
10-6 x 12-6

pantry

walk-in
closet

d UTIL
7-8 x
w 8-10

DINING RM.
12-8 x 12-0

GREAT RM.
14-6 x 21-2
(cathedral ceiling)

cl

cl

BED RM.
11-6 x 10-4

Width 65'-10"
Depth 59'-8"

fireplace

FOYER
8-4 x 6-8

skylights

bath

PORCH

© 1994 Donald A. Gardner Architects, Inc.

BED RM./
STUDY
11-4 x 12-0

cl

(cathedral ceiling)

DESIGN BY
*Donald A. Gardner
Architects, Inc.*

EDGE

This home, as shown in the photographs, may differ from the actual blueprints. For more detailed information, please check the floor plans carefully.

Photos by Riley & Riley Photography, Inc.

DESIGN BY
Donald A. Gardner Architects, Inc.

© 1993 Donald A. Gardner Architects, Inc.

Width 70'-0"
Depth 79'-2"

GARAGE
22-4 x 21-4

spa

DECK

covered breezeway

clerestory with arched window

(cathedral ceiling)
GREAT RM.
19-8 x 19-2

BRKFST.
9-8 x 10-6

UTIL.
8-0 x 9-4

fireplace

walk-in closet

skylight

master bath

cab.

balcony above

pantry

wet bar

KITCHEN
13-0 x 16-4

MASTER BED RM.
13-0 x 15-4

bath

cl

up

BED RM./STUDY
12-0 x 11-0

FOYER
5-0 x 13-6

DINING
12-0 x 13-2

PORCH
30-4 x 8-0

Rear View

great room below

railing

balcony

down

bath

BED RM.
12-8 x 14-10

lin.

cl cl

BED RM.
12-0 x 12-6

PLAN 9703

First Floor: 1,783 square feet
Second Floor: 611 square feet
Total: 2,394 square feet

Bedrooms: 4
Bathrooms: 3

Onlookers will delight in the symmetry of the arched windows and dormers of this Edge or Village design. This open plan is also packed with the latest features, including the kitchen's amenities: a cooktop island counter and a spacious breakfast area that opens to the outdoors. A flex room off the foyer easily converts from a study to a guest suite. Nearby, the master suite boasts a generous bath with a skylight, walk-in closet and garden tub. A spacious rear deck and front covered porch offer a warm invitation to enjoy the outdoors.

VILLAGE EDGE

Periwinkle Way

An engaging blend of Old South comfort and modern style balance past and present with this carefree Edge or Village design. Horizontal siding complements an insulated metal roof to create a charming look that calls up a sense of 19th-Century style. At the heart of the home, the two-story great room features a corner fireplace, an angled entertainment center and an eating bar shared with the gourmet kitchen. Upstairs, an expansive deck captures panoramic views and serves the sounds of the sea to a secondary bedroom.

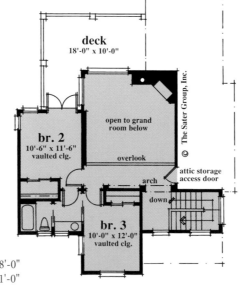

Rear View

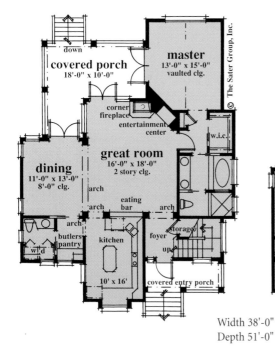

Width 38'-0"
Depth 51'-0"

DESIGN BY
©*The Sater Design Collection*

PLAN 6683

First Floor: 1,290 square feet
Second Floor: 548 square feet
Total: 1,838 square feet

Bedrooms: 3
Bathrooms: 2½

VILLAGE   EDGE

P revailing summer breezes find their way through many joyful rooms in this Neoclassical Revival design. Inspired by 19th-Century Key West houses, the exterior is heart-stoppingly beautiful with Doric columns, lattice and fretwork, and a glass-paneled entry. The mid-level foyer eases the trip from ground level to living and dining areas, which offer flexible space for planned events or cozy gatherings. Two sets of French doors lead out to the gallery and sun deck, and a tall picture window invites natural light. A computer loft offers built-in desk space and a balcony overlook.

Rear View

PLAN 6689

Main Level: 1,642 square feet
Upper Level: 1,165 square feet
Lower Level: 150 square feet
Total: 2,957 square feet

Bedrooms: 5
Bathrooms: 3½

VILLAGE   EDGE

DESIGN BY
©*The Sater Design Collection*

Main Level

© The Sater Group, Inc.

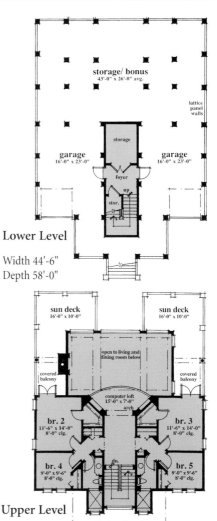

Lower Level

Width 44'-6"
Depth 58'-0"

Upper Level

© The Sater Group, Inc.

This handsome Edge design has a heart of gold: a gourmet kitchen and an open living area with a morning nook and two sets of French doors to the rear deck. A spacious guest bedroom leads to the side porch. The dramatic front hall leads to a flex room and a formal dining room, then to a large great room. Upstairs, the master suite is a spacious retreat, complete with a private study or sitting room. A second-floor guest suite has its own access to the morning nook and kitchen via a rear staircase. This home is designed with a basement foundation.

Homeowner's Option: This garage may be customized to provide a rear entry.

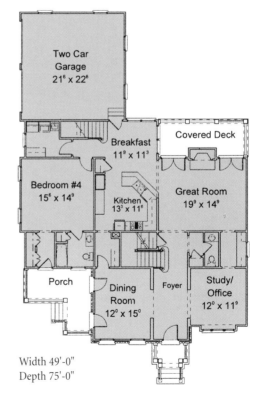

PLAN T245

First Floor: 1,886 square feet
Second Floor: 2,076 square feet
Total: 3,962 square feet

Bedrooms: 5
Bathrooms: 4½

Width 49'-0"
Depth 75'-0"

DESIGN BY
©*Stephen Fuller,*
American Home Gallery

Distinctive windows, round columns and stone piers complement a stone chimney on this Edge design. Inside, the living room provides access to the wraparound porch, creating a space that's both intimate and grand. The great room and the porch beyond provide a natural indoor/outdoor flow. The staircase—a focal point in the foyer—is in the Arts and Crafts style and features built-in display spaces. The bonus room has its own entry, making it perfect for guests or a home office. This home is designed with a basement foundation.

Homeowner's Option: This garage may be customized to provide a rear entry.

PLAN T247

First Floor: 1,652 square feet
Second Floor: 1,460 square feet
Total: 3,112 square feet
Bonus Room: 256 square feet

Bedrooms: 4
Bathrooms: 3½

DESIGN BY
©*Stephen Fuller,*
American Home Gallery

Future Bonus Room
12⁶ x 22⁶

WIC

Master Suite
14⁰ x 21⁵

Master Bath

Bedroom #4
13⁶ x 12⁹

Bedroom #2
13⁶ x 12⁹

Bedroom #3
13⁶ x 11⁶

Two Car Garage
22³ x 21³

Porch

Kitchen
14⁶ x 13⁰

Breakfast
14⁸ x 12⁰

Great Room
16⁰ x 19³

Office

Foyer

Dining Room
12³ x 15⁹

Living Room
13⁶ x 13⁶

Covered Porch

Width 48'-0"
Depth 78'-4"

EDGE

Sweet Birch Lane

T he sweetly relaxed, slightly rambling composition of this lovely Edge home gives it all the warmth of Southern Vernacular style. The regional materials have a country flavor but the stone piers, lap siding and wood-trimmed walls provide classical details, such as the retreating columns on the extended front porch. Guests enter the home through a two-story foyer, and the front parlor easily converts to a formal dining room or study. This home is designed with a basement foundation.

Homeowner's Option: This garage may be customized to provide a rear entry.

PLAN T246

First Floor: 2,090 square feet
Second Floor: 1,160 square feet
Total: 3,250 square feet

Bedrooms: 4
Bathrooms: 3½

Width 70'-6"
Depth 79'-9"

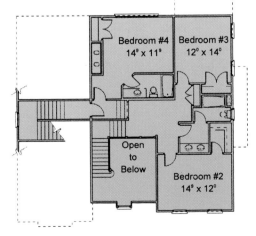

DESIGN BY
©*Stephen Fuller,*
American Home Gallery

EDGE

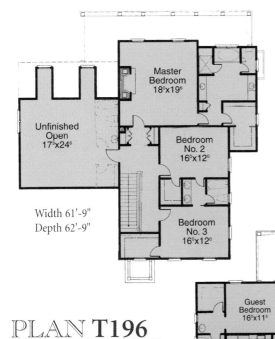

Width 61'-9"
Depth 62'-9"

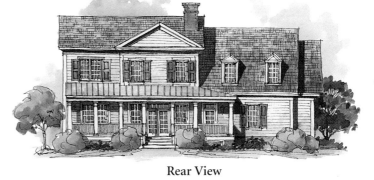

Rear View

PLAN **T196**

First Floor: 1,959 square feet
Second Floor: 1,408 square feet
Total: 3,367 square feet

Bedrooms: 4
Bathrooms: 3½

Inspired by Federal-style residences in the Northeast, this Edge design features a monumental front gable and a columned, balustrade-topped covered entrance. Inside, the foyer opens to formal rooms that offer quiet elegance for planned events and traditional festivities. Casual living space to the rear of the plan features a fireplace and opens to a hospitable rear porch. A U-shaped gourmet kitchen shares natural light from wide windows in the breakfast room. Upstairs, a gallery hall leads from the master suite to two family bedrooms, each with a walk-in closet. This home is designed with a basement foundation.

DESIGN BY
©*Stephen Fuller,*
American Home Gallery

EDGE

Strong traditional lines, graceful columns and a triplet of dormers lend a sense of history to this lovely Edge design. Formal rooms frame the foyer and provide the perfect environment for entertaining. A spacious great room features a fireplace and French doors to a covered porch. Positioned for privacy, the first-floor master suite is designed to pamper, with three walk-in closets, an island whirlpool tub and a separate shower. Upstairs, three bedrooms share a full bath, while the fourth bedroom has its own, making it a perfect guest suite. Please specify basement, crawlspace or slab foundation when ordering.

PLAN Y001

First Floor: 2,202 square feet
Second Floor: 1,192 square feet
Total: 3,394 square feet
Bonus Room: 396 square feet

Bedrooms: 5
Bathrooms: 3½

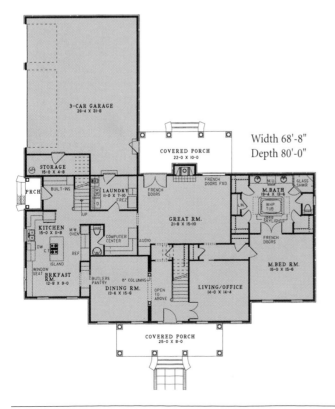

Width 68'-8"
Depth 80'-0"

DESIGN BY
©*Michael E. Nelson*
Nelson Design Group, LLC

EDGE

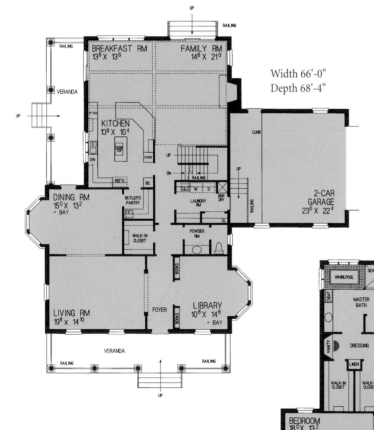

DESIGN BY
©Home Planners

This lovely stone farmhouse, reminiscent of the solid, comfortable homes once prevalent throughout America, will fit the Edge or Village areas of the neighborhood. The foyer leads to the formal rooms, including a spacious library. The family room and breakfast room have beam ceilings and open to the kitchen. On the second floor are four bedrooms, including a guest room with a private bath. The master suite has a fireplace and a fine bath with a whirlpool tub. A covered veranda leads to a side yard and invites enjoyment of the outdoors.

Width 66'-0"
Depth 68'-4"

PLAN 3502

First Floor: 2,086 square feet
Second Floor: 2,040 square feet
Total: 4,126 square feet

Bedrooms: 4
Bathrooms: 3½

L D

$ QUOTE ONE®

Cost to build? See page 182
to order complete cost estimate
to build this house in your area!

Honeyberry Lane

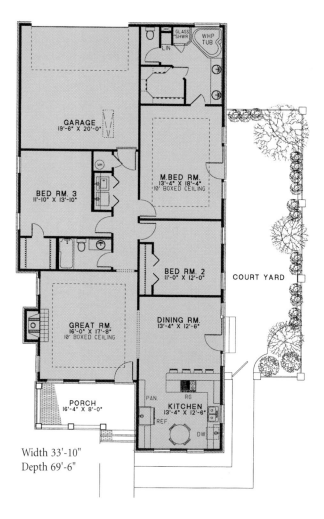

Width 33'-10"
Depth 69'-6"

PLAN Y077

Square Footage: 1,660

Bedrooms: 3
Bathrooms: 2

This lovely brick facade is set off with a dormer window and stately square columns to create a look that's welcome in the Village. A tray ceiling enhances the great room, which is warmed by a hearth. The corner kitchen provides a snack counter, a sizable pantry and casual dining space. The dining room leads outdoors to a side courtyard and is easily served by the eat-in kitchen. Two family bedrooms share a hall bath—one bedroom has a walk-in closet. The master suite has a luxurious bath with a walk-in closet, plus its own access to the courtyard.

DESIGN BY
©*Michael E. Nelson*
Nelson Design Group, LLC

PLAN Y066

Square Footage: 1,915

Bedrooms: 3
Bathrooms: 2

Simple accents such as decorative columns, a gable roof and charming dormer give this Town home a straight-forward, honest appeal. The great room has a built-in media center and a focal-point fire-place. The U-shaped kitchen features a cor-ner walk-in pantry, a snack counter and a view of three windows, which also brighten the dining room. The master suite has a box ceiling, walk-in closet and heavenly private bath. The dining room leads to a kid's nook and a grilling porch, with steps down to the side property. Please specify crawlspace or slab foundation when ordering.

DESIGN BY
©*Michael E. Nelson*
Nelson Design Group, LLC

Width 39'-0"
Depth 72'-0"

GARAGE
19'-4" X 19'-0"

WHP TUB
GLASS SHWR

M.BATH
16'-6" X 13'-0"

MASTER SUITE
16'-8" X 15'-0"

11' BOXED CEILING

LAU.
7'-0" X 6'-5"

W   D

GRILLING PORCH
8'-4" X 8'-11"

KID'S NOOK

PANTRY

REF

BENCH W/ STORAGE

BEDROOM 2
13'-4" X 12'-1"

KITCHEN
13'-2" X 12'-1"

DW

DINING
11'-6" X 11'-9"

8" COLUMNS

LIN

COMPUTER AREA

MEDIA CENTER

GREAT ROOM
17'-8" X 17'-0"

FOYER

3' GAS FIREPLACE

BEDROOM 3 / STUDY
13'-4" X 12'-0"

8" COLUMNS

COVERED PORCH
25'-0" X 8'-0"

TOWN

Harbor Bend Road

Photo by ©Jeffrey Jacobs/Mims Studios

This home, as shown in the photograph, may differ from the actual blueprints.

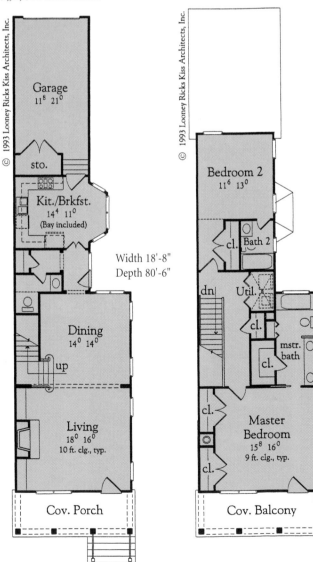

© 1993 Looney Ricks Kiss Architects, Inc.

Garage
11⁸ 21⁰

sto.

Kit./Brkfst.
14⁴ 11⁰
(Bay included)

Width 18'-8"
Depth 80'-6"

Dining
14⁰ 14⁰

up

Living
18⁰ 16⁰
10 ft. clg., typ.

Cov. Porch

© 1993 Looney Ricks Kiss Architects, Inc.

Bedroom 2
11⁶ 13⁰

cl. Bath 2

dn   Util.

cl.

mstr.
bath

cl.

cl.

Master
Bedroom
15⁸ 16⁰
9 ft. clg., typ.

cl.

Cov. Balcony

This lovely Town design is much more than just a pretty face. A row of symmetrical exteriors creates a stunning streetscape but the real beauty is within each home. A well-organized interior arranges the formal rooms to accommodate gatherings both grand and cozy. A centered fireplace lends warmth and a sense of comfort to the living room, and shares its glow with the formal dining room. A U-shaped kitchen overlooks a breakfast bay with three windows. Upstairs, the master suite provides a covered balcony and a double-bowl vanity.

DESIGN BY
©*Looney Ricks Kiss
Architects, Inc.*

PLAN W507

First Floor: 804 square feet
Second Floor: 835 square feet
Total: 1,639 square feet

Bedrooms: 2
Bathrooms: 2½

TOWN

Town Center

Main Street, Row Houses and the Village Commons

For many people, actively participating in the public realm is what community life is all about.

Unique Spaces for In-town Living

Willamette Court

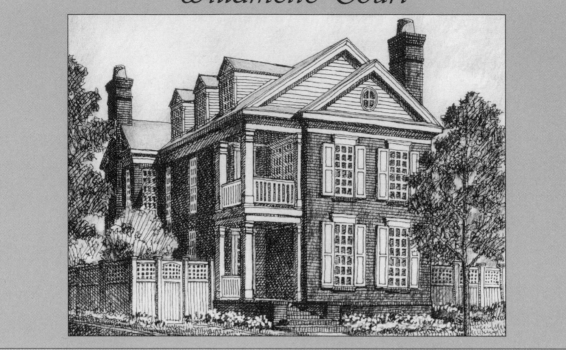

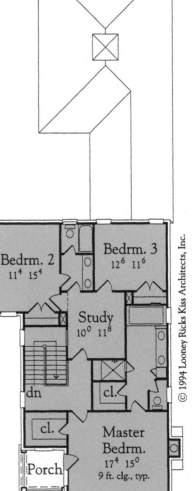

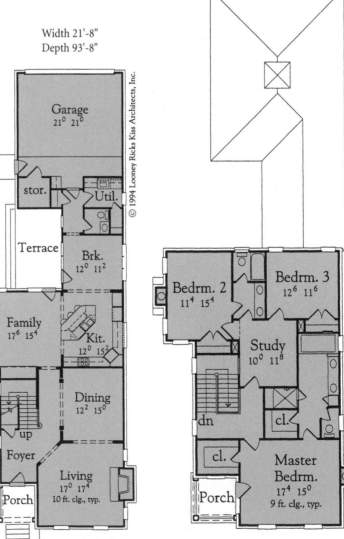

Box-paneled shutters add a touch of class to this Town design—a home that is simply the ultimate in comfort and style. A winding staircase highlights a refined foyer that sets the pace for the entire home. Fireplaces warm the formal and casual rooms, which can accommodate all occasions. The well-organized kitchen provides a snack bar for easy meals and serves the formal dining room with ease. Upstairs, two secondary bedrooms share a full bath and a study that could be used as a computer room. The master suite boasts two walk-in closets, an indulgent bath and a private porch.

PLAN W511

First Floor: 1,587 square feet
Second Floor: 1,191 square feet
Total: 2,778 square feet

Bedrooms: 3
Bathrooms: 2½

DESIGN BY
*©Looney Ricks Kiss
Architects, Inc.*

Width 21'-8"
Depth 93'-8"

© 1994 Looney Ricks Kiss Architects, Inc.

© 1994 Looney Ricks Kiss Architects, Inc.

Garage
21⁰ 21⁰

stor.

Util.

Terrace

Brk.
12⁰ 11²

Family
17⁶ 15⁴

Kit.
12⁰ 15²

Dining
12² 15⁰

up

Foyer

Porch

Living
17⁰ 17⁴
10 ft. clg., typ.

Bedrm. 2
11⁴ 15⁴

Bedrm. 3
12⁶ 11⁶

Study
10⁰ 11⁸

dn

cl.

cl.

Porch

Master
Bedrm.
17⁴ 15⁰
9 ft. clg., typ.

TOWN

South Bluffs Circle

This home, as shown in the photographs, may differ from the actual blueprints.

Photos by ©Jeffrey Jacobs/Mims Studios

PLAN W509

First Floor: 1,135 square feet
Second Floor: 1,092 square feet
Total: 2,227 square feet

Bedrooms: 3
Bathrooms: 2½

Width 28'-8"
Depth 74'-2"

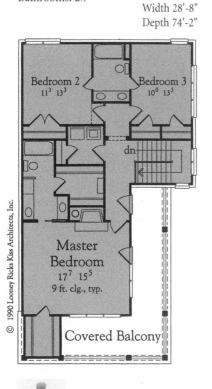

Bedroom 2
11³ 13³

Bedroom 3
10⁰ 13³

dn

Master
Bedroom
17⁷ 15⁵
9 ft. clg., typ.

Covered Balcony

© 1990 Looney Ricks Kiss Architects, Inc.

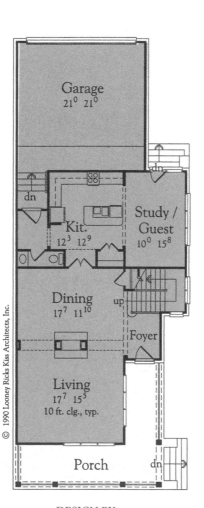

Garage
21⁰ 21⁰

dn

Kit.
12³ 12⁹

Study /
Guest
10⁰ 15⁸

Dining
17⁷ 11¹⁰

up

Foyer

Living
17⁷ 15⁵
10 ft. clg., typ.

Porch

dn

© 1990 Looney Ricks Kiss Architects, Inc.

DESIGN BY
©Looney Ricks Kiss
Architects, Inc.

Stylish square columns line the porch and portico of this Town home, which has received the Builder's Choice National Design and Planning Award and the Award of Merit in Architecture. Inside, an open arrangement of the formal rooms is partially defined by a through-fireplace. Brightened by a triple window, the breakfast nook is an inviting place for family and friends to gather. A single door opens to the outside, where steps lead down to the rear property—a good place to start a walk into town. The kitchen features a food prep island and a sizable pantry. Upstairs, the master suite offers a fireplace and access to the portico.

A simple balustrade complements box-panel accents on this award-winning Town home.

Mill Bay Commons

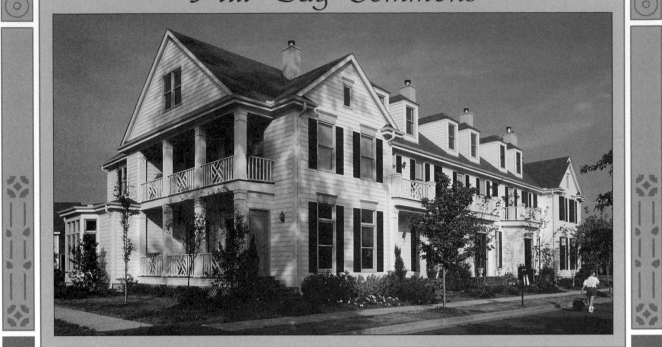

Photo by ©Jeffrey Jacobs/Mims Studios

This home, as shown in the photograph, may differ from the actual blueprints.

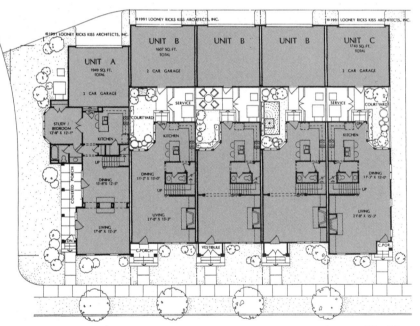

Row houses offer unique solutions for narrow-lot spaces and provide a sense of unity to the Town Center. The middle three units (Unit B) provide identical floor plans, with an entry porch or vestibule that opens to a living room with a centerpiece fireplace. The second floor includes a family bedroom with bath, and a master suite with a balcony. Unit A, a corner home, is enhanced by a covered front porch and balcony, and features a through-fireplace shared by the dining and living rooms. A flex room easily converts to a study or bedroom with its own bath. Unit C, also a corner home, provides open views from the open living and dining rooms and, upstairs, a generous master suite.

PLAN W508

(Units A/B/C)

First Floor: 1,063/836/904 square feet
Second Floor: 886/771/839 square feet
Total: 1,949/1,607/1,743 square feet

Bedrooms: 3/2
Bathrooms: 3/2½

DESIGN BY
*©Looney Ricks Kiss
Architects, Inc.*

Width 22'-6"
Depth 76'-9"

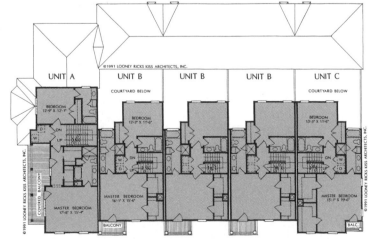

TOWN

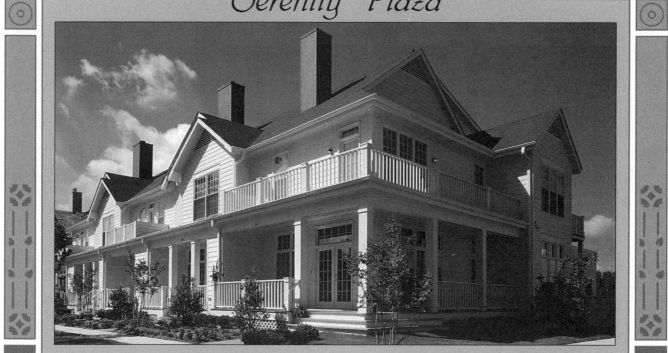

Serenity Plaza

This home, as shown in the photograph, may differ from the actual blueprints.

Photo by ©Jeffrey Jacobs/Mims Studios

Wide porches, set off by charming French doors, provide plenty of opportunities for greeting passersby and enjoying the outdoor spaces of these captivating row houses. The corner home, Unit A, offers a walk-through kitchen that leads to the dining area. The second floor includes a spacious master suite with access to a private deck. Unit B, represented twice in this arrangement, includes a U-shaped kitchen. Upstairs, the master suite boasts a rear deck. Unit C provides a vaulted master suite on the second floor. The open formal rooms of Unit D, a corner home, lead outdoors to a wraparound porch. Upstairs, the master suite has a private deck.

PLAN W510

(Units A/B/C/D)

First Floor: 772/772/772/839 square feet
Second Floor: 735/784/768/787 square feet
Total: 1,507/1,556/1,540/1,626 square feet

Bedrooms: 2
Bathrooms: 2½

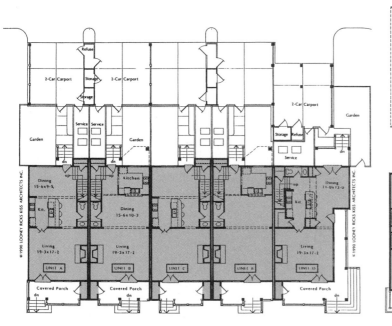

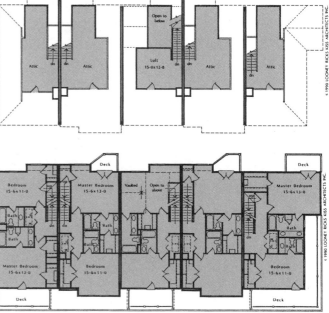

Width 22'-11"
Depth 46'-6" (without carport)

DESIGN BY
©*Looney Ricks Kiss*
Architects, Inc.

Lake Newport Drive

PLAN Y075

First Floor: 1,295 square feet
Second Floor: 664 square feet
Total: 1,959 square feet

Bedrooms: 4
Bathrooms: 2½

A gracious facade of columns, shuttered windows, gabled rooflines, a long porch and balcony make this home seem like an established landmark. The great room boasts a media center, gas fireplace and views toward the front property. A well-planned kitchen serves a snack counter and enjoys vistas through the formal dining room. A secluded master suite has a computer center, tray ceiling and a vanity with two lavatories. On the second floor, three bedrooms share access to a balcony that other family members can enjoy. Please specify basement, crawlspace or slab foundation when ordering.

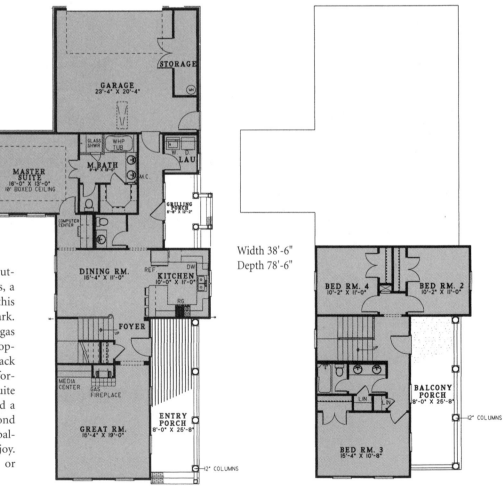

Width 38'-6"
Depth 78'-6"

DESIGN BY
©*Michael E. Nelson*
Nelson Design Group, LLC

TOWN

Edison Park Lane

The "single-house" style represented here is simply one-room wide with a two-story piazza that runs the depth of the home—a perfect arrangement for the narrow lots of the Town Center. Inside, the foyer opens to a parlor, which offers a hearth. The formal dining room has its own door to the piazza and courtyard, while the kitchen and breakfast room open to a private porch and terrace. Upstairs, sleeping quarters include three secondary bedrooms and a spacious master suite with a centered hearth. A third floor holds a guest bedroom and a study.

PLAN 2660

First Floor: 1,479 square feet
Second Floor: 1,501 square feet
Third Floor: 912 square feet
Activities Room: 556 square feet
Total: 4,448 square feet

Bedrooms: 5
Bathrooms: 4½ + ½

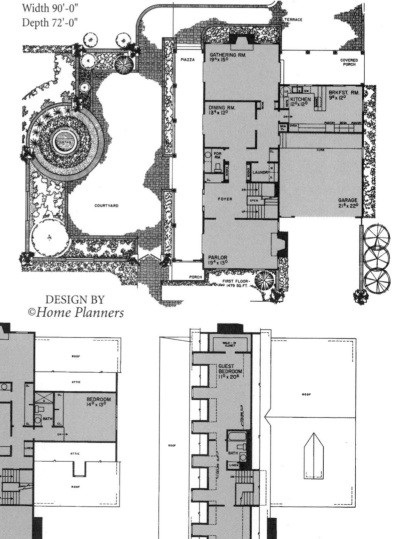

Width 90'-0"
Depth 72'-0"

DESIGN BY
©Home Planners

TOWN   VILLAGE

Brighton Corner

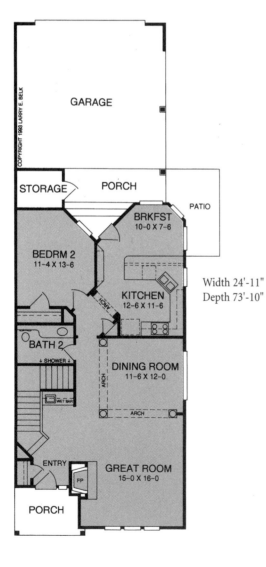

GARAGE

COPYRIGHT 1993 LARRY E. BELK

STORAGE

PORCH

PATIO

BRKFST
10-0 X 7-6

BEDRM 2
11-4 X 13-6

KITCHEN
12-6 X 11-6

Width 24'-11"
Depth 73'-10"

BATH 2

↓ SHOWER ↓

ARCH

DINING ROOM
11-6 X 12-0

ARCH

WET BAR

ARCH

ENTRY

GREAT ROOM
15-0 X 16-0

FP

PORCH

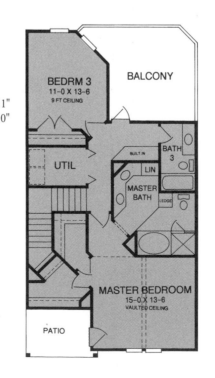

BEDRM 3
11-0 X 13-6
9 FT CEILING

BALCONY

BUILT IN

BATH
3

UTIL

LIN

MASTER
BATH

LEDGE

MASTER BEDROOM
15-0 X 13-6
VAULTED CEILING

PATIO

This charming clapboard home is loaded with character and perfect for a narrow lot. High ceilings throughout give the home an open, spacious feeling. The great room and the dining room are defined by columns with connecting arches. A bedroom and a bath are conveniently located for guests on the first floor. Upstairs, the master bedroom features a vaulted ceiling and a luxurious master bath. Access to a covered patio from the master bedroom provides a relaxing outdoor retreat. Please specify crawlspace or slab foundation when ordering.

PLAN 8051

First Floor: 1,078 square feet
Second Floor: 921 square feet
Total: 1,999 square feet

Bedrooms: 3
Bathrooms: 3

L

DESIGN BY
©*Larry E. Belk Designs*

TOWN   VILLAGE

St. Jacques Circle

Width 50'-2"
Depth 69'-3"

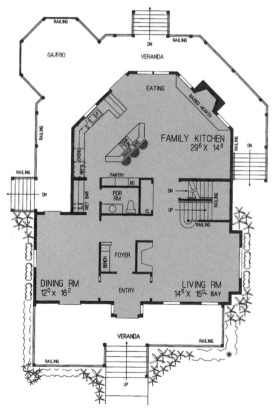

PLAN 3382

First Floor: 1,366 square feet
Second Floor: 837 square feet
Third Floor: 363 square feet
Total: 2,566 square feet

Bedrooms: 3
Bathrooms: 3½

L D

QUOTE ONE®

Cost to build? See page 182
to order complete cost estimate
to build this house in your area!

A simple but charming Queen Anne Victorian, this enchanting three-story home will fit the Town or Village areas of the neighborhood. The well-planned interior includes a formal living room with a fireplace, a spacious family kitchen with its own hearth, and casual eating space. The dining room leads to the wraparound veranda, which provides a charming gazebo. The second floor holds two bedrooms, one a master suite with grand bath. A guest suite tucked away on the third floor provides additional linen storage.

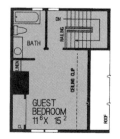

DESIGN BY
©Home Planners

Hope River Lane

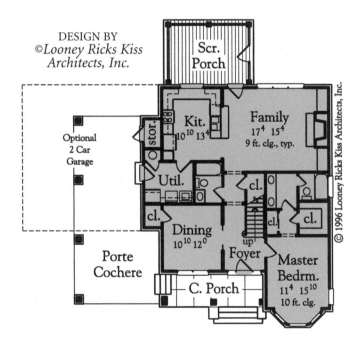

DESIGN BY
©Looney Ricks Kiss
Architects, Inc.

Scr. Porch

Optional 2 Car Garage

Kit. 10¹⁰ 13⁴

stor.

Family 17⁴ 15⁴
9 ft. clg., typ.

Util.

cl.

Porte Cochere

Dining 10¹⁰ 12⁰

Foyer
up

C. Porch

Master Bedrm. 11⁴ 15¹⁰
10 ft. clg.

cl.
cl.

© 1996 Looney Ricks Kiss Architects, Inc.

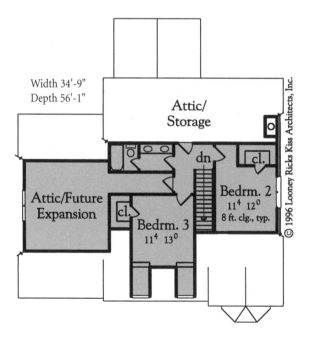

Width 34'-9"
Depth 56'-1"

Attic/ Storage

Attic/Future Expansion

cl.

Bedrm. 3 11⁴ 13⁰

dn

cl.

Bedrm. 2 11⁴ 12⁰
8 ft. clg., typ.

© 1996 Looney Ricks Kiss Architects, Inc.

Arches, dormers, a bay window and porch columns set off this lovely Town or Village home. The varied vernacular of this stunning design promotes the eclectic nature of the neighborhood. Inside, the foyer directs guests to the formal dining room or to the rear of the plan to warm their hands by the hearth in the family room. The screened porch offers a summertime retreat and great indoor/outdoor flow. A master suite, thoughtfully placed just off the foyer, provides a bay window and a compartmented bath.

PLAN W516

First Floor: 1,235 square feet
Second Floor: 541 square feet
Total: 1,776 square feet

Bedrooms: 3
Bathrooms: 3

TOWN   VILLAGE

Avenue Montpelier

Grand arch-top windows set off the lovely facade of this gently French design, and promote the presence of natural light within. The open formal rooms blend traditional style with supreme comfort, with a centered fireplace and French doors to the covered porch. A secluded study or secondary bedroom has a splendid bath with a dressing area and a walk-in closet. Upstairs, an additional bedroom has its own door to the covered balcony. The master suite includes two walk-in closets and access to the balcony.

DESIGN BY
©*Looney Ricks Kiss
Architects, Inc.*

PLAN W517

First Floor: 1,660 square feet
Second Floor: 943 square feet
Total: 2,603 square feet

Bedrooms: 3
Bathrooms: 3½

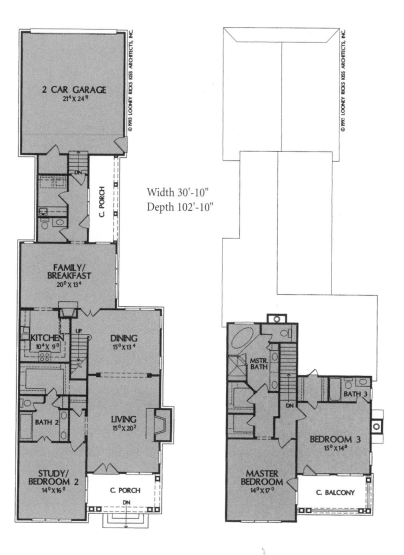

Width 30'-10"
Depth 102'-10"

TOWN   VILLAGE

Laurel Park Place

Tall, elegant windows and a stately chimney deck out the facade of this stunning Town home. The robust mix of Colonial balance and natural symmetry lends an inviting look to the exterior. Inside, a row of columns sets off the dining area, which provides views to the side courtyard. Informal spaces share a door to the side property—a great place to linger or start a walk into town. The secluded master suite provides a dressing area and two walk-in closets. Upstairs, a cluster of secondary bedrooms share a spacious hall bath.

DESIGN BY
©Looney Ricks Kiss Architects, Inc.

PLAN W512

First Floor: 1,792 square feet
Second Floor: 899 square feet
Total: 2,691 square feet

Bedrooms: 4
Bathrooms: 2½

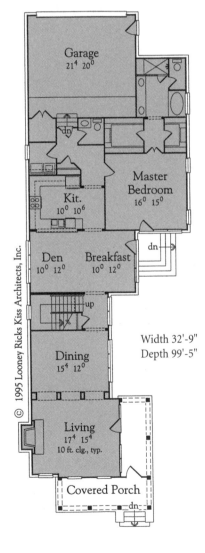

Garage
21⁴ 20⁰

Master Bedroom
16⁰ 15⁰

Kit.
10⁰ 10⁶

Den
10⁰ 12⁰

Breakfast
10⁰ 12⁰

Dining
15⁴ 12⁰

Living
17⁴ 15⁴
10 ft. clg., typ.

Covered Porch

Width 32'-9"
Depth 99'-5"

© 1995 Looney Ricks Kiss Architects, Inc.

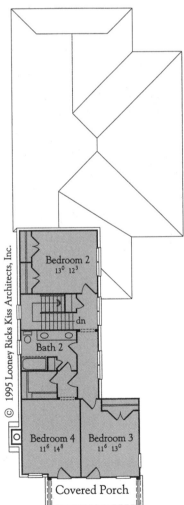

Bedroom 2
13⁰ 12³

Bath 2

Bedroom 4
11⁶ 14⁸

Bedroom 3
11⁶ 13⁰

Covered Porch

© 1995 Looney Ricks Kiss Architects, Inc.

TOWN

Strasbourg Lane

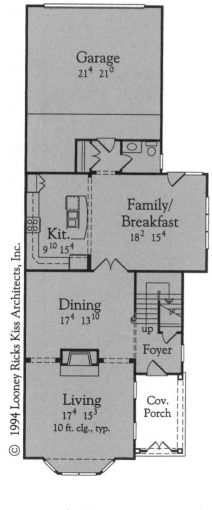

Garage
21⁴ 21⁰

Kit.
9¹⁰ 15⁴

**Family/
Breakfast**
18² 15⁴

Dining
17⁴ 13¹⁰

up

Foyer

Living
17⁴ 15³
10 ft. clg., typ.

**Cov.
Porch**

© 1994 Looney Ricks Kiss Architects, Inc.

Width 29'-4"
Depth 73'-0"

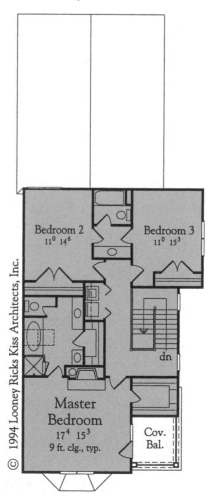

Bedroom 2
11⁰ 14⁶

Bedroom 3
11⁰ 15³

dn

**Master
Bedroom**
17⁴ 15³
9 ft. clg., typ.

**Cov.
Bal.**

© 1994 Looney Ricks Kiss Architects, Inc.

The curb appeal of this Town or Village home can be found in the dazzling details: a bay window, twin sconces illuminating a columned porch, a pretty portico and classic shutters. The foyer opens to the formal living and dining rooms, subtly defined by a through-fireplace. The gourmet kitchen overlooks a spacious family/breakfast area, which leads outdoors. The second floor includes a lavish master suite with a spa-style tub and a private covered balcony. The secondary sleeping area is connected by a gallery hall and a stair landing.

DESIGN BY
©*Looney Ricks Kiss
Architects, Inc.*

PLAN W513

First Floor: 1,237 square feet
Second Floor: 1,098 square feet
Total: 2,335 square feet

Bedrooms: 3
Bathrooms: 2½

TOWN **VILLAGE**

Georgetown Square

DESIGN BY
©*Looney Ricks Kiss
Architects, Inc.*

PLAN W514

First Floor: 1,545 square feet
Second Floor: 933 square feet
Total: 2,478 square feet

Bedrooms: 4
Bathrooms: 2½

A porch can be the beginning of a congenial relationship between a home and the neighborhood. Shuttered windows and square columns adorn this facade and offer a warm, welcoming greeting to guests and family. Inside, the formal living room features a centered hearth and opens to a spacious dining room. The family/breakfast room adjoins a well-planned kitchen that offers a pantry area. The master suite offers a garden tub, walk-in closet and knee-space vanity. Upstairs, a sitting area between the three bedrooms serves as a study or media area.

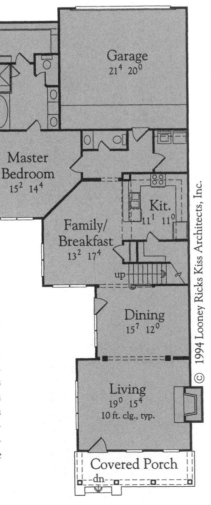

Garage
21⁴ 20⁰

Master
Bedroom
15² 14⁴

Kit.
11¹ 11⁰

Family/
Breakfast
13² 17⁴

up

Dining
15⁷ 12⁰

Living
19⁰ 15⁴
10 ft. clg., typ.

Covered Porch
dn

© 1994 Looney Ricks Kiss Architects, Inc.

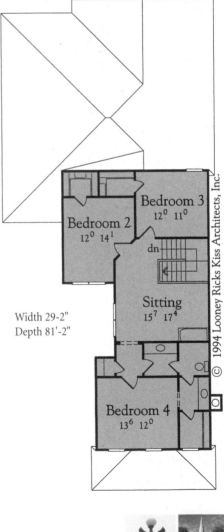

Width 29-2"
Depth 81'-2"

Bedroom 2
12⁰ 14¹

Bedroom 3
12⁰ 11⁰

dn

Sitting
15⁷ 17⁴

Bedroom 4
13⁶ 12⁰

© 1994 Looney Ricks Kiss Architects, Inc.

TOWN | VILLAGE

La Prairie Circle

The lovely facade of this Town or Village home is beautifully decorated with a double portico. A front bay window provides a stunning accent to the traditional exterior, while allowing natural light within. The formal living room features a fireplace and opens to the dining room, which leads outdoors. The gourmet kitchen has a walk-in pantry. The master suite is a relaxing space that includes a sitting bay, access to the side grounds, walk-in closet and soothing bath. A winding staircase offers an overlook to the living room.

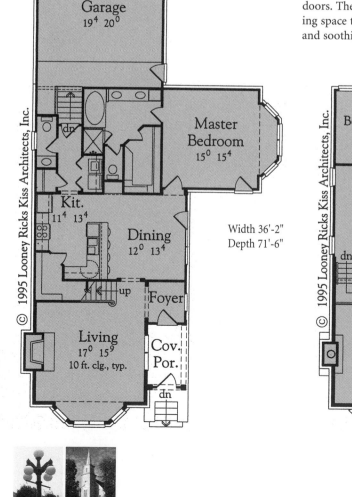

© 1995 Looney Ricks Kiss Architects, Inc.

Garage
19⁴ 20⁰

Master Bedroom
15⁰ 15⁴

Kit.
11⁴ 13⁴

Dining
12⁰ 13⁴

Width 36'-2"
Depth 71'-6"

Living
17⁰ 15⁹
10 ft. clg., typ.

Foyer

Cov. Por.

dn

up

dn

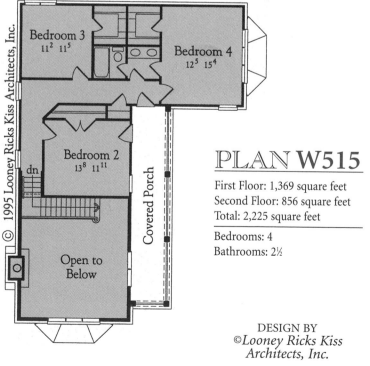

© 1995 Looney Ricks Kiss Architects, Inc.

Bedroom 3
11² 11⁵

Bedroom 4
12⁵ 15⁴

Bedroom 2
13⁸ 11¹¹

Open to Below

Covered Porch

dn

PLAN W515

First Floor: 1,369 square feet
Second Floor: 856 square feet
Total: 2,225 square feet

Bedrooms: 4
Bathrooms: 2½

DESIGN BY
©*Looney Ricks Kiss Architects, Inc.*

TOWN   VILLAGE

Westminster Lane

Shuttered windows and gabled rooflines prove that traditional style is timeless. The living room provides a fireplace, which is framed by views of the side property. The kitchen includes a walk-in pantry and easily serves the breakfast/family area. The master suite boasts two walk-in closets and an oversized corner shower. Three family bedrooms and a study/guest room are located upstairs and share two full baths.

PLAN W539

First Floor: 1,832 square feet
Second Floor: 1,164 square feet
Total: 2,996 square feet

Bedrooms: 4 or 5
Bathrooms: 3½

DESIGN BY
©*Looney Ricks Kiss Architects, Inc.*

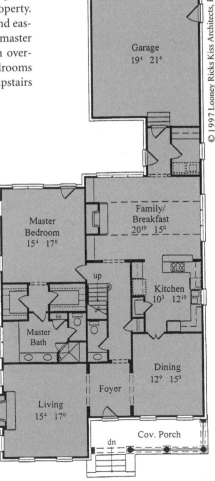

© 1997 Looney Ricks Kiss Architects, Inc.

Garage
19⁴ 21⁴

Family/
Breakfast
20¹⁰ 15⁰

Master
Bedroom
15⁴ 17⁰

Kitchen
10³ 12¹⁰

Master
Bath

up

Dining
12⁹ 15⁰

Living
15⁴ 17⁰

Foyer

Cov. Porch

dn

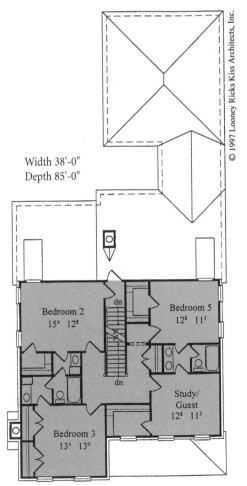

© 1997 Looney Ricks Kiss Architects, Inc.

Width 38'-0"
Depth 85'-0"

Bedroom 2
15⁴ 12⁸

Bedroom 5
12⁸ 11³

dn

dn

Study/
Guest
12⁸ 11³

Bedroom 3
13⁴ 13⁰

Town Village

Aldergrove Circle

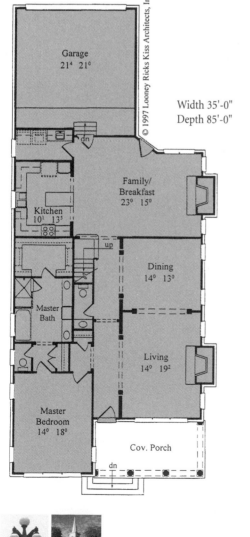

Garage
21⁴ 21⁰

Width 35'-0"
Depth 85'-0"

Family/
Breakfast
23⁰ 15⁰

Kitchen
10¹ 13⁵

Dining
14⁰ 13⁰

Master
Bath

Living
14⁰ 19²

Master
Bedroom
14⁰ 18⁰

Cov. Porch

© 1997 Looney Ricks Kiss Architects, Inc.

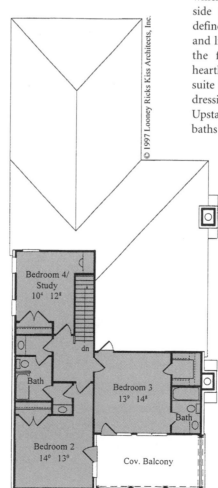

© 1997 Looney Ricks Kiss Architects, Inc.

Bedroom 4/
Study
10⁴ 12⁸

Bath

Bedroom 3
13⁹ 14⁸

Bath

Bedroom 2
14⁰ 13⁰

Cov. Balcony

A variety of window treatments creates a striking facade on this Town home. A gallery hall opens to the living room, which has a fireplace and wide views of the side property. Decorative columns help to define the spacious area between the dining and living rooms. Set to the rear of the plan, the family/breakfast area enjoys its own hearth, framed by tall windows. The master suite features a walk-in closet, two vanities, a dressing area and additional linen storage. Upstairs, three family bedrooms share two baths and a covered balcony.

PLAN W538

First Floor: 1,887 square feet
Second Floor: 899 square feet
Total: 2,786 square feet

Bedrooms: 4
Bathrooms: 3½

DESIGN BY
©*Looney Ricks Kiss
Architects, Inc.*

TOWN VILLAGE

East Prospect Place

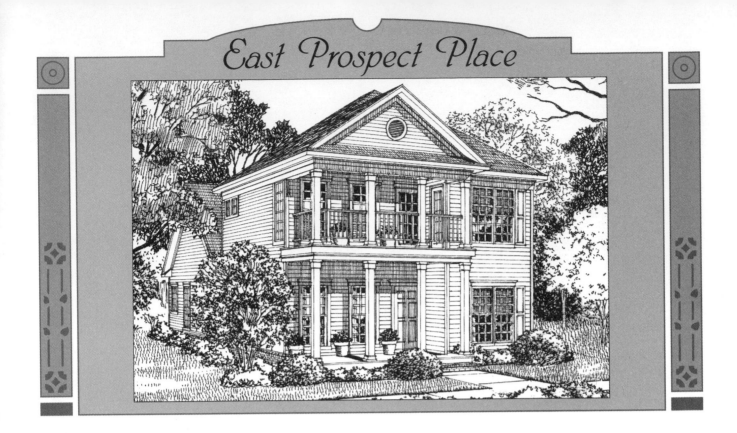

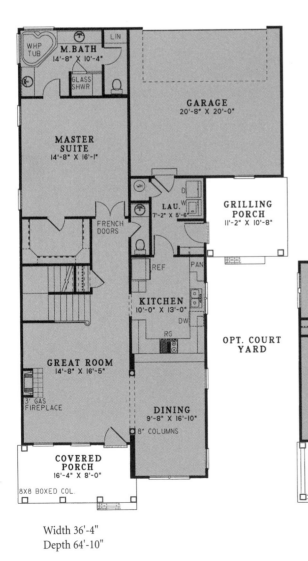

Width 36'-4"
Depth 64'-10"

This stunning double portico displays a classic touch to a Town facade with a sweet, slightly Southern personality. A paneled entry leads to a spacious great room, complete with a gas fireplace and extended-tile hearth. With the spacious dining room to the right, entertaining is a cinch. The master suite is thoughtfully placed to the rear and provides French doors to the gallery hall. On the second floor, two family bedrooms share a full bath and enjoy a porch and computer desk. Please specify crawlspace or slab foundation when ordering.

PLAN Y059

First Floor: 1,298 square feet
Second Floor: 624 square feet
Total: 1,922 square feet

Bedrooms: 3
Bathrooms: 2½

DESIGN BY
©*Michael E. Nelson*
Nelson Design Group, LLC

TOWN

Weybosset Street

Transoms and muntin windows deck out this Town facade, enhanced by a welcoming covered porch. The interior begins with an open arrangement of the formal living and dining rooms, subtly defined by a through-fireplace shared with the family room. The windows of this home have been thoughtfully oriented to one side of the plan for privacy. Upstairs, two family bedrooms share a bath, while the master suite makes splendid use of space with a walk-in closet and compartment bath.

DESIGN BY
©*Park House*
Properties, LLC

PLAN E503

First Floor: 752 square feet
Second Floor: 782 square feet
Total: 1,534 square feet

Bedrooms: 3
Bathrooms: 2½

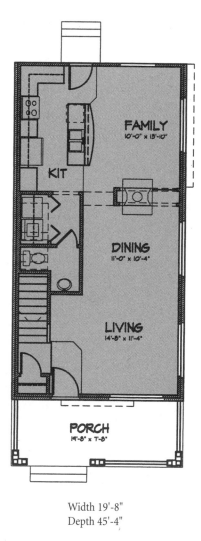

FAMILY
10'-0" x 15'-10"

KIT

DINING
11'-0" x 10'-4"

LIVING
14'-8" x 11'-4"

PORCH
14'-8" x 7'-8"

Width 19'-8"
Depth 45'-4"

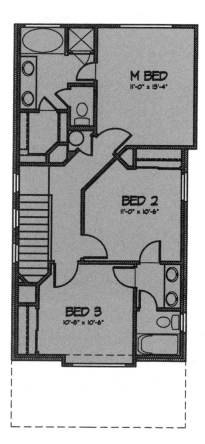

M BED
11'-0" x 15'-4"

BED 2
11'-0" x 10'-6"

BED 3
10'-8" x 10'-6"

TOWN

Sweet Marian Lane

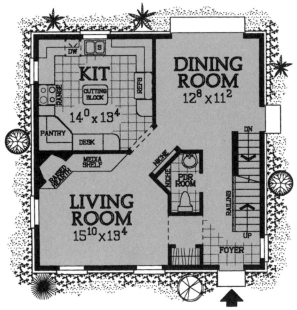

Width 28'-8"
Depth 28'-8"

Perfect for a small lot, this attractive brick home offers Colonial detailing and a practical floor plan. The living room features a raised-hearth fireplace and built-in media shelf, while the dining room offers access to the backyard. The kitchen includes a built-in desk, pantry and cutting-block island. The second floor consists of two bedrooms: a master suite offering a walk-in closet, garden tub and linen closet, and a family bedroom with its own bath.

DESIGN BY
©*Home Planners*

PLAN 3524

First Floor: 822 square feet
Second Floor: 766 square feet
Total: 1,588 square feet
Bonus Room: 405 square feet

Bedrooms: 2
Bathrooms: 2½

L

QUOTE ONE®
Cost to build? See page 182
to order complete cost estimate
to build this house in your area!

TOWN | VILLAGE

Chester Hill Drive

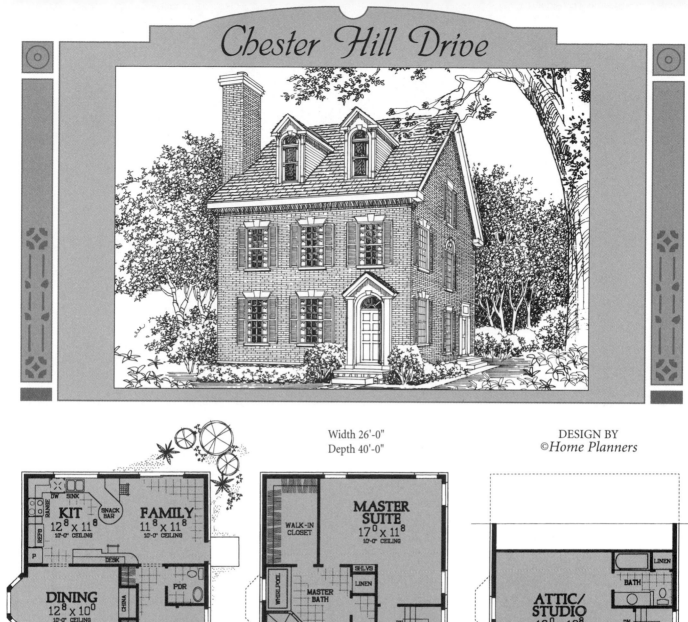

Width 26'-0"
Depth 40'-0"

DESIGN BY
©Home Planners

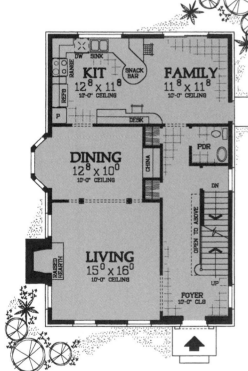

KIT 12⁸ x 11⁸ 10'-0" CEILING

FAMILY 11⁸ x 11⁸ 10'-0" CEILING

DW SINK SNACK BAR RANGE REFG P DESK

DINING 12⁸ x 10⁰ 10'-0" CEILING

CHINA PDR

DN OPEN TO ABOVE

LIVING 15⁰ x 16⁰ 10'-0" CEILING

RAISED HEARTH

UP

FOYER 10'-0" CL8

WALK-IN CLOSET

MASTER SUITE 17⁰ x 11⁸ 10'-0" CEILING

SHLVS LINEN

WHIRLPOOL

MASTER BATH

S

BATH

DN RAILING OPEN TO BELOW UP

BEDROOM 15⁰ x 10⁸ 10'-0" CEILING

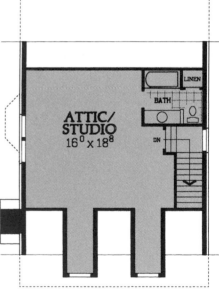

ATTIC/ STUDIO 16⁰ x 18⁸

LINEN BATH DN

TOWN   VILLAGE

Capstones and cornices lend Colonial charm to this quaint Town or Village design—and efficient floor planning makes it very livable. The foyer opens to a formal living room with a raised-hearth fireplace. Decorative columns help to define the dining room, which has a bay window. The family room and kitchen share a snack bar and views of the rear property. On the second floor, a secluded master suite boasts a sumptuous bath with a whirlpool tub, two vanities and a sizable walk-in closet. A third-floor studio with plans for a full bath offers twin window dormers.

PLAN 3523

First Floor: 1,068 square feet
Second Floor: 982 square feet
Third Floor: 548 square feet
Total: 2,598 square feet

Bedrooms: 3
Bathrooms: 3½

L D

Market Square

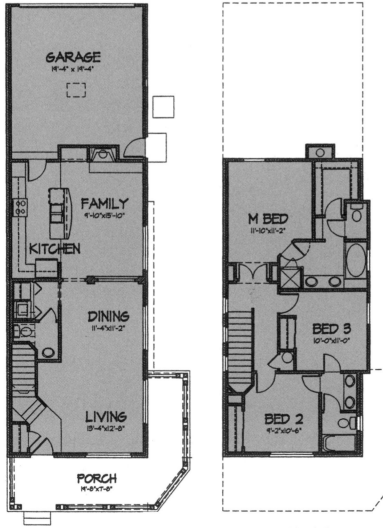

GARAGE
19'-4" x 19'-4"

FAMILY
9'-10"x15'-10"

KITCHEN

DINING
11'-4"x11'-2"

LIVING
13'-4"x12'-8"

PORCH
14'-8"xT-8"

M BED
11'-10"x11'-2"

BED 3
10'-0"x11'-0"

BED 2
9'-2"x10'-6"

Gabled rooflines and a brick facade accentuate the exterior of this traditional home, while a wrap-around porch lends a "welcome home" feeling. The open living and dining rooms complement casual living space that's thoughtfully placed to the rear of the plan. The family room is catered to by a well-organized kitchen. Upstairs, two family bedrooms share a compartmented bath that has two vanities. The master suite enjoys an entry of lovely French doors, a lavish bath with separate tub and shower, and a walk-in closet.

PLAN E532

First Floor: 830 square feet
Second Floor: 797 square feet
Total: 1,627 square feet

Bedrooms: 3
Bathrooms: 2½

DESIGN BY
©*Park House Properties, LLC*

Plans are not to be sold or built within the state of Arkansas.

Width 25'-8"
Depth 70'-8"

TOWN

Macy Rock Lane

A brick-and-siding facade, double-hung windows and a "welcome home" porch determine the comfortable look and feel of this Town facade. Windows are placed on one side of the plan to promote privacy yet permit plenty of natural light inside. The living and dining areas invite entertaining on a grand or small scale. The family room is warmed by a fireplace and the fragrant aromas of home cooking in the nearby kitchen. The master suite employs double doors that sweep open to the private bath, walk-in closet and dressing area.

PLAN E506

First Floor: 830 square feet
Second Floor: 797 square feet
Total: 1,627 square feet

Bedrooms: 3
Bathrooms: 2½

DESIGN BY
©Park House
Properties, LLC

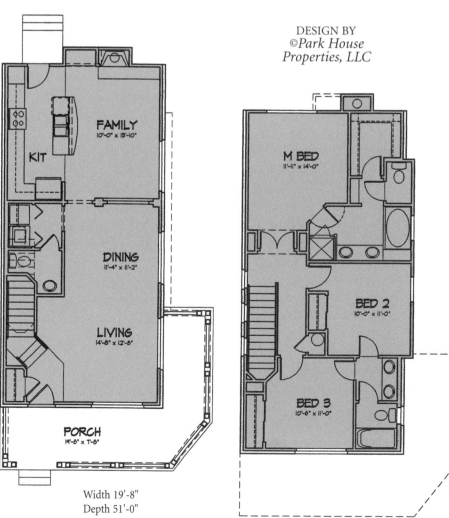

KIT

FAMILY
10'-0" x 15'-10"

DINING
11'-4" x 11'-2"

LIVING
14'-8" x 12'-8"

PORCH
19'-8" x 7'-8"

Width 19'-8"
Depth 51'-0"

M BED
11'-11" x 14'-0"

BED 2
10'-0" x 11'-0"

BED 3
10'-6" x 11'-0"

TOWN

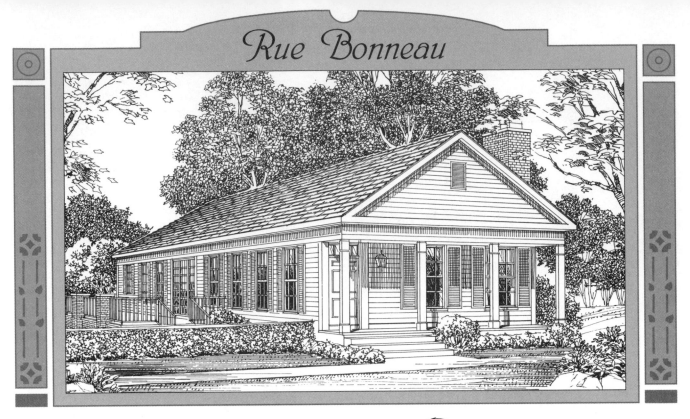

Rue Bonneau

PLAN 2698

Square Footage: 1,700

Bedrooms: 2
Bathrooms: 2

Here is the quintessential narrow-lot house, based on the "shotgun" house, a popular style found in 19th-Century New Orleans and many other Southern towns. To meet the demands of today's homeowner, this version forsakes the rear door in favor of two full baths. A spacious interior offers formal rooms as well as casual space, each with a fireplace. The kitchen serves a snack counter and is just a few steps away from the formal dining room. The family room leads outdoors to an entertainment terrace.

DESIGN BY
©Home Planners

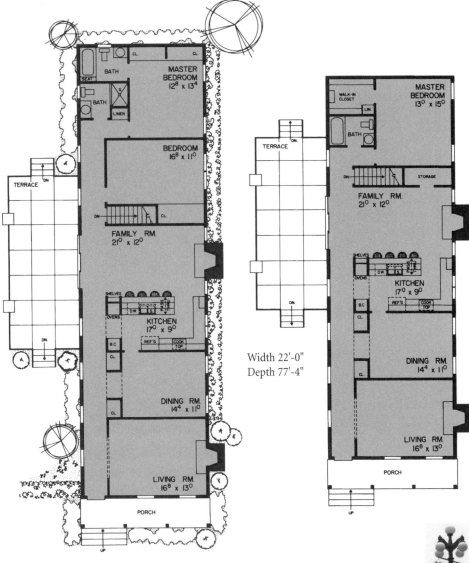

Width 22'-0"
Depth 77'-4"

TOWN

White Rock Way

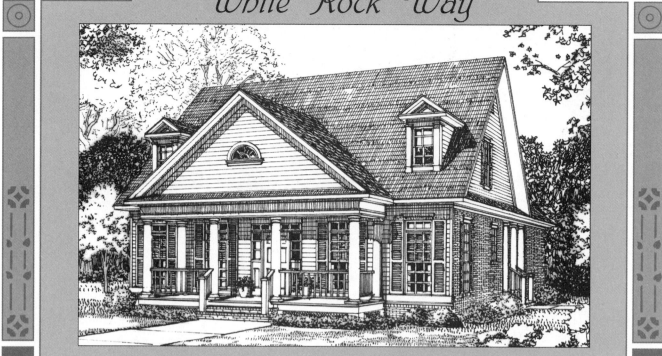

A protruding porch with decorative columns and a stunning pediment complements twin dormers and shuttered windows on this Town home. Inside, a very comfortable interior begins with a large foyer, which directs traffic to either the formal dining room set off by decorative columns or the office/study through elegant French doors. A pampering master bath includes a compartmented toilet, shower, separate garden tub, dual vanities and a walk-in closet. Please specify crawlspace or slab foundation when ordering.

PLAN Y058

First Floor: 1,698 square feet
Second Floor: 533 square feet
Total: 2,231 square feet
Bonus Room: 394 square feet

Bedrooms: 4
Bathrooms: 2½

DESIGN BY
©*Michael E. Nelson*
Nelson Design Group, LLC

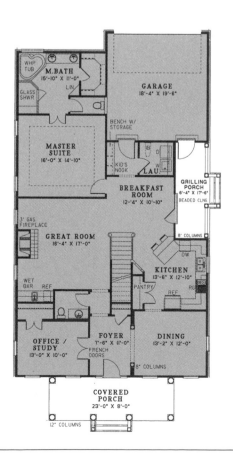

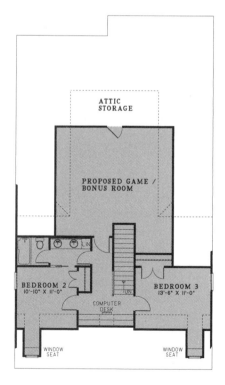

Width 35'-4"
Depth 71'-6"

TOWN

Maple Falls Circle

The front covered porch of this Town home has a sweet disposition, set off by a charming single dormer. Inside, a spacious great room with an optional gas fireplace can handle a crowd and still be cozy enough for just the family. Casual dining will take place in the breakfast room or at the snack bar, served by the U-shaped kitchen. The family bedrooms to one side of the home share a full hall bath. Please specify crawlspace or slab foundation when ordering.

PLAN Y054

Square Footage: 985

Bedrooms: 2

Bathrooms: 1

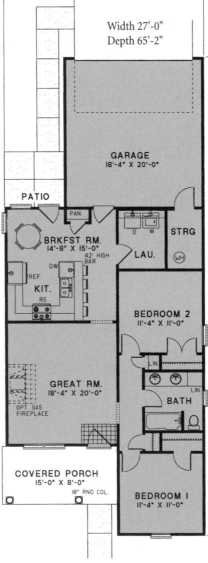

Width 27'-0"
Depth 65'-2"

GARAGE
18'-4" X 20'-0"

PATIO

PAN

STRG

BRKFST RM.
14'-8" X 15'-0"

42" HIGH
BAR

D   W

LAU.

WH

DW

REF.

KIT.

RG

BEDROOM 2
11'-4" X 11'-0"

LIN

GREAT RM.
18'-4" X 20'-0"

LIN

OPT. GAS
FIREPLACE

BATH

COVERED PORCH
15'-0" X 8'-0"

10" RND COL.

BEDROOM 1
11'-4" X 11'-0"

DESIGN BY
©*Michael E. Nelson*
Nelson Design Group, LLC

TOWN

Clemence Avenue

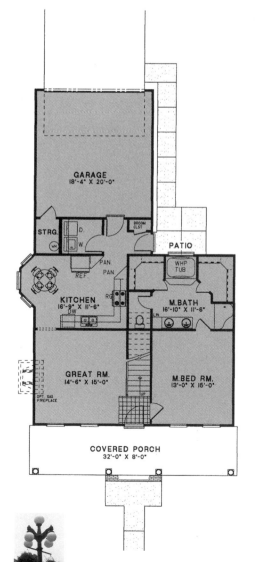

Width 34'-8"
Depth 61'-10"

GARAGE
18'-4" X 20'-0"

STRG.

BROOM CLST

PAN. PAN

PATIO

REF.

WHP TUB

KITCHEN
16'-8" X 11'-6"

M.BATH
16'-10" X 11'-6"

GREAT RM.
14'-6" X 15'-0"

M.BED RM.
13'-0" X 15'-0"

OPT. GAS FIREPLACE

UP

COVERED PORCH
32'-0" X 8'-0"

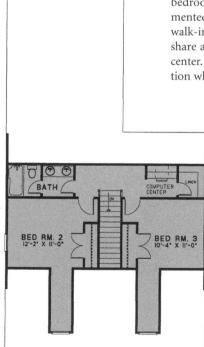

BATH

COMPUTER CENTER

LINEN

DN

BED RM. 2
12'-2" X 11'-0"

BED RM. 3
10'-4" X 11'-0"

This quaint cottage greets guests with a columned porch and tall windows. Inside, the great room features an optional gas fireplace and accommodates crowd-size get-togethers or a quiet evening at home. The eat-in kitchen provides plenty of natural light through a bay window. The master bedroom includes two vanities, a compartmented toilet, separate shower and tub, and two walk-in closets. Upstairs, secondary bedrooms share a full hall bath and space for a computer center. Please specify crawlspace or slab foundation when ordering.

PLAN Y076

First Floor: 990 square feet
Second Floor: 551 square feet
Total: 1,541 square feet

Bedrooms: 3
Bathrooms: 2

DESIGN BY
©Michael E. Nelson
Nelson Design Group, LLC

TOWN

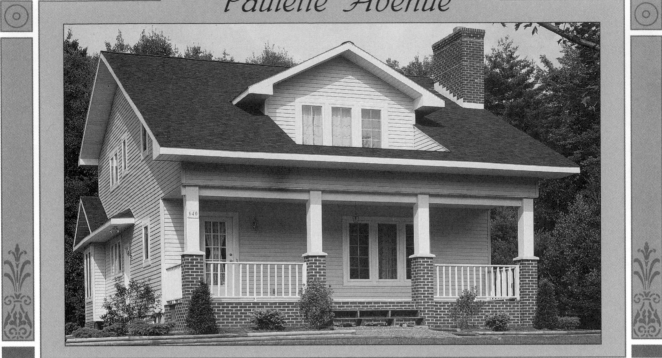

Paulette Avenue

This home, as shown in the photograph, may differ from the actual blueprints. For more detailed information, please check the floor plans carefully.

PLAN 3316

First Floor: 1,111 square feet
Second Floor: 886 square feet
Total: 1,997 square feet

Bedrooms: 3
Bathrooms: 2½

L

This charming Village plan offers three bedrooms and a spacious living area. An open arrangement of the formal rooms provides space for planned events or family gatherings, and makes it cozy with a fireplace. Other welcome amenities include: box-bay windows in the breakfast and dining rooms, a planning desk and pass-through snack bar in the kitchen, and an open two-story foyer. On the second floor, the master suite boasts a dressing room, twin vanities and a whirlpool tub. Two secondary bedrooms enjoy great views and share a bath.

Width 34'-1"
Depth 50'-0"

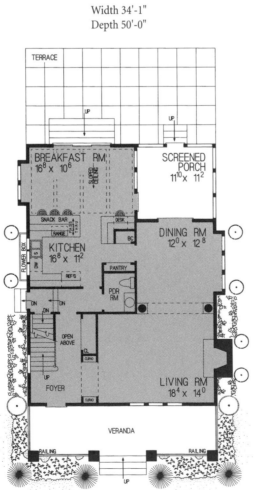

DESIGN BY
©*Home Planners*

QUOTE ONE®

Cost to build? See page 182
to order complete cost estimate
to build this house in your area!

VILLAGE

Midtown Village

Parks, Promenades and Distinctive Houses

Human-scale elements such as columns and porches mix amiably with diverse architectural styles.

Versatile Plans for Singles, Couples and Families

Tupelo Avenue

This charming Village design has plenty of curb appeal with a covered porch that welcomes guests. An open foyer continues the warm welcome and announces the grand interior. The great room features a built-in media center and fireplace. The master suite has a luxurious bath with walk-in closet, knee-space vanity, compartmented toilet, whirlpool tub and separate shower. A guest/study accesses a full bath. Upstairs, two family bedrooms share a full hall bath. Please specify basement, crawlspace or slab foundation when ordering.

DESIGN BY
©*Michael E. Nelson*
Nelson Design Group, LLC

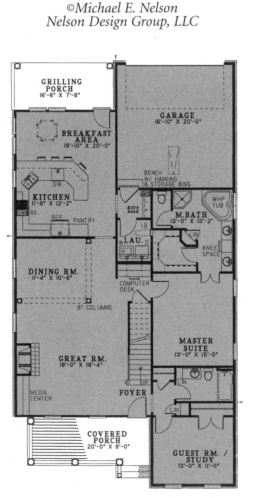

GRILLING PORCH
16'-6" X 7'-8"

GARAGE
18'-10" X 20'-0"

BREAKFAST AREA
18'-10" X 20'-0"

BENCH W/ HANGING & STORAGE BINS

KITCHEN
11'-8" X 12'-2"

DW.

REF. PANTRY

KID'S NOOK

M.BATH
13'-0" X 13'-2"

WHP TUB

LAU.

KNEE SPACE

DINING RM.
11'-4" X 10'-6"

COMPUTER DESK

8" COLUMNS

GREAT RM.
18'-0" X 18'-4"

MASTER SUITE
13'-0" X 15'-0"

MEDIA CENTER

FOYER

COVERED PORCH
20'-0" X 8'-0"

GUEST RM. / STUDY
13'-0" X 11'-0"

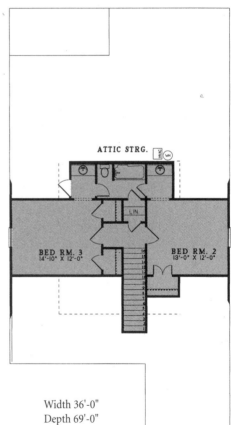

ATTIC STRG.

BED RM. 3
14'-10" X 12'-0"

LIN.

BED RM. 2
13'-0" X 12'-0"

Width 36'-0"
Depth 69'-0"

PLAN Y040

First Floor: 1,694 square feet
Second Floor: 558 square feet
Total: 2,252 square feet

Bedrooms: 3
Bathrooms: 3

VILLAGE

Mark Twain Drive

Tall windows, charming planters, a columned L-shaped porch and dormers make this home a pleasure to look upon. The great room overlooks the wraparound porch and features a gas fireplace. There are no catering obstacles from the gourmet kitchen, which includes a snack bar close to the breakfast nook and dining room. The master suite offers bath amenities, including a large walk-in closet, whirlpool tub, separate shower and dual vanities. Two secondary bedrooms share a full bath. Please specify crawlspace or slab foundation when ordering.

PLAN Y067

Square Footage: 1,845
Bonus Room: 1,191 square feet

Bedrooms: 3
Bathrooms: 2

DESIGN BY
©*Michael E. Nelson*
Nelson Design Group, LLC

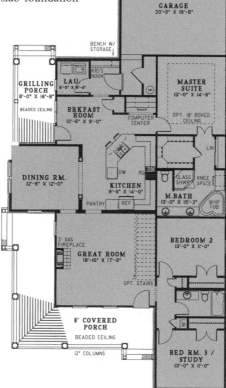

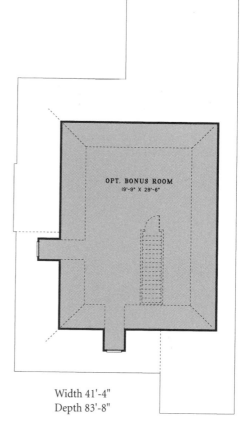

Width 41'-4"
Depth 83'-8"

VILLAGE

Newsom Circle

DESIGN BY
©Michael E. Nelson
Nelson Design Group, LLC

Width 45'-6"
Depth 56'-10"

PLAN Y078

Square Footage: 1,289

Bedrooms: 3
Bathrooms: 2

Unusual rooflines, shuttered windows, double gables and a columned porch accent this home. The foyer leads to the great room which has a boxed ceiling and gas fireplace. The dining room is placed near the U-shaped kitchen with snack bar. The private master bedroom is located in the front of the home with a walk-in closet and full bath. Two family bedrooms share a full hall bath and both have walk-in closets. Please specify basement, crawlspace or slab foundation when ordering.

Floor plan labels

GARAGE 17'-8" X 19'-4"

LAU. 6'-6" X 6'-10"

DINING 9'-4" X 11'-0"

GRILLING PORCH 6'-0" X 13'-0"

PAN.

REF.

KIT. 11'-0" X 12'-0"

RG.

DW

BEDROOM 2 10'-4" X 10'-6"

GREAT RM. 16'-2" X 15'-6" 10' BOXED CEILING

GAS FIREPLACE

WH

BATH

LIN

FOYER 4'-8" X 10'-2"

BEDROOM 3 / OFFICE 10'-4" X 10'-6"

MASTER SUITE 11'-2" X 12'-0" 10' BOXED CEILING

COVERED PORCH 15'-8" X 6'-6"

8" COLUMNS

VILLAGE

Enfield Drive

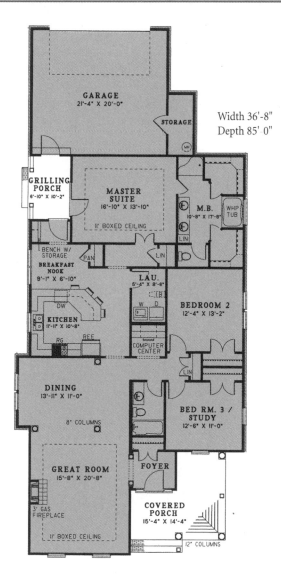

GARAGE
21'-4" X 20'-0"

STORAGE

Width 36'-8"
Depth 85'-0"

WH

GRILLING PORCH
6'-10" X 10'-2"

MASTER SUITE
16'-10" X 13'-10"

11' BOXED CEILING

M.B.
10'-8" X 17'-8"

WHP TUB

LIN

BENCH W/ STORAGE

PAN

LIN

BREAKFAST NOOK
9'-1" X 6'-10"

LAU.
5'-4" X 8'-6"

DW

W D

KITCHEN
11'-11" X 10'-8"

RG   REF

BEDROOM 2
12'-4" X 13'-2"

COMPUTER CENTER

LIN

DINING
13'-11" X 11'-0"

8" COLUMNS

BED RM. 3 / STUDY
12'-6" X 11'-0"

GREAT ROOM
15'-8" X 20'-8"

FOYER

3' GAS FIREPLACE

11' BOXED CEILING

COVERED PORCH
15'-4" X 14'-4"

12" COLUMNS

Decorative lintels and stylish shuttered windows complement the columned L-shaped porch and gables, for a simple traditional look. The entryway reveals the great room with boxed ceiling and gas fireplace and leads to an open dining room defined by columns. The master suite includes a whirlpool tub, separate shower, dual vanities, compartmented toilet and two walk-in closets. The two family bedrooms share a full hall bath. Please specify crawlspace or slab foundation when ordering.

PLAN Y068

Square Footage: 1,934

Bedrooms: 3
Bathrooms: 2

DESIGN BY
©*Michael E. Nelson*
Nelson Design Group, LLC

VILLAGE

Howard Avenue

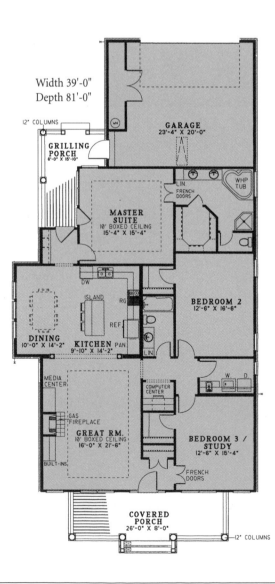

This brick-and-siding exterior offers a columned porch and dormers that highlight this traditional home. Inside, the great room boasts a built-in media center and fireplace and opens to the dining room and gourmet kitchen. The master suite enjoys a walk-in closet and luxurious bath. Bedroom 2 provides a walk-in closet and leads to a hall bath. Nearby, a flex room easily converts to a study or a guest bedroom. Please specify crawlspace or slab foundation when ordering.

PLAN Y055

Square Footage: 1,832

Bedrooms: 3
Bathrooms: 2

DESIGN BY
©*Michael E. Nelson*
Nelson Design Group, LLC

Width 39'-0"
Depth 81'-0"

12' COLUMNS

GARAGE
23'-4" X 20'-0"

GRILLING PORCH
6'-0" X 15'-10"

WH

LIN

FRENCH DOORS

WHP TUB

MASTER SUITE
10' BOXED CEILING
15'-4" X 15'-4"

DW

ISLAND

RG

REF

DINING
10'-0" X 14'-2"

KITCHEN
9'-10" X 14'-2"

PAN

LIN

BEDROOM 2
12'-6" X 16'-6"

MEDIA CENTER

COMPUTER CENTER

W. D.

GAS FIREPLACE

GREAT RM.
10' BOXED CEILING
16'-0" X 21'-6"

BUILT-INS

BEDROOM 3 / STUDY
12'-6" X 15'-4"

FRENCH DOORS

COVERED PORCH
26'-0" X 8'-0"

12' COLUMNS

VILLAGE

Woodstock Lane

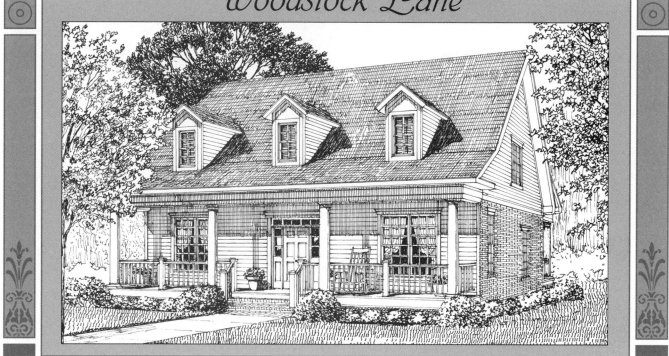

This well-balanced design includes three dormers, a columned porch and a charming brick-and-siding exterior. The foyer ushers guests into the formal dining room or through the French doors of the study/guest room. The master suite provides a walk-in closet, whirlpool tub, separate shower and twin vanities. The great room is enhanced by a focal-point fireplace and built-in media center. Upstairs, two family bedrooms share a walk-through bath. Please specify basement, crawlspace or slab foundation when ordering.

Width 37'-0"
Depth 73'-0"

PLAN Y041

First Floor: 1,713 square feet
Second Floor: 610 square feet
Total: 2,323 square feet
Bonus Room: 384 square feet

Bedrooms: 3
Bathrooms: 3

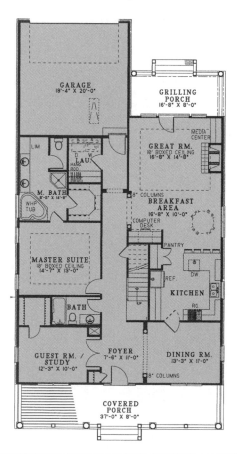

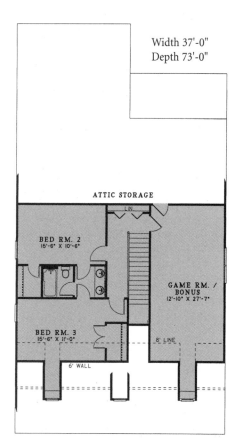

DESIGN BY
©*Michael E. Nelson*
Nelson Design Group, LLC

TOWN   VILLAGE

Coatsworth Drive

Traditional lines allow this home to fit into an established neighborhood seamlessly yet with an exceptional presence. The open interior includes a spacious great room, made cozy with a gas fireplace. The formal dining area is easily served by the well-planned galley kitchen. An attractive box ceiling highlights the master suite, placed to the rear of the plan. Two family bedrooms share a full hall bath with two lavatories. Please specify basement, crawlspace or slab foundation when ordering.

PLAN Y057

Square Footage: 1,317

Bedrooms: 3
Bathrooms: 2

DESIGN BY
©Michael E. Nelson
Nelson Design Group, LLC

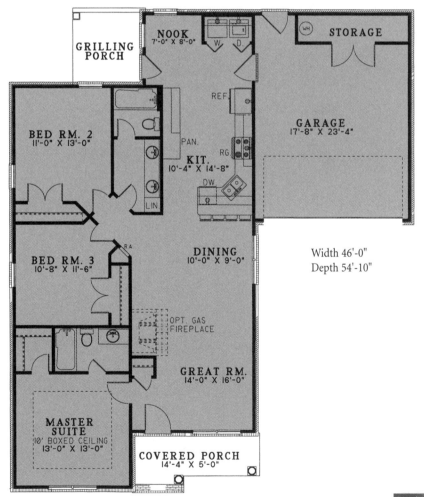

GRILLING PORCH

NOOK
7'-0" X 8'-0"

STORAGE

REF.

GARAGE
17'-8" X 23'-4"

BED RM. 2
11'-0" X 13'-0"

PAN.

RG.

KIT.
10'-4" X 14'-8"

DW.

LIN

BED RM. 3
10'-8" X 11'-6"

DINING
10'-0" X 9'-0"

Width 46'-0"
Depth 54'-10"

OPT. GAS FIREPLACE

GREAT RM.
14'-0" X 16'-0"

MASTER SUITE
10' BOXED CEILING
13'-0" X 13'-0"

COVERED PORCH
14'-4" X 5'-0"

VILLAGE

Holly Hill Circle

Distinctive accents such as decorative lintels, shuttered windows, a double-gabled roof and a charming entry porch adorn this home. The foyer introduces the formal dining room, defined by decorative columns, and the great room, which provides a gas fireplace. The kitchen sports a snack bar for meals on-the-run. The secluded master suite offers a boxed ceiling, walk-in closet, whirlpool tub and separate shower. Please specify crawlspace or slab foundation when ordering.

PLAN Y074

Square Footage: 1,627

Bedrooms: 3
Bathrooms: 2

DESIGN BY
©Michael E. Nelson
Nelson Design Group, LLC

MASTER BATH
15'-8" X 8'-4"

WHP TUB

MASTER SUITE
10' BOXED CEILING
15'-8" X 12'-0"

GRILLING PORCH
11'-4" X 8'-0"

LAU.
7'-6" X 5'-6"

STORAGE
6'-8" X 5'-6"

BRKFAST RM.
11'-0" X 8'-10"

BED RM. 2
10'-6" X 12'-4"

BED RM. 3
10'-6" X 13'-10"

GARAGE
19'-0" X 20'-0"

KITCHEN
11'-0" X 13'-8"

PANTRY

REF.

DW

RG

FOYER

GREAT RM.
10' BOXED CEILING
15'-0" X 18'-4"

GAS FIREPLACE

ENTRY PORCH

DINING RM.
10' CEILING
10'-8" X 11'-6"

8" COLUMNS

10" COLUMNS

Width 52'-8"
Depth 60'-6"

Worcester Avenue

© 1996 Donald A. Gardner Architects, Inc.

This compact plan offers plenty of space for families just starting out or empty-nesters scaling down. The great room's cathedral ceiling, combined with the openness of the adjoining dining room and kitchen, create a sense of spaciousness beyond this plan's modest square footage. The dining room is enlarged by a bay window, while a picture window with arched top allows light into the great room. The master suite features ample closet space and a skylit bath that boasts a double-sink vanity.

PLAN 7749

Square Footage: 1,372

Bedrooms: 3
Bathrooms: 2

DESIGN BY
*Donald A. Gardner
Architects, Inc.*

Width 46'-0"
Depth 61'-10"

© 1996 Donald A. Gardner Architects, Inc.

VILLAGE

West Mary Lane

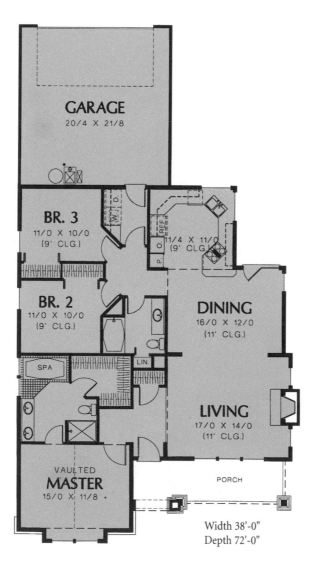

GARAGE
20/4 X 21/8

BR. 3
11/0 X 10/0
(9' CLG.)

BR. 2
11/0 X 10/0
(9' CLG.)

DINING
16/0 X 12/0
(11' CLG.)

11/4 X 11/0
(9' CLG.)

W. D.

P.O. REF

SPA

LIN.

LIVING
17/0 X 14/0
(11' CLG.)

VAULTED MASTER
15/0 X 11/8 +

PORCH

Width 38'-0"
Depth 72'-0"

This charming cottage-style home offers a spacious living room with a focal-point fireplace and plenty of transoms to let in the light. The U-shaped kitchen provides an angled double sink and easily serves the formal dining room, which leads outdoors. A secluded master suite features a lavish bath with a spa-style tub and a walk-in closet. Two secondary bedrooms reside to the rear of the plan and share a full hall bath.

PLAN 7465

Square Footage: 1,520

Bedrooms: 3
Bathrooms: 2

DESIGN BY
©*Alan Mascord Design Associates, Inc.*

VILLAGE

Stonington Road

PLAN E512

Square Footage: 1,976

Bedrooms: 4
Bathrooms: 2

Width 44'-8"
Depth 54'-0"

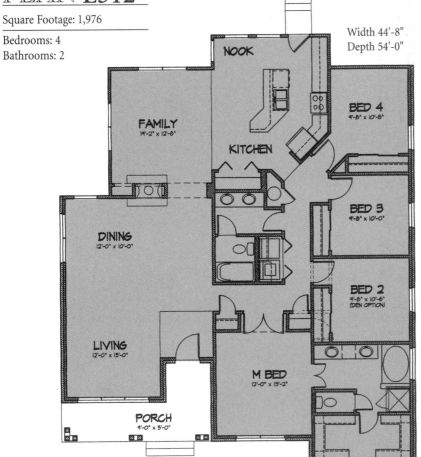

NOOK

FAMILY
14'-2" x 12'-8"

KITCHEN

BED 4
9'-8" x 10'-8"

DINING
12'-0" x 10'-0"

BED 3
9'-8" x 10'-0"

BED 2
9'-8" x 10'-6"
(DEN OPTION)

LIVING
12'-0" x 15'-0"

M BED
12'-0" x 15'-2"

PORCH
9'-0" x 5'-0"

Clerestory windows and balanced dormers catch the eye and add appeal as well as function. The recessed entry leads guests into the formal living room, which flows into the open dining area. The family room shares a see-through fireplace with the dining room and is easily served by the nearby island kitchen. Three family bedrooms share a full hall bath. The master bedroom greets its occupants with French doors to both the bedroom and a bath that includes a walk-in closet, separate tub and shower, dual vanities and compartmented toilet.

DESIGN BY
©*Park House
Properties, LLC*

Plans are not to be sold or built within the state of Arkansas.

VILLAGE   EDGE

Somerville Place

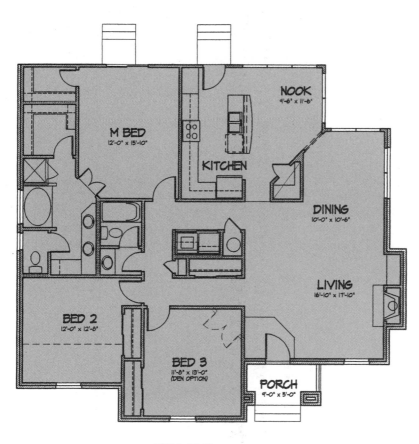

Width 47'-0"
Depth 46'-0"

M BED
12'-0" x 15'-10"

NOOK
9'-6" x 11'-6"

KITCHEN

DINING
10'-0" x 10'-6"

LIVING
16'-10" x 17'-10"

BED 2
12'-0" x 12'-8"

BED 3
11'-8" x 13'-0"
(DEN OPTION)

PORCH
9'-0" x 5'-0"

PLAN E519

Square Footage: 1,716

Bedrooms: 3
Bathrooms: 2

This rustic facade complements its natural surroundings and introduces a thoroughly modern interior, complete with a morning nook and gourmet kitchen. Many windows and walls of glass promote natural light, offer wide views and provide great indoor/outdoor flow. A foyer greets the living/dining area, which is warmed by the fireplace or sunshine through the windows. A large island kitchen has a pantry and breakfast nook. The master bedroom has two walk-in closets and a spacious bath with French doors.

DESIGN BY
©*Park House*
Properties, LLC

VILLAGE

Roxbury Lane

PLAN W519

First Floor: 1,680 square feet
Second Floor: 950 square feet
Total: 2,630 square feet

Bedrooms: 3
Bathrooms: 2½

The timeless structural elements of simpler times, such as the exposed rafters, enhance the quiet curb appeal of this Craftsman-style Village home. A covered entry porch topped with a quaint balustrade announces the sophisticated but casual nature of this comfortable interior. Elegant columns help to define the formal dining room. The family/living room enjoys a focal-point fireplace and provides access to a rear covered porch. On the second floor, each of the two secondary bedrooms has its own door to a shared bath. The family will enjoy gathering on the rear covered porch.

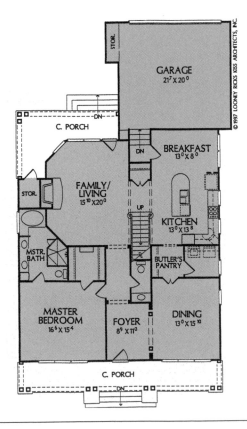

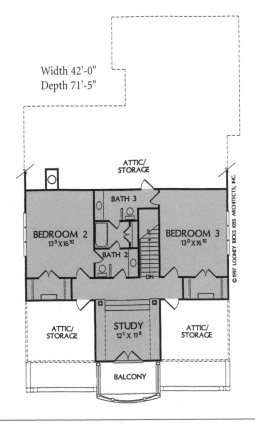

Width 42'-0"
Depth 71'-5"

DESIGN BY
©*Looney Ricks Kiss Architects, Inc.*

Wildwood Circle

Here's a home that marries the best of past and present. A stunning facade displays Craftsman characteristics and leads to an amenity-packed interior, complete with a butler's pantry, gourmet kitchen and second-floor study. The foyer extends a warm welcome to guests and leads to the formal dining room, which enjoys front-property views. A family room with a fireplace provides access to a rear covered porch. The master suite boasts a walk-in closet, dual basins, and separate tub and shower. Upstairs, two secondary bedrooms share a full bath. An open study is a great place for a quiet read or homework.

Width 41'-8"
Depth 71'-2"

DESIGN BY
©*Looney Ricks Kiss Architects, Inc.*

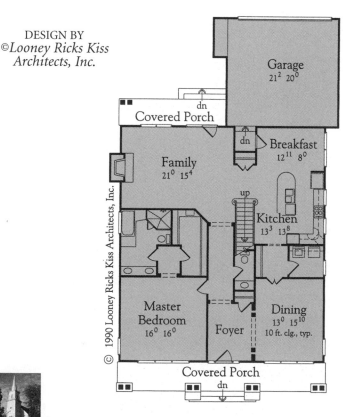

© 1990 Looney Ricks Kiss Architects, Inc.

Garage
21² 20⁰

dn

Covered Porch

dn

Breakfast
12¹¹ 8⁰

Family
21⁰ 15⁴

up

Kitchen
13³ 13⁸

Master Bedroom
16⁰ 16⁰

Foyer

Dining
13⁰ 15¹⁰
10 ft. clg., typ.

Covered Porch

dn

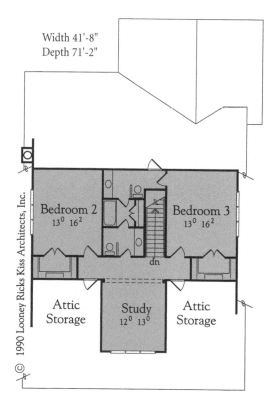

© 1990 Looney Ricks Kiss Architects, Inc.

Bedroom 2
13⁰ 16²

Bedroom 3
13⁰ 16²

dn

Attic Storage

Study
12⁰ 13⁰

Attic Storage

PLAN W520

First Floor: 1,790 square feet
Second Floor: 860 square feet
Total: 2,650 square feet

Bedrooms: 3
Bathrooms: 2½

VILLAGE

Traditional Neighborhood Home Plans 75

Lopez Island Way

PLAN 3496

Square Footage: 2,033

Bedrooms: 3
Bathrooms: 2

L

Get more out of your home-building dollars with this unique one-story bungalow. A covered front porch provides sheltered entry into a spacious living room. A built-in bookshelf and a decorative column are special touches here. The dining room enjoys a sloped ceiling, a wet bar and direct access to the rear covered patio. The master suite provides a sitting area, patio access and a luxurious bath. Two secondary bedrooms share a full hall bath.

DESIGN BY
©*Home Planners*

QUOTE ONE®
Cost to build? See page 182
to order complete cost estimate
to build this house in your area!

Width 47'-6"
Depth 61'-6"

Victoria Circle

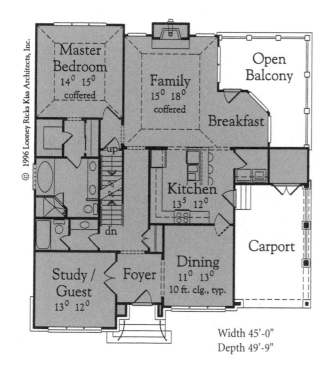

Master Bedroom
14⁰ 15⁰
coffered

Family
15⁰ 18⁰
coffered

Open Balcony

Breakfast

up

Kitchen
13⁵ 12⁰

dn

Carport

Study / Guest
13⁰ 12⁰

Foyer

Dining
11⁰ 13⁰
10 ft. clg., typ.

© 1996 Looney Ricks Kiss Architects, Inc.

Width 45'-0"
Depth 49'-9"

DESIGN BY
©*Looney Ricks Kiss Architects, Inc.*

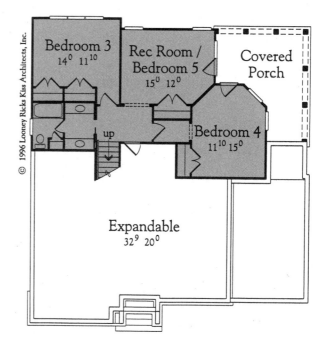

Bedroom 3
14⁰ 11¹⁰

Rec Room / Bedroom 5
15⁰ 12⁰

Covered Porch

up

Bedroom 4
11¹⁰ 15⁰

Expandable
32⁹ 20⁰

© 1996 Looney Ricks Kiss Architects, Inc.

PLAN W518

Main Level: 1,586 square feet
Lower Level: 767 square feet
Total: 2,353 square feet

Bedrooms: 5
Bathrooms: 3

VILLAGE

Double gables and a charming dormer set off the sweet sophistication of this spacious Village home. An arch-top window complements the arched entry, which leads to an open foyer. Formal rooms enjoy front-property views and plenty of natural light. A gallery hall leads to casual living space, which is warmed by a fireplace framed by tall windows. An open balcony is accessible through the breakfast area. The master bedroom boasts a walk-in closet, separate tub and shower, and dual vanities.

Prospect Avenue

Exterior accents such as decorative woodwork and columns along the covered porch, plus dormers and clerestory windows, add charm to this home. The formal living room and dining area are open and share a see-through fireplace with the family room. The galley-style kitchen easily serves the breakfast, dining and family areas. Each of two family bedrooms has a walk-in closet and access to a shared bath. The master bedroom opens through French doors to the bath, which is packed with amenities and includes a walk-in closet.

PLAN E509

Square Footage: 1,954

Bedrooms: 3
Bathrooms: 2

DESIGN BY
©*Park House
Properties, LLC*

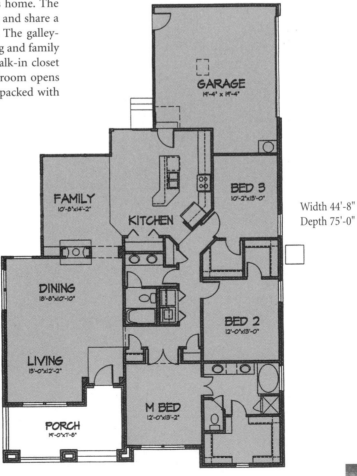

GARAGE
19'-4" x 19'-4"

FAMILY
10'-8"x14'-2"

KITCHEN

BED 3
10'-2"x13'-0"

Width 44'-8"
Depth 75'-0"

DINING
18'-8"x10'-10"

BED 2
12'-0"x13'-0"

LIVING
13'-0"x12'-2"

M BED
12'-0"x13'-2"

PORCH
14'-0"x7'-8"

Plans are not to be sold or built within the state of Arkansas.

VILLAGE EDGE

Elizabeth Place

Shingles, shutters and a flower box below the kitchen window dress up this winsome country composition. Inside, the open foyer and formal dining room are defined by decorative columns. A spacious great room is enhanced by a warming fireplace and access to the rear patio. Two family bedrooms and a bath-and-a-half complete the first floor. Upstairs, the deluxe master bath is highlighted by a relaxing garden tub.

Width 52'-0"
Depth 49'-0"

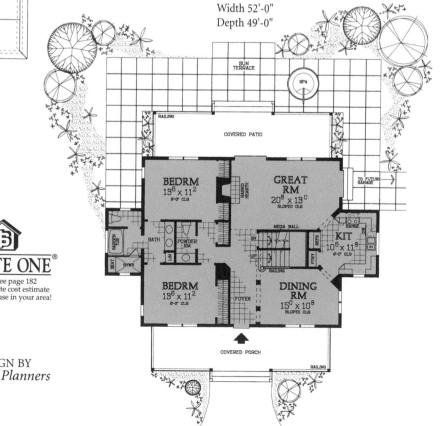

PLAN 3678

First Floor: 1,393 square feet
Second Floor: 487 square feet
Total: 1,880 square feet

Bedrooms: 3
Bathrooms: 2½

L

QUOTE ONE®

Cost to build? See page 182
to order complete cost estimate
to build this house in your area!

DESIGN BY
©Home Planners

VILLAGE | EDGE

Keenan Road

© 1996 Donald A. Gardner Architects, Inc.

This two-story home is a great starter for a young family with plans to grow or for empty-nesters with a need for guest rooms. Two additional bedrooms and a shared bath on the second floor could easily convert to a home office. The foyer opens through a columned entrance to the great room, which has a cathedral ceiling and fireplace. The dining room offers access to the deck—a perfect arrangement for entertaining. The master bedroom is located at the rear of the home for privacy and features a walk-in closet and corner whirlpool tub. A basement or crawlspace foundation is available.

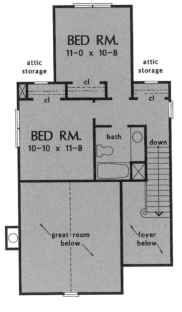

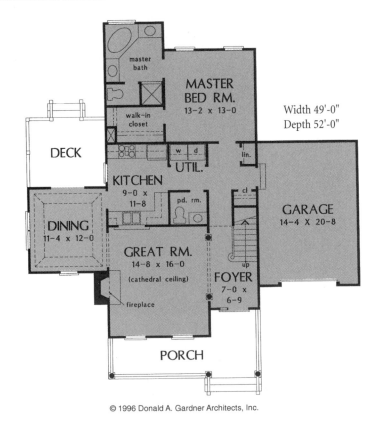

© 1996 Donald A. Gardner Architects, Inc.

Width 49'-0"
Depth 52'-0"

PLAN 7613

First Floor: 1,116 square feet
Second Floor: 442 square feet
Total: 1,558 square feet

Bedrooms: 3
Bathrooms: 2½

DESIGN BY
Donald A. Gardner
Architects, Inc.

Hurst Park Way

PLAN 3674

PLAN 3673/3674

First Floor: 1,086 square feet
Second Floor: 554 square feet
Total: 1,640 square feet

Bedrooms: 3
Bathrooms: 2

L **D**

QUOTE ONE®
Cost to build? See page 182
to order complete cost estimate
to build this house in your area!

A touch of tradition (Design 3674) and a charming Victorian vogue (Design 3673) provide alternate exterior styles for this delightful farmhouse. A welcoming entry and a tiled foyer lead to a thoughtful floor plan, starting with a built-in seat with shoe storage. The two-story great room is the heart of the plan and offers an extended-hearth fireplace framed by grand picture windows. The secluded master suite features private access to the wraparound porch. Skylights brighten the balcony hall that connects two second-floor family bedrooms and a full bath.

Width 52'-0"
Depth 43'-0"

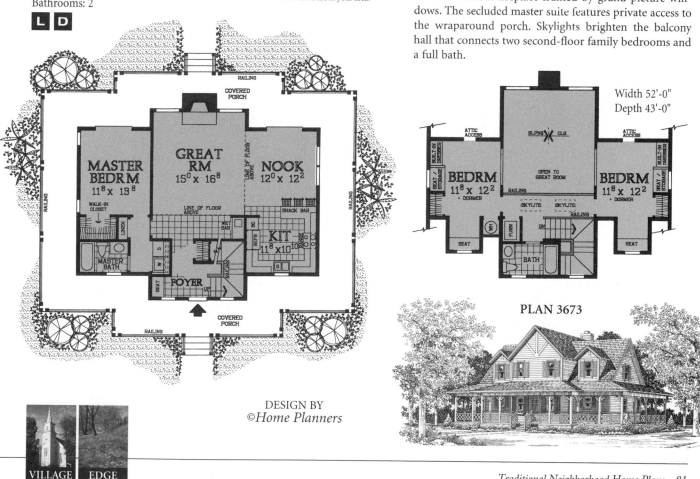

DESIGN BY
©*Home Planners*

PLAN 3673

VILLAGE **EDGE**

Fairbury Lane

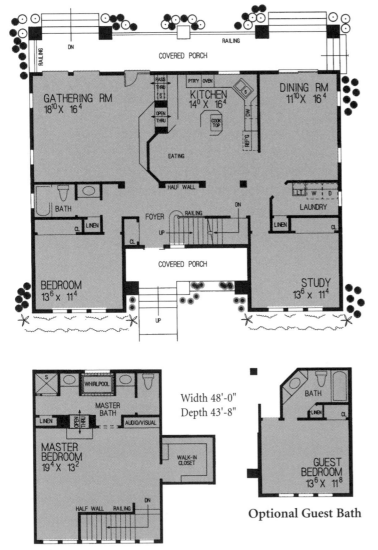

Details make the difference in this darling two-bedroom (or three-bedroom) bungalow. From the covered front porch to the covered rear porch, this is a fine floor plan. The living area includes a gathering room with a through-fireplace and its own access to the rear porch. A pass-through counter to the kitchen allows snacks and a kick-your-shoes-off atmosphere in the gathering room. To the front of the plan, a bedroom and study can easily serve as formal rooms. Upstairs, the master bedroom features a through-fireplace that it shares with the bath.

PLAN 3318

First Floor: 1,557 square feet
Second Floor: 540 square feet
Total: 2,097 square feet

Bedrooms: 2
Bathrooms: 2

L **D**

Width 48'-0"
Depth 43'-8"

Optional Guest Bath

QUOTE ONE®
Cost to build? See page 182
to order complete cost estimate
to build this house in your area!

DESIGN BY
©*Home Planners*

VILLAGE **EDGE**

San Juan Circle

Width 64'-0"
Depth 50'-0"

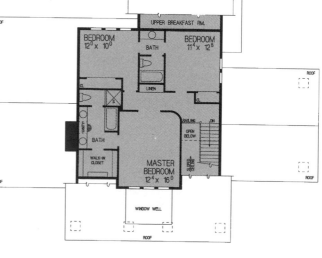

Cozy living abounds in this comfortable two-story bungalow. The foyer opens to a spacious living room, which features a fireplace. A U-shaped kitchen offers a snack bar, a planning desk and easy access to the formal dining room. The family room features a fireplace and entry to a screened porch. Second-floor bedrooms offer ample closet space and direct access to a shared bath. The master suite includes a walk-in closet, double-bowl vanity and compartmented shower.

PLAN 3313

First Floor: 1,482 square feet
Second Floor: 885 square feet
Total: 2,367 square feet

Bedrooms: 3
Bathrooms: 2½

L

Cost to build? See page 182 to order complete cost estimate to build this house in your area!

QUOTE ONE®

DESIGN BY
© Home Planners

VILLAGE EDGE

Yesler Terrace Road

PLAN E522

PLAN E523

This Village design provides a choice of two facades. Both feature porches, distinctive gables and unique window treatments. Decorative columns and balustrades line the wraparound porch of Plan E522, while thick columns and wide gables with exposed rafters give E523 a more grounded appeal. Inside, the foyer opens to all areas of the first floor. A study with French doors complements a two-story living room, which provides a fireplace and access to the rear property. On the second floor, two family bedrooms share a full hall bath and lead to a loft area that's just right for computers.

PLAN E522/E523

First Floor: 1,287 square feet
Second Floor: 913 square feet
Total: 2,200 square feet

Bedrooms: 3
Bathrooms: 3

Plans are not to be sold or built within the state of Arkansas.

Width 40'-0"
Depth 64'-8"

DESIGN BY
©*Park House
Properties, LLC*

VILLAGE

PLAN E524

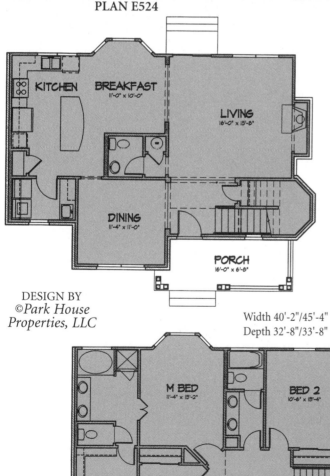

KITCHEN

BREAKFAST
11'-0" x 10'-0"

LIVING
16'-0" x 15'-8"

DINING
11'-4" x 11'-0"

PORCH
16'-0" x 6'-8"

DESIGN BY
©*Park House
Properties, LLC*

Width 40'-2"/45'-4"
Depth 32'-8"/33'-8"

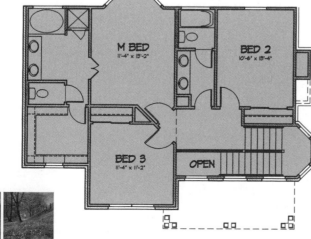

M BED
11'-4" x 19'-2"

BED 2
10'-6" x 13'-4"

BED 3
11'-4" x 11'-2"

OPEN

PLAN E526

A traditional facade is employed with Plan E524—gabled rooflines, transom and clerestory windows—while plan E526 uses Craftsmen elements, such as exposed rafters and a deep porch to enhance its appeal. Just off the foyer, a dining room is ready to seat guests, easily served by a well-organized gourmet kitchen, which also serves a breakfast bay. The living room features a focal-point fireplace and offers views of the rear grounds. Upstairs, two secondary bedrooms share a hall bath with compartmented toilet. The master bedroom boasts a sitting bay and French doors.

PLAN E524/E526

First Floor: 965/951 square feet
Second Floor: 856 square feet
Total: 1,821/1,807 square feet

Bedrooms: 3
Bathrooms: 2½

Plans are not to be sold or built within the state of Arkansas.

VILLAGE EDGE

Wing Luke Circle

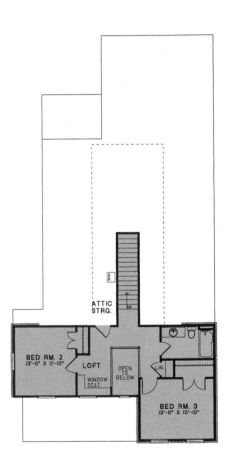

DESIGN BY
©*Michael E. Nelson*
Nelson Design Group, LLC

Shuttered windows and a gabled roofline define this home's traditional style. A columned porch invites friends and family alike into the foyer, which sets off the great room with accenting columns. Built-in shelves, a fireplace and a computer center complement this space. The dining room, open to the great room, is easily served from the U-shaped kitchen. The master suite enjoys a tray ceiling, spacious walk-in closet and French doors. Upstairs, two family bedrooms share a full bath and a loft that has a window seat. Please specify basement, crawlspace or slab foundation when ordering.

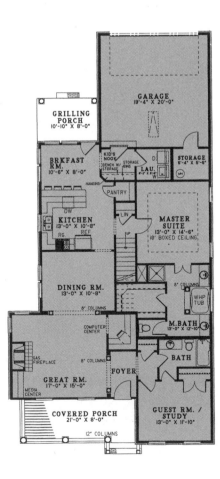

PLAN Y060

First Floor: 1,558 square feet
Second Floor: 429 square feet
Total: 1,987 square feet

Bedrooms: 3
Bathrooms: 3

Width 36'-4"
Depth 73'-6"

VILLAGE

Embury Circle

PLAN E530

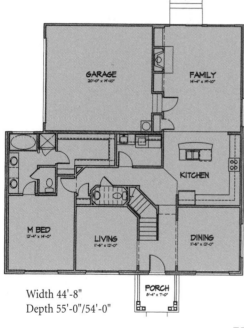

Width 44'-8"
Depth 55'-0"/54'-0"

PLAN E531

DESIGN BY
©*Park House
Properties, LLC*

PLAN E530/E531

First Floor: 1,582/1,542 square feet
Second Floor: 746/721 square feet
Total: 2,328/2,263 square feet

Bedrooms: 4
Bathrooms: 2½

Beautiful fenestration, natural materials, a columned porch and other elements of Arts and Crafts style catch the eye and stop the stroller for a better look at this stunning home. The entryway leads to the formal rooms or to the informal spaces upstairs and to the rear of the plan. The kitchen serves both the dining area and the large family room, which has a fireplace and a door to the garage. The secluded master suite provides amenities such as a walk-in closet, a compartmented toilet, double basins, and separate shower and tub.

VILLAGE

Plans are not to be sold or built within the state of Arkansas.

Cabot Place

Traditional styling distinguishes this narrow-lot home. The foyer provides superb interior vistas to the living and dining rooms—both with volume ceilings. A flex room easily converts from a home office or study to a guest suite. The kitchen features a pass-through counter to the living room. A roomy covered porch is accessed from the breakfast room and provides space for outdoor entertaining. Upstairs, the master suite has all the amenities, including a door to a private second-story covered porch.

PLAN 8278

First Floor: 1,233 square feet
Second Floor: 824 square feet
Total: 2,057 square feet

Bedrooms: 3
Bathrooms: 3

DESIGN BY
©*Larry E. Belk Designs*

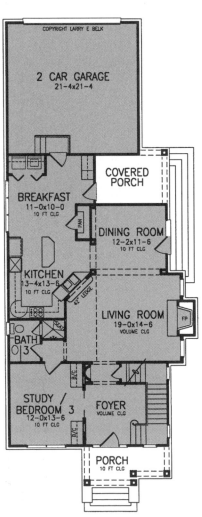

COPYRIGHT LARRY E BELK

2 CAR GARAGE
21-4x21-4

COVERED PORCH

BREAKFAST
11-0x10-0
10 FT CLG

DINING ROOM
12-2x11-6
10 FT CLG

KITCHEN
13-4x13-6
10 FT CLG

LIVING ROOM
19-0x14-6
VOLUME CLG

FP

BATH 3

STUDY / BEDROOM 3
12-0x13-6
10 FT CLG

FOYER
VOLUME CLG

PORCH
10 FT CLG

HERS HIS

COVERED PORCH
9 FT CLG

MASTER BEDROOM
14-0x15-0
9 FT CLG

MSTR BATH
9 FT CLG

BATH 2
9 FT CLG

OPEN TO LIVING ROOM BELOW

BALCONY

BEDROOM 2
10-0x14-6
9 FT CLG

OPEN TO FOYER BELOW

Width 31'-10"
Depth 77'-10"

TOWN   VILLAGE

Biddeford Lane

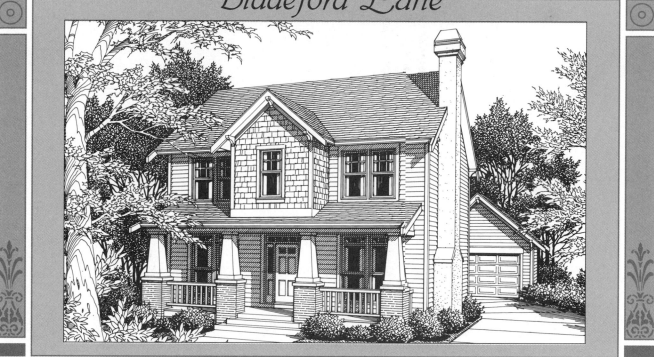

PLAN 7564

First Floor: 1,158 square feet
Second Floor: 1,044 square feet
Total: 2,202 square feet

Bedrooms: 4
Bathrooms: 2½

DESIGN BY
©*Alan Mascord Design Associates, Inc.*

Width 54'-0"
Depth 51'-0"

GARAGE
19/4 X 19/4

NOOK
9/0 X 8/0

FAMILY
12/0 X 17/6 +/-

7/6 X 14/4

REF

DINING
10/8 X 12/2
(9' CLG)

DEN
12/2 X 10/6
(9' CLG)

PARLOR
12/2 X 12/0
(9' CLG)

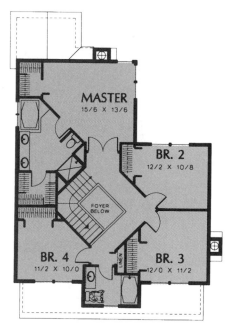

MASTER
15/6 X 13/6

BR. 2
12/2 X 10/8

FOYER
BELOW

BR. 4
11/2 X 10/0

LINEN

BR. 3
12/0 X 11/2

Strong square pillars, a combination of shingles and siding, and stylish window detailing dress up this fine Craftsman-style home. A den at the front of the plan provides space for quiet studying or working at home. The spacious family room is convenient to the L-shaped kitchen and offers a fireplace. Upstairs, three secondary bedrooms share a full hall bath, while the master suite features many luxuries. Completing this suite are two walk-in closets, a large and pampering bath and plenty of sunshine from the corner windows.

VILLAGE

Brittany Bay Road

Photos by ©Jeffrey Jacobs/Mims Studios

This home, as shown in the photographs, may differ from the actual blueprints.

Rear View

PLAN W521

First Floor: 1,482 square feet
Second Floor: 1,142 square feet
Total: 2,624 square feet

Bedrooms: 2 or 3
Bathrooms: 3

DESIGN BY
©*Looney Ricks Kiss
Architects, Inc.*

With beautiful lines and a look that is both contemporary and traditional, this home boasts two covered porches and a balcony. On the first floor, a study/guest room with private access to a full bath is available to use as a flex room. A well-organized island kitchen serves the breakfast and dining areas. On the second floor, a secondary bedroom has a box-bay window and private bath. The master suite features a fireplace, raised bedroom area, spacious balcony and walk-in closet.

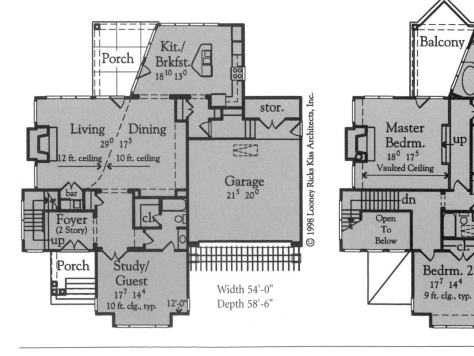

© 1998 Looney Ricks Kiss Architects, Inc.

Width 54'-0"
Depth 58'-6"

Amherst Circle

This home, as shown in the photograph, may differ from the actual blueprints.

Photo by ©Wickford Point/Bayshore Ventures

PLAN W522

First Floor: 1,041 square feet
Second Floor: 998 square feet
Total: 2,039 square feet

Bedrooms: 3
Bathrooms: 2½

This sweet facade pays homage to the architectural symmetry of simpler times. A deep front porch welcomes guests and complements a triplet of charming windows. Inside, formal rooms frame the foyer, which provides a discreet staircase. Upstairs, two secondary bedrooms have plenty of closet space and share a full bath. The master suite features two walk-in closets, a double-bowl vanity, and a separate shower and bath. A garage is placed to the rear of the plan.

DESIGN BY
©*Looney Ricks Kiss Architects, Inc.*

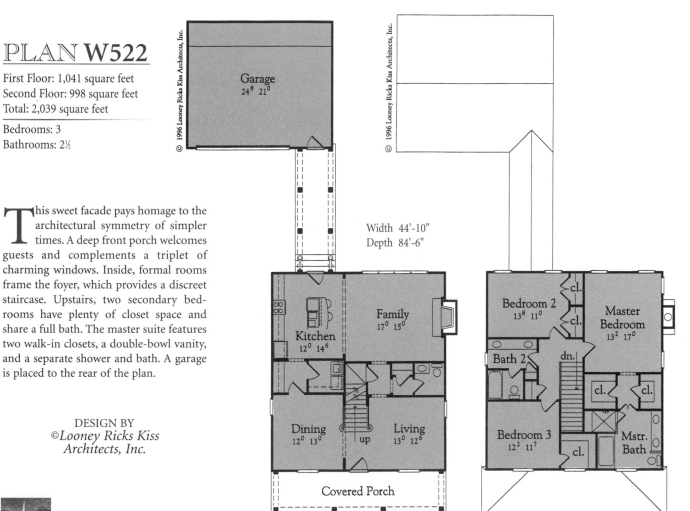

Width 44'-10"
Depth 84'-6"

VILLAGE

Shady Bay Grove

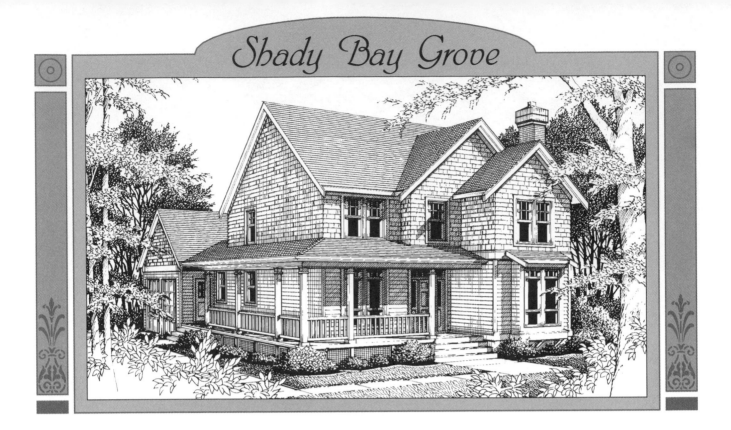

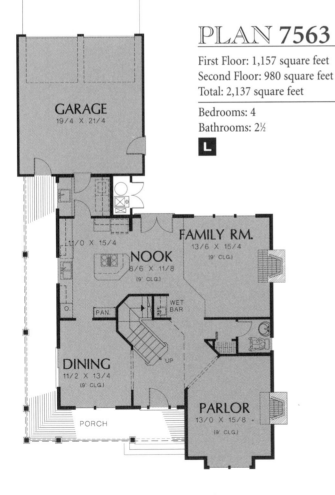

PLAN 7563

First Floor: 1,157 square feet
Second Floor: 980 square feet
Total: 2,137 square feet

Bedrooms: 4
Bathrooms: 2½

L

Country style comes home in this great farmhouse with a front porch that welcomes guests. The dramatic two-story foyer features an angled stairway that creates a highlight as well as forms the circulation hub for this efficient home. A large parlor with fireplace will be the center of all entertaining, with the kitchen merely steps away. Upstairs, a large master suite includes a spa tub, large shower and walk-in closet. Three other bedrooms share a full hall bath and complete the second floor.

GARAGE
19/4 X 21/4

11/0 X 15/4

FAMILY RM.
13/6 X 15/4
(9' CLG.)

NOOK
8/6 X 11/8
(9' CLG.)

O.

PAN.

WET BAR

UP

DINING
11/2 X 13/4
(9' CLG.)

PARLOR
13/0 X 15/8 +
(9' CLG.)

PORCH

BR. 3
10/0 X 12/0

BR.4
10/0 X 10/0

LINEN

DN.

BR. 2
11/2 X 12/0

FOYER BELOW

PLANT SHELF

VAULTED

MASTER
13/0 X 15/0

Width 54'-0"
Depth 38'-0"

DESIGN BY
©*Alan Mascord Design
Associates, Inc.*

VILLAGE | EDGE

Otter Creek Circle

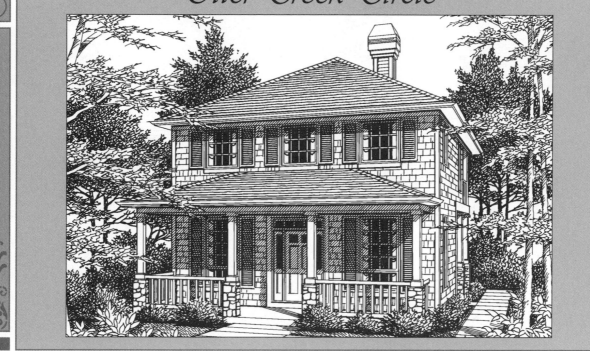

Perfect for a narrow lot, this two-story home has plenty to offer. The entryway opens directly into the two-story great room/dining area, where a built-in media center and a fireplace make this a room to truly relax in. The C-shaped kitchen offers plenty of counter and cabinet space and has an adjacent nook with built-in shelves. Upstairs, two secondary bedrooms share a full hall bath with a dual-bowl vanity, while the master suite features a walk-in closet and private deck.

PLAN 7495

First Floor: 860 square feet
Second Floor: 845 square feet
Total: 1,705 square feet

Bedrooms: 3
Bathrooms: 2½

DESIGN BY
©*Alan Mascord Design Associates, Inc.*

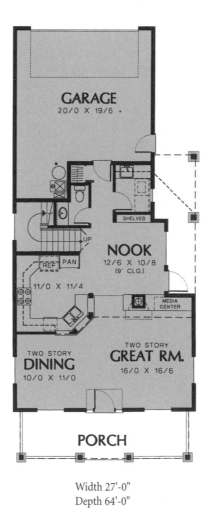

GARAGE
20/0 X 19/6 +

SHELVES

NOOK
12/6 X 10/8
(9' CLG.)

UP

REF | PAN

11/0 X 11/4

MEDIA CENTER

TWO STORY
DINING
10/0 X 11/0

TWO STORY
GREAT RM.
16/0 X 16/6

PORCH

Width 27'-0"
Depth 64'-0"

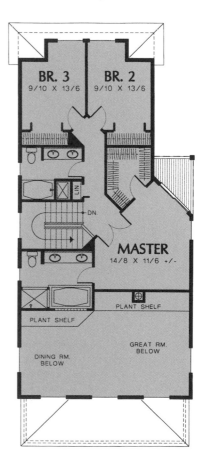

BR. 3
9/10 X 13/6

BR. 2
9/10 X 13/6

LIN

DN.

MASTER
14/8 X 11/6 +/-

PLANT SHELF

PLANT SHELF

GREAT RM.
BELOW

DINING RM.
BELOW

VILLAGE

Willowbrook Lane

© 1996 Donald A. Gardner Architects, Inc.

Double gables and a covered porch give this narrow-lot home a storybook beginning. A rear deck expands outdoor living space from the great room, which is open to a center island kitchen. Formal dining is enhanced by a bay window and a columned entry that graces this room. The second floor contains a relaxing master suite that features a private bath filled with amenities and two family bedrooms that share a full bath.

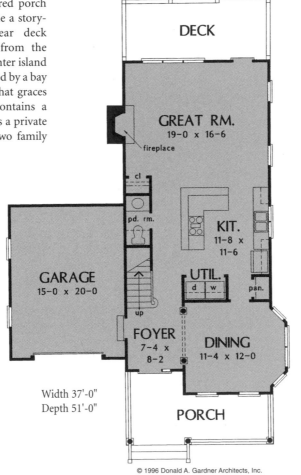

DECK

GREAT RM.
19-0 x 16-6

fireplace

cl

pd. rm.

KIT.
11-8 x
11-6

GARAGE
15-0 x 20-0

UTIL.
d   w

pan.

up

FOYER
7-4 x
8-2

DINING
11-4 x 12-0

PORCH

Width 37'-0"
Depth 51'-0"

© 1996 Donald A. Gardner Architects, Inc.

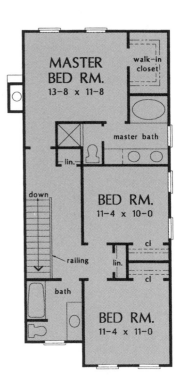

MASTER
BED RM.
13-8 x 11-8

walk-in
closet

master bath

lin.

down

BED RM.
11-4 x 10-0

railing

cl

lin.

cl

bath

BED RM.
11-4 x 11-0

DESIGN BY
*Donald A. Gardner
Architects, Inc.*

PLAN 7612

First Floor: 875 square feet
Second Floor: 814 square feet
Total: 1,689 square feet

Bedrooms: 3
Bathrooms: 2½

VILLAGE

Waverly Drive

The perfect blend of country and traditional, this family home would fit nicely on a narrow lot. Columns define the entry to the dining room, while the kitchen, breakfast bay and great room provide a casual atmosphere. A half bath and utility room are conveniently located nearby. Upstairs, the master suite has a luxurious bath with a sunny bay window. Two additional bedrooms share a skylit bath.

PLAN 7642

First Floor: 1,113 square feet
Second Floor: 960 square feet
Total: 2,073 square feet
Bonus Room: 338 square feet

Bedrooms: 3
Bathrooms: 2

Width 49'-4"
Depth 58'-10"

DESIGN BY
Donald A. Gardner Architects, Inc.

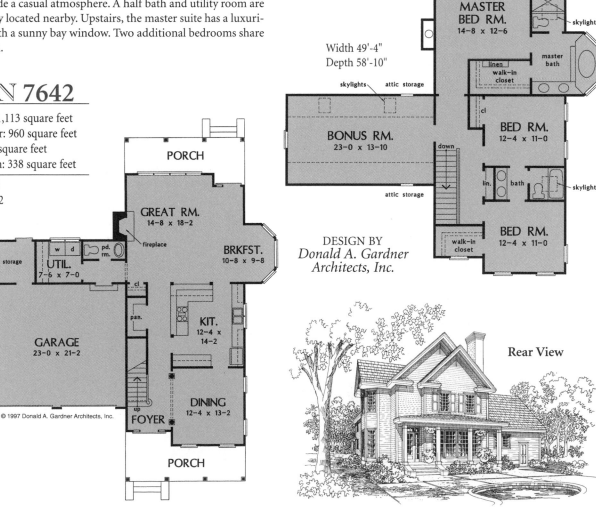

Rear View

VILLAGE

Mount Pleasant Place

P erfect for a narrow site, this historic adaptation is in "temple form"—the gable end of the house faces the street, an element of Greek Revival style. Three chimneys support four fireplaces—in the living room, study, kitchen and master bedroom. Family members and guests will love the huge country kitchen, with room for relaxing, a snack bar for quick meals and access to the terrace. The master suite has a deluxe bath and a private balcony. Three bedrooms and two full baths complete the plan.

PLAN 2979

First Floor: 1,440 square feet
Second Floor: 1,394 square feet
Total: 2,834 square feet

Bedrooms: 4
Bathrooms: 3½

DESIGN BY
©*Home Planners*

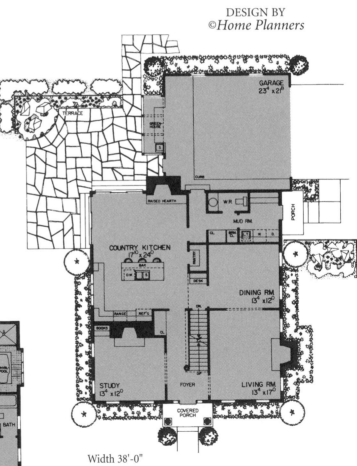

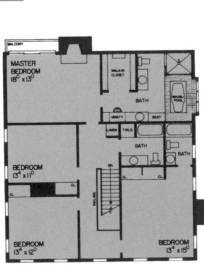

Width 38'-0"
Depth 62'-0"

Reidville Circle

© 1995 Donald A. Gardner Architects, Inc.

Width 52'-6"
Depth 42'-8"

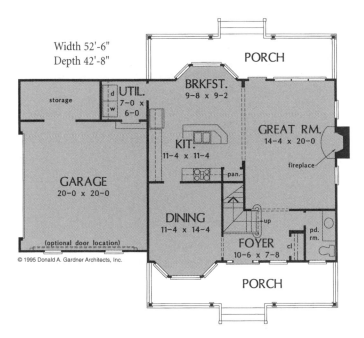

storage

UTIL.
7-0 x
6-0

d
w

BRKFST.
9-8 x 9-2

PORCH

KIT.
11-4 x 11-4

GREAT RM.
14-4 x 20-0

fireplace

GARAGE
20-0 x 20-0

pan.

DINING
11-4 x 14-4

up

FOYER
10-6 x 7-8

cl

pd.
rm.

(optional door location)

© 1995 Donald A. Gardner Architects, Inc.

PORCH

A large, center front gable and a covered porch set the tone for a down-home country welcome. The formal dining room is filled with light from a bay window and has direct access to an island kitchen. A matching bay is found in the breakfast room, furnishing the perfect location for a leisurely cup of morning tea. Active families will enjoy the large great room, graced with a warming fireplace and an abundance of windows. An L-shaped staircase leads to the second floor, which includes a master suite filled with amenities. A basement or crawlspace foundation is available.

DESIGN BY
*Donald A. Gardner
Architects, Inc.*

PLAN 7600

First Floor: 959 square feet
Second Floor: 833 square feet
Total: 1,792 square feet
Bonus Room: 344 square feet

Bedrooms: 3
Bathrooms: 2½

attic storage

BED RM.
10-4 x 10-0

bath

MASTER
BED RM.
13-6 x 15-8

BONUS RM.
20-0 x 14-2

cl

down

attic
storage

walk-in
closet

master
bath

BED RM.
11-4 x 11-10

walk-in
closet

VILLAGE EDGE

Stephen's Retreat

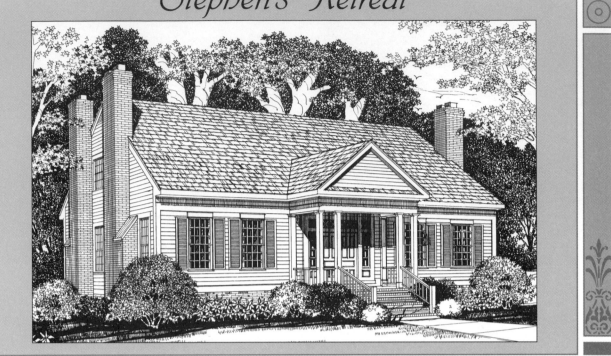

PLAN 3517

First Floor: 1,536 square feet
Second Floor: 679 square feet
Total: 2,215 square feet

Bedrooms: 3
Bathrooms: 2½

L D

DESIGN BY
©*Home Planners*

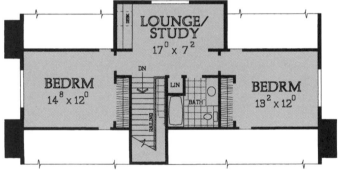

Width 53'-0"
Depth 44'-0"

There is much more to this Early American home than a warm, inviting exterior. Inside, first-floor fireplaces enhance the living room, country kitchen and master bedroom. To the right of the foyer, the master suite is enhanced by a walk-in closet and a pampering bath. The country kitchen provides an L-shaped food preparation area and an island snack counter that's perfect for informal gatherings. The second floor holds two family bedrooms, a full bath and a lounge/study with a built-in desk.

QUOTE ONE®

Cost to build? See page 182
to order complete cost estimate
to build this house in your area!

VILLAGE

Plymouth Square

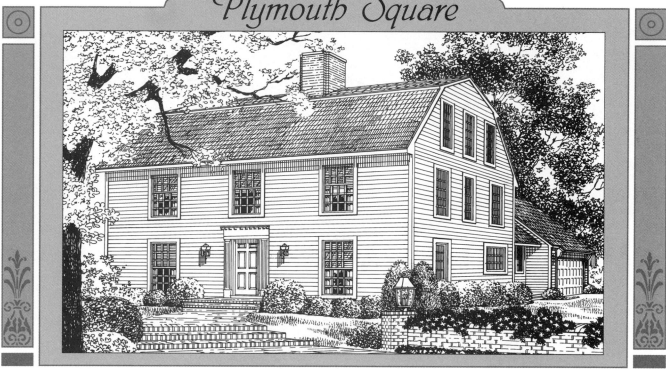

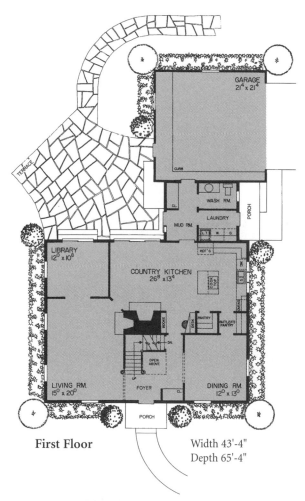

First Floor

Width 43'-4"
Depth 65'-4"

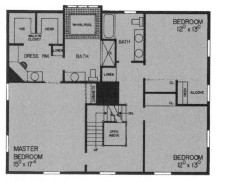

Second Floor

The Nathaniel Hawthorne house, constructed in Salem, Massachusetts, around 1730, was the inspiration for this two-story gambrel-roofed design. This modern version shows off its interior space with a family-pleasing country kitchen—with an island and a built-in desk—a library, and formal living and dining rooms. The highlight of the second floor is the luxurious master suite, with two walk-in closets and a heavenly whirlpool spa-style tub. The third floor accommodates a guest bedroom and a large exercise room or studio.

PLAN **2978**

First Floor: 1,451 square feet
Second Floor: 1,268 square feet
Third Floor: 746 square feet
Total: 3,465 square feet

Bedrooms: 4
Bathrooms: 3½

DESIGN BY
©*Home Planners*

Third Floor

VILLAGE EDGE

Salemburg Lane

PLAN 9691

First Floor: 1,044 square feet
Second Floor: 719 square feet
Total: 1,763 square feet

Bedrooms: 3
Bathrooms: 2½

Colonial through and through, this charming design features an added attraction—an addition containing a family room complete with a fireplace and access to a rear deck and spa. The formal living room has a second fireplace and opens through pillars to a formal dining room for ease in entertaining. Upstairs, three bedrooms include a sumptuous master suite with a pampering bath and walk-in closet. A bonus room offers the possibility of a hobby or recreation room.

GARAGE
21-4 x 21-4

spa

covered breezeway

DECK

KITCHEN
14-0 x 10-8

DINING
12-0 x 13-10

BRKFST./
FAMILY RM.
14-0 x 20-0
fireplace

d w

pd. rm.

LIVING RM.
15-8 x 12-4
fireplace

FOYER
6-10 x 5-4
up

Width 45'-0"
Depth 63'-2"

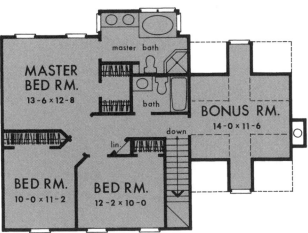

MASTER
BED RM.
13-6 x 12-8

master bath

bath

lin

down

BONUS RM.
14-0 x 11-6

BED RM.
10-0 x 11-2

BED RM.
12-2 x 10-0

DESIGN BY
*Donald A. Gardner
Architects, Inc.*

VILLAGE

Saint George Circle

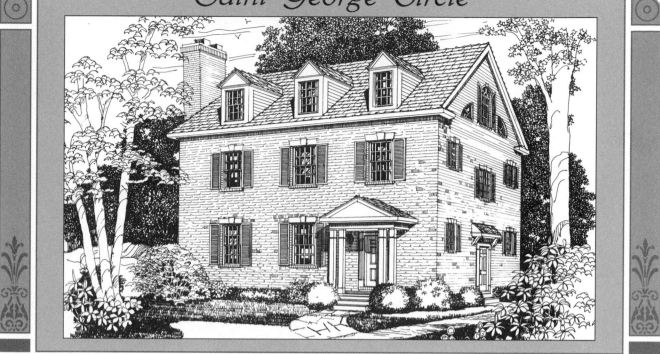

PLAN 3526

First Floor: 1,056 square feet
Second Floor: 960 square feet
Total: 2,016 square feet
Attic: 659 square feet

Bedrooms: 3
Bathrooms: 2½

L **D**

Borrowing from the historic designs of Williamsburg, Virginia, this home is graceful and timeless. Classic floor planning is a must for such a home: living areas on the first floor and sleeping quarters on the second floor. The living room is large enough and appealing enough for both casual and formal occasions. Separated from it by niches, the formal dining room has a bay window. The island kitchen and an attached nook are found to the rear of the plan. A stunning second-floor master suite features a fireplace and a bath with dual lavatories.

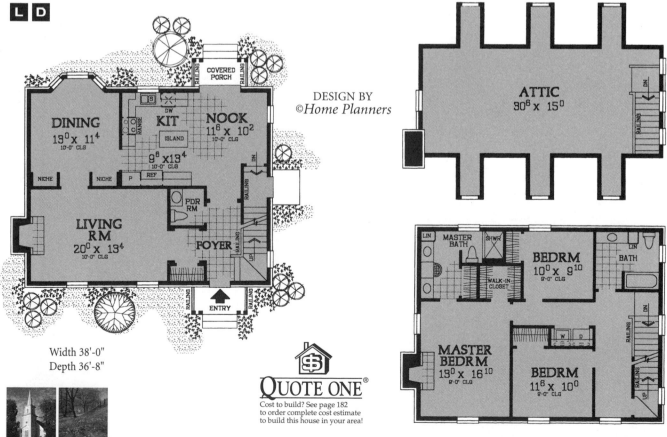

DESIGN BY
©Home Planners

Width 38'-0"
Depth 36'-8"

QUOTE ONE®
Cost to build? See page 182
to order complete cost estimate
to build this house in your area!

VILLAGE | EDGE

Jamestown Drive

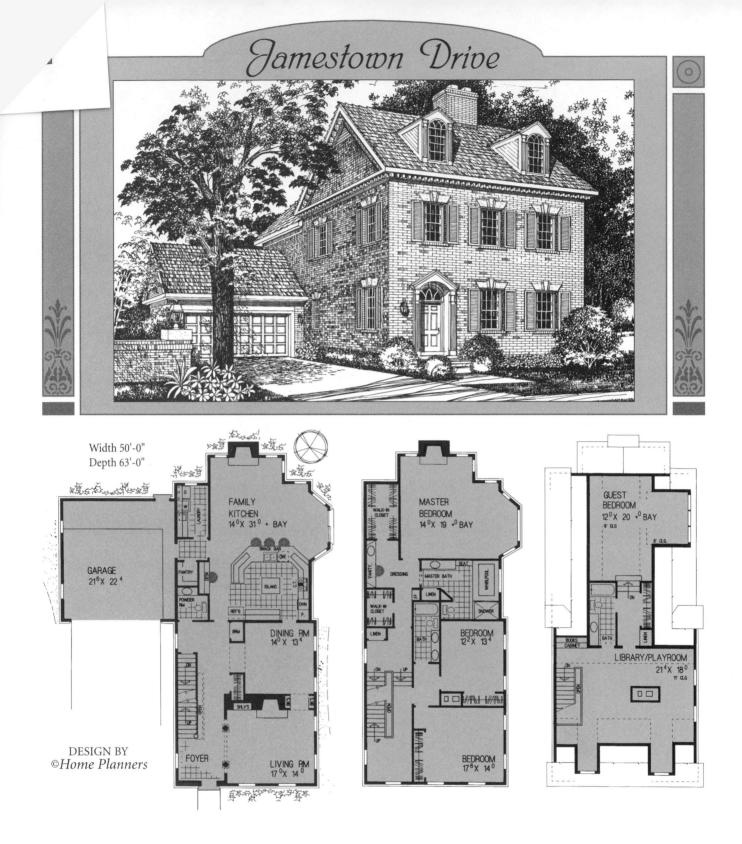

Width 50'-0"
Depth 63'-0"

GARAGE
21⁶ X 22⁴

FAMILY KITCHEN
14⁰ X 31⁰ + BAY

PANTRY

POWDER RM

REF'G

BRM

DINING RM
14⁰ X 13⁴

SNACK BAR

ISLAND

OVN

FOYER

LIVING RM
17⁰ X 14⁰

DESIGN BY
©Home Planners

WALK-IN CLOSET

MASTER BEDROOM
14⁰ X 19 +⁰ BAY

VANITY

DRESSING

MASTER BATH

SEAT

WHIRLPOOL

LINEN

SHOWER

WALK-IN CLOSET

LINEN

BATH

BEDROOM
12² X 13⁴

BEDROOM
17⁶ X 14⁰

GUEST BEDROOM
12⁰ X 20 +⁰ BAY
9' CLG.

8' CLG.

BOOKS CABINET

BATH

LINEN

LIBRARY/PLAYROOM
21⁴ X 18⁰
11' CLG.

PLAN 3503

First Floor: 1,748 square feet
Second Floor: 1,748 square feet
Third Floor: 1,100 square feet
Total: 4,596 square feet

Bedrooms: 4
Bathrooms: 3½

L D

This Early American brick exterior serves as a quaint introduction to a thoroughly modern floor plan. The tiled foyer opens through decorative columns to the formal living room, which offers a fireplace framed by built-in cabinetry. Second-floor sleeping quarters offer a master suite with its own fireplace, a bumped-out bay window and a lavish bath with a whirlpool tub. Two family bedrooms share a full bath with a double-bowl vanity. A sumptuous guest suite shares the third floor with a library or playroom.

QUOTE ONE®

Cost to build? See page 182
to order complete cost estimate
to build this house in your area!

VILLAGE

Windham Garden Lane

First Floor

QUOTE ONE®

Cost to build? See page 182 to order complete cost estimate to build this house in your area!

DESIGN BY
©*Home Planners*

Width 38'-0"
Depth 44'-0"

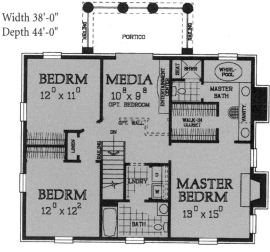

Second Floor

PLAN 3516

First Floor: 1,140 square feet
Second Floor: 1,120 square feet
Lower Floor: 964 square feet
Total: 3,224 square feet

Bedrooms: 3
Bathrooms: 2½

An exquisitely detailed portico sets the classical character of this home, as well as providing a sheltered front entry. The foyer is flanked by the formal dining room and the parlor, which has a commanding fireplace. The L-shaped kitchen includes an island cooktop counter with cabinets below, a pantry and planning desk. On the second floor, the media room allows space for an entertainment center and provides access to the upper railed portico. The lower level offers a guest bedroom and spacious activities room with a mini-kitchen.

Lower Floor

VILLAGE EDGE

Brinton's Mill

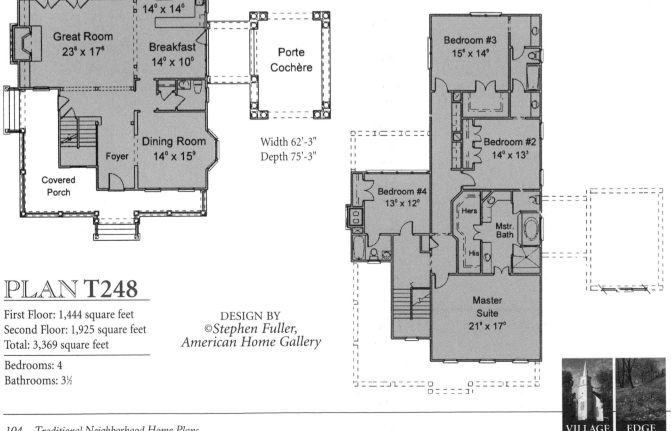

When warm weather comes and the wraparound porch becomes an extended living room, this home can feel almost twice its already spacious size. The heart of this lovely Edge design is the generous great room, which opens to the back porch, while the central hall leads to the side porch. Just off the foyer, the formal dining room easily converts to a living room. The second floor includes a master suite and three generous bedrooms, one with its own bath. This home is designed with a basement foundation.

Homeowner's Option: This garage may be customized to provide a rear entry.

Two Car Garage
22⁶ x 21⁹

Covered Porch

Kitchen
14⁰ x 14⁰

Great Room
23⁶ x 17⁶

Breakfast
14⁰ x 10⁰

Porte Cochère

Dining Room
14⁰ x 15⁹

Foyer

Covered Porch

Width 62'-3"
Depth 75'-3"

Bedroom #3
15⁶ x 14⁹

Bedroom #2
14⁰ x 13³

Bedroom #4
13⁰ x 12⁰

Hers

Mstr. Bath

His

Master Suite
21⁹ x 17⁰

PLAN T248

First Floor: 1,444 square feet
Second Floor: 1,925 square feet
Total: 3,369 square feet

Bedrooms: 4
Bathrooms: 3½

DESIGN BY
©*Stephen Fuller,*
American Home Gallery

VILLAGE EDGE

Boxwood Lane

Symmetry is everything in the Georgian style, and Boxwood Lane is a classic Georgian in both plan and elevation. The facade as a whole balances a one-story extended porch under a two-story hipped roof box. Inside, a traditional foyer with central staircase is flanked by the living/dining rooms on one side and the great room on the other. Rear stairs allow private access to a secluded guest suite over the garage. This home is designed with a basement foundation.

Homeowner's Option: This garage may be customized to provide a rear entry.

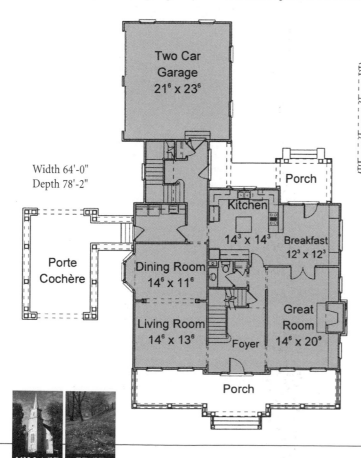

Width 64'-0"
Depth 78'-2"

Two Car Garage 21⁶ x 23⁶

Porte Cochère

Kitchen 14³ x 14³

Porch

Breakfast 12³ x 12³

Dining Room 14⁶ x 11⁶

Living Room 14⁶ x 13⁶

Foyer

Great Room 14⁶ x 20⁹

Porch

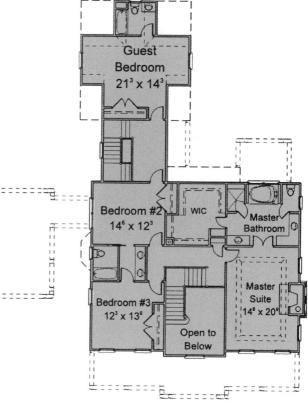

Guest Bedroom 21³ x 14³

Bedroom #2 14⁶ x 12³

WIC

Master Bathroom

Bedroom #3 12³ x 13⁶

Open to Below

Master Suite 14⁶ x 20⁹

PLAN T249

First Floor: 1,670 square feet
Second Floor: 1,741 square feet
Total: 3,411 square feet

Bedrooms: 4
Bathrooms: 3½

DESIGN BY
©*Stephen Fuller,*
American Home Gallery

VILLAGE EDGE

Avon Place

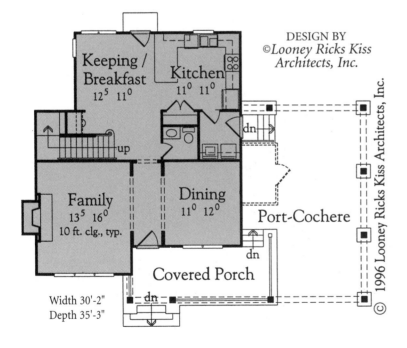

DESIGN BY
©*Looney Ricks Kiss Architects, Inc.*

Keeping / Breakfast
12⁵ 11⁰

Kitchen
11⁰ 11⁰

up

Family
13⁵ 16⁰
10 ft. clg., typ.

dn

Dining
11⁰ 12⁰

dn

Port-Cochere

Covered Porch

dn

Width 30'-2"
Depth 35'-3"

© 1996 Looney Ricks Kiss Architects, Inc.

Bedroom 2
10⁶ 11⁰

Bedroom 3
10⁶ 12⁴

dn

Master Bedroom
13⁵ 16⁰
coffered

© 1996 Looney Ricks Kiss Architects, Inc.

PLAN W525

First Floor: 935 square feet
Second Floor: 880 square feet
Total: 1,815 square feet

Bedrooms: 3
Bathrooms: 2½

A cozy covered porch leads down to a stunning porte cochere on this spacious Village home. The family room features a lovely triple window and a fireplace that's easily enjoyed from the dining room. The U-shaped kitchen opens to a breakfast/keeping room, which has its own door to the rear yard. Upstairs, two secondary bedrooms share a hall bath, and Bedroom 3 has a walk-in closet. The master suite enjoys a view of the front property and features a dressing area, two walk-in closets and a whirlpool tub.

VILLAGE

La Jolla Cove

Width 37'-11"
Depth 66'-4"

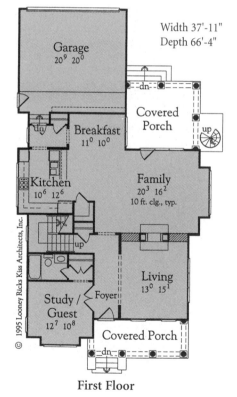

First Floor

Garage
20⁹ 20⁰

Covered Porch

Breakfast
11⁰ 10⁰

Kitchen
10⁶ 12⁶

Family
20³ 16²
10 ft. clg., typ.

Study / Guest
12⁷ 10⁸

Foyer

Living
13⁰ 15¹

Covered Porch

© 1995 Looney Ricks Kiss Architects, Inc.

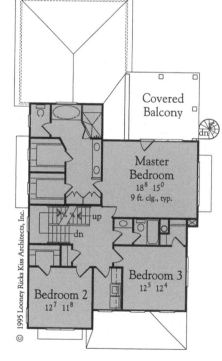

Second Floor

Covered Balcony

Master Bedroom
18⁸ 15⁰
9 ft. clg., typ.

Bedroom 2
12⁷ 11⁸

Bedroom 3
12⁵ 12⁴

© 1995 Looney Ricks Kiss Architects, Inc.

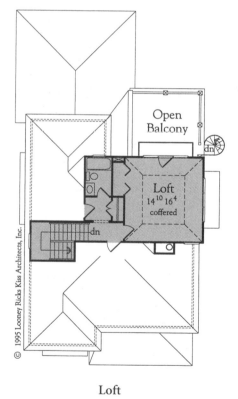

Loft

Open Balcony

Loft
14¹⁰ 16⁴
coffered

© 1995 Looney Ricks Kiss Architects, Inc.

DESIGN BY
©*Looney Ricks Kiss Architects, Inc.*

PLAN W526

First Floor: 1,344 square feet
Second Floor: 1,260 square feet
Loft: 393 square feet
Total: 2,997 square feet

Bedrooms: 3 or 4
Bathrooms: 4

This unique stucco facade is gently flavored with Mediterranean elements, such as the arched decorative columns and hip standing-seam roof. A well-defined foyer announces the formal rooms, including a flex study or guest room, and a living room, which shares its through-fireplace with the casual living area. On the second floor, the master suite is positively spoiled by two walk-in closets and a sumptuous bath. Each of the secondary bedrooms has a walk-in closet.

VILLAGE

Princeton Place

This home, as shown in the photograph, may differ from the actual blueprints.

Asymmetrical gables and wide muntin windows create curb appeal and more than just a little dazzle with this Village plan. A shallow porch leads to the foyer, while a nearby study easily converts to a secluded guest suite. The living room with fireplace provides access to the rear porch and is convenient to the formal dining room and kitchen. Upstairs, two family bedrooms share a full bath. The master suite features vaulted ceilings, a fireplace, private balcony, two walk-in closets and a spacious bath with compartmented toilet.

PLAN W523

First Floor: 1,473 square feet
Second Floor: 1,455 square feet
Total: 2,928 square feet

Bedrooms: 3 or 4
Bathrooms: 3

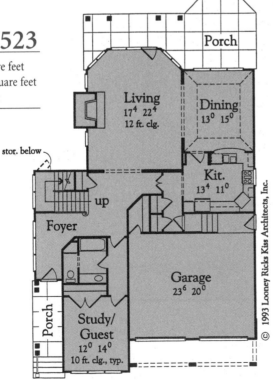

stor. below

Porch

Living
17⁴ 22⁴
12 ft. clg.

Dining
13⁰ 15⁰

Kit.
13⁴ 11⁰

Foyer

up

Garage
23⁶ 20⁰

Porch

Study/
Guest
12⁰ 14⁰
10 ft. clg., typ.

© 1993 Looney Ricks Kiss Architects, Inc.

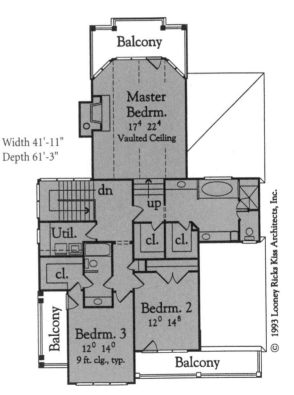

Width 41'-11"
Depth 61'-3"

Balcony

Master
Bedrm.
17⁴ 22⁴
Vaulted Ceiling

dn

up

Util.

cl.

cl.   cl.

Balcony

Bedrm. 3
12⁰ 14⁰
9 ft. clg., typ.

Bedrm. 2
12⁰ 14⁸

Balcony

© 1993 Looney Ricks Kiss Architects, Inc.

DESIGN BY
©Looney Ricks Kiss
Architects, Inc.

VILLAGE

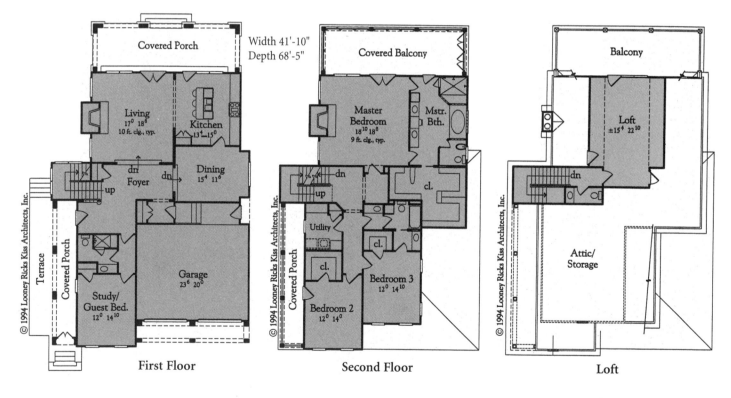

Covered Porch

Width 41'-10"
Depth 68'-5"

Covered Balcony

Balcony

Living
17⁰ 18⁸
10 ft. clg., typ.

Kitchen
13⁴ 15⁰

Master
Bedroom
18¹⁰ 18⁸
9 ft. clg., typ.

Mstr.
Bth.

Loft
±15⁴ 22¹⁰

dn

dn

Dining
15⁴ 11⁶

Foyer

up

dn

up

dn

cl.

dn

Utility

Covered Porch

cl.

cl.

Attic/
Storage

Terrace

Covered Porch

Garage
23⁶ 20⁰

Bedroom 3
12⁰ 14¹⁰

Study/
Guest Bed.
12⁰ 14¹⁰

Bedroom 2
12⁰ 14⁰

© 1994 Looney Ricks Kiss Architects, Inc.

© 1994 Looney Ricks Kiss Architects, Inc.

© 1994 Looney Ricks Kiss Architects, Inc.

First Floor

Second Floor

Loft

DESIGN BY
©*Looney Ricks Kiss*
Architects, Inc.

PLAN **W536**

First Floor: 1,379 square feet
Second Floor: 1,593 square feet
Loft: 410 square feet
Total: 3,382 square feet

Bedrooms: 3 or 4
Bathrooms: 3½

This stately facade displays enchanting elements, such as a piazza, an upper portico and charming shutters. The entryway, set off the covered porch, leads one step down to the formal dining room or living room, which has a fireplace. The gourmet kitchen serves a convenient snack counter, while a study/guest room and nearby hall bath complete this floor. The splendid master suite has its own hearth, a lavish bath and private balcony. A staircase leads up to a loft area—a perfect space for a home office.

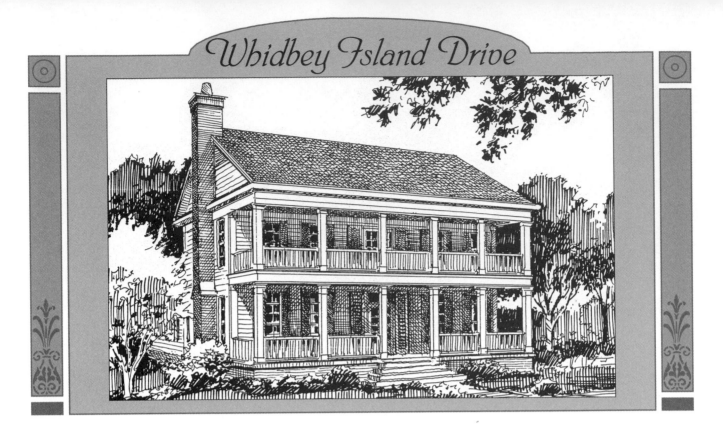

Whidbey Island Drive

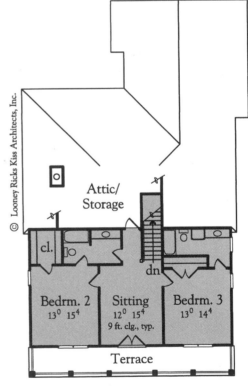

Decorative columns and charming balustrades set off this historical facade and reveal the sweet disposition of the spacious and thoroughly modern interior. The formal dining room opens just off the foyer and leads to the gourmet kitchen through a convenient butler's pantry. The living room features a focal-point fireplace and rear-porch access. The master bedroom includes a walk-in closet and whirlpool tub. Upstairs, two family bedrooms share a spacious sitting area. An upper-level terrace allows quiet conversation and stargazing on summer evenings.

PLAN W527

First Floor: 1,630 square feet
Second Floor: 881 square feet
Total: 2,511 square feet

Bedrooms: 3
Bathrooms: 3½

DESIGN BY
©*Looney Ricks Kiss Architects, Inc.*

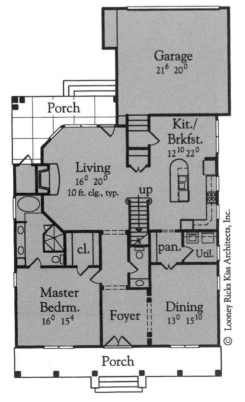

Garage
21⁶ 20⁰

Porch

Kit./
Brkfst.
12¹⁰ 22⁰

Living
16⁰ 20⁰
10 ft. clg., typ.

up

pan.

Util.

cl.

Master
Bedrm.
16⁰ 15⁴

Foyer

Dining
13⁰ 15¹⁰

Porch

© Looney Ricks Kiss Architects, Inc.

Attic/
Storage

cl.

dn

Bedrm. 2
13⁰ 15⁴

Sitting
12⁰ 15⁴
9 ft. clg., typ.

Bedrm. 3
13⁰ 14⁴

Terrace

Width 42'-1"
Depth 71'-5"

© Looney Ricks Kiss Architects, Inc.

VILLAGE

South Newport Circle

© 1996 Looney Ricks Kiss Architects, Inc.

Breakfast / Kitchen
15⁵ 19²

Garage
21⁰ 20⁹

Dining
12⁹ 14⁰

Study / Guest
11⁰ 11¹⁰

up

Living
17⁴ 15⁴
10 ft. clg., typ.

Courtyard

Covered Porch

dn

Width 38'-4"
Depth 64'-1"

© 1996 Looney Ricks Kiss Architects, Inc.

Bedroom 3
12⁰ 13⁸

dn

Bedroom 4
11⁷ 13⁵

Master Bedroom
17⁴ 14⁰
9 ft. clg., typ.

Covered Porch

PLAN W528

First Floor: 1,150 square feet
Second Floor: 1,194 square feet
Total: 2,344 square feet

Bedrooms: 3 or 4
Bathrooms: 3

This eye-catching facade is dominated by Colonial elements, such as the double portico and classic pediment. The well-planned interior begins with an open arrangement of the living and dining rooms. The kitchen serves the breakfast room and dining area with ease. A study/guest room has use of a hall bath. Upstairs, two family bedrooms enjoy walk-in closets and share a bath. The master suite provides two walk-in closets and a private balcony.

DESIGN BY
©*Looney Ricks Kiss Architects, Inc.*

TOWN VILLAGE

Glorietta Bay Drive

Width 39'-8"
Depth 51'-9"

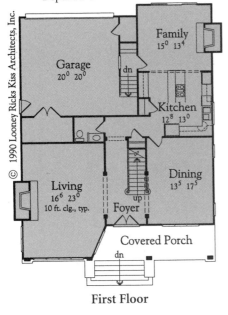

First Floor

Garage
20⁰ 20⁰

Family
15⁰ 13⁴

dn

Kitchen
12⁸ 13⁰

Living
16⁶ 23⁰
10 ft. clg., typ.

Foyer

up

Dining
13⁵ 17⁵

Covered Porch

dn

© 1990 Looney Ricks Kiss Architects, Inc.

Second Floor

Bedroom 3
18¹ 13⁴

up

dn

Master
Bedroom
16⁶ 23⁰
9 ft. clg., typ.

Bedroom 2
13⁵ 17⁵

Covered Balcony

© 1990 Looney Ricks Kiss Architects, Inc.

Loft

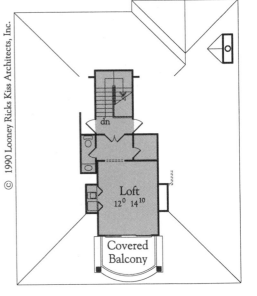

dn

Loft
12⁰ 14¹⁰

Covered
Balcony

© 1990 Looney Ricks Kiss Architects, Inc.

PLAN W524

First Floor: 1,318 square feet
Second Floor: 1,810 square feet
Loft: 250 square feet
Total: 3,378 square feet

Bedrooms: 3
Bathrooms: 3½ + ½

A raised porch with two-story columns, a covered balcony and a third-story portico create great outdoor spaces with this stunning Village or Edge design. The living room has a fireplace and a wall of windows to allow plenty of natural light within. The family room is also equipped with a fireplace, which shares its warmth with the L-shaped kitchen. On the second floor, each of two family bedrooms has its own full bath. The master suite is equipped with a fireplace, a double walk-in closet and separate vanities in the bath. The third floor provides a loft and a private balcony.

DESIGN BY
©Looney Ricks Kiss
Architects, Inc.

VILLAGE   EDGE

Prideaux Lane

© 1998 Donald A. Gardner, Inc.

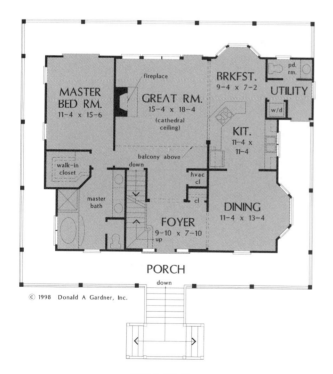

MASTER BED RM.
11-4 x 15-6

fireplace

GREAT RM.
15-4 x 18-4
(cathedral ceiling)

BRKFST.
9-4 x 7-2

UTILITY

w/d

pd. rm.

KIT.
11-4 x 11-4

walk-in closet

balcony above

down

hvac cl

cl

master bath

DINING
11-4 x 13-4

FOYER
9-10 x 7-10
up

PORCH

down

© 1998 Donald A Gardner, Inc.

Width 49'-4"
Depth 44'-10"

great room below

attic storage

attic storage

BED RM.
11-4 x 11-2

down

railing

BED RM.
11-4 x 11-2

cl

cl

bath

cl

cl

attic sto.

foyer below

attic storage

An enchanting wraparound porch, delightful dormers and bright bay windows create excitement inside and out for this Village or Edge home. The large center dormer brightens the vaulted foyer, while the great room with cathedral ceiling enjoys a trio of rear clerestory windows. A balcony dividing the second-floor bedrooms overlooks the great room and visually connects the two floors. The master suite features rear-porch access, a walk-in closet and private bath with a garden tub and separate shower. The second-floor bedrooms share a full bath.

PLAN 7759

First Floor: 1,362 square feet
Second Floor: 481 square feet
Total: 1,843 square feet

Bedrooms: 3
Bathrooms: 2½

DESIGN BY
*Donald A. Gardner
Architects, Inc.*

VILLAGE   EDGE

Runaway Bay

This two-story home's pleasing exterior is complemented by its warm character and decorative "widow's walk." The covered entry—with its dramatic transom window—leads to a spacious great room highlighted by a warming fireplace. To the right, the dining room and kitchen combine to provide a delightful place for mealtimes. Two bedrooms and a full bath complete the first floor. The upper-level master suite affords privacy to the homeowner and features a walk-in closet, separate dressing area and relaxing bath.

Rear View

PLAN 6616

Main Level: 1,136 square feet
Upper Level: 636 square feet
Total: 1,772 square feet

Bedrooms: 2 or 3
Bathrooms: 2

L

DESIGN BY
©*The Sater Design
Collection*

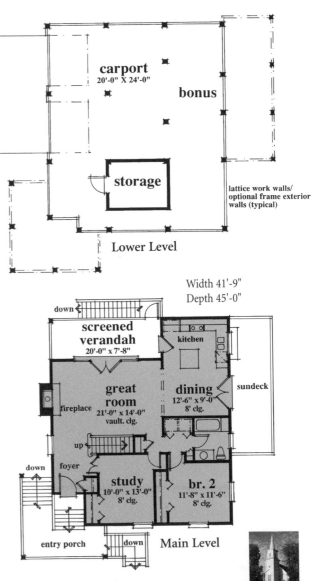

carport
20'-0" X 24'-0"

bonus

storage

lattice work walls/
optional frame exterior
walls (typical)

Lower Level

Width 41'-9"
Depth 45'-0"

down

**screened
verandah**
20'-0" x 7'-8"

kitchen

**great
room**
21'-0" x 14'-0"
vault. clg.

fireplace

dining
12'-6" x 9'-0"
8' clg.

sundeck

up

down

foyer

study
10'-0" x 13'-0"
8' clg.

br. 2
11'-8" x 11'-6"
8' clg.

entry porch   down   Main Level

**master
suite**
12'-3" x 20'-0"
8' clg.

open to
below

down

loft

w.i.c.

Upper Level

VILLAGE

Tradewind Court

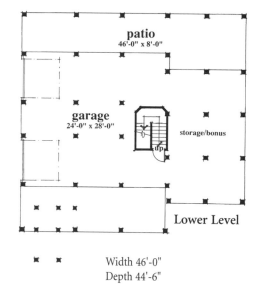

patio
46'-0" x 8'-0"

garage
24'-0" x 28'-0"

storage/bonus

up

Lower Level

H ere's a seaside retreat with an easy-going style. This island-flavored Floridian-style Village plan offers a master suite with a lofty vantage point. The heart of the home opens through lovely French doors to a screened veranda, which is served by a gourmet kitchen. A relaxed attitude is carried throughout the home with carefully designed living spaces and a soothing style. The entry leads through a well-lit foyer to an expansive great room, warmed by a fireplace. A roomy sun deck opens from the dining room and hosts casual meals, morning coffees and afternoon teas.

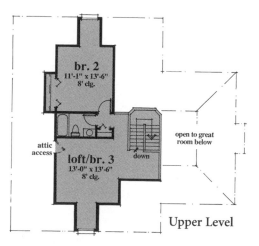

Rear View

DESIGN BY
©*The Sater Design
Collection*

Width 46'-0"
Depth 44'-6"

PLAN 6617

Main Level: 1,189 square feet
Upper Level: 575 square feet
Total: 1,764 square feet

Bedrooms: 3
Bathrooms: 2½

L

br. 2
11'-1" x 13'-6"
8' clg.

attic
access

loft/br. 3
13'-0" x 13'-6"
8' clg.

down

open to great
room below

Upper Level

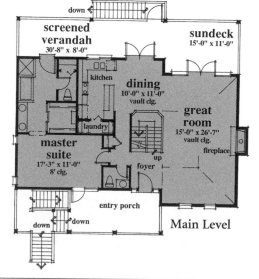

down

**screened
verandah**
30'-8" x 8'-0"

sundeck
15'-0" x 11'-0"

kitchen

dining
10'-0" x 11'-0"
vault clg.

**great
room**
15'-0" x 26'-7"
vault clg.

laundry

fireplace

**master
suite**
17'-3" x 11'-0"
8' clg.

up

foyer

entry porch

down   down

Main Level

Cayman Court

A blend of Southern comfort and Gulf Coast style sets this home apart. A covered porch runs the width of the home, creating a haven for family gatherings. Inside, decorative arches and columns mark the grand entrance to the living and dining areas, while the gourmet kitchen provides a pass-through to the dining room. On cold nights, a fireplace warms the great room, and on warm evenings, French doors to the porch let in cool breezes. Thoughtfully placed to the rear of the plan, the master suite has private access to a sun deck, and French doors open to the covered porch. This plan includes pier and crawlspace foundation options.

PLAN 6694

Square Footage: 1,792

Bedrooms: 2
Bathrooms: 2

DESIGN BY
©*The Sater Design Collection*

Rear View

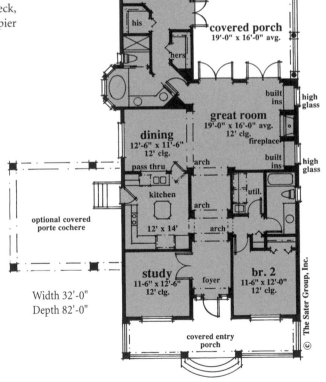

© The Sater Group, Inc.

master
12'-0" x 16'-6"
12' clg.

sundeck

his

hers

covered porch
19'-0" x 16'-0" avg.

built ins

high glass

great room
19'-0" x 16'-0" avg.
12' clg.

fireplace

dining
12'-6" x 11'-6"
12' clg.

arch

built ins

high glass

pass thru

kitchen
12' x 14'

arch

util.

arch

optional covered porte cochere

arch

study
11-6" x 12'-6"
12' clg.

foyer

br. 2
11-6" x 12'-0"
12' clg.

Width 32'-0"
Depth 82'-0"

covered entry porch

VILLAGE

Southampton Bay

A charming porte cochere sets off a perfect blend of Southern Cracker comfort and Gulf Coast style with this seaside retreat. Exposed rafters, lattice panels and a deep covered porch make a strong architectural statement that's tuned to a 1940s personality. Ocean breezes flow through the raised living area, which rallies a full palette of living spaces within a modest footprint. A secluded master suite nestles to the back of the plan, with private access to a sun deck and French doors to the covered porch. The sitting bay offers space for reading and adds plenty of sunlight to the homeowner's retreat.

PLAN 6684

Main Level: 2,385 square feet
Lower Level: 80 square feet
Total: 2,465 square feet

Bedrooms: 3
Bathrooms: 2½

DESIGN BY
©*The Sater Design
Collection*

Width 60'-4"
Depth 59'-4

Main Level

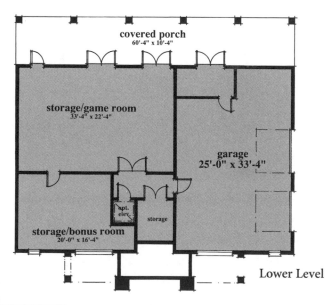

Lower Level

Rear View

Monticello Place

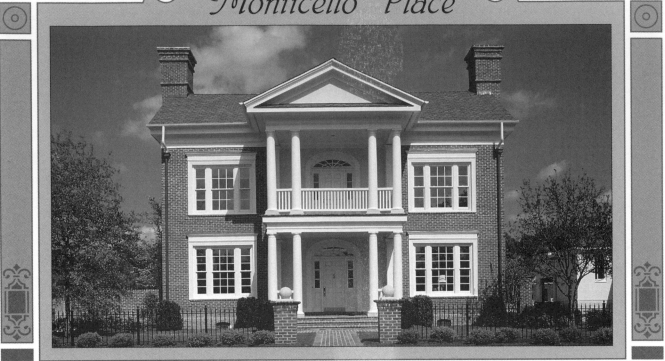

Photo by ©Jeffrey Jacobs/Architectural Photography

This home, as shown in the photograph, may differ from the actual blueprints.

PLAN W530

First Floor: 3,504 square feet
Second Floor: 1,725 square feet
Total: 5,229 square feet

Bedrooms: 6
Bathrooms: 4½

DESIGN BY
©Looney Ricks Kiss
Architects, Inc.

Width 56'-9"
Depth 122'-0"

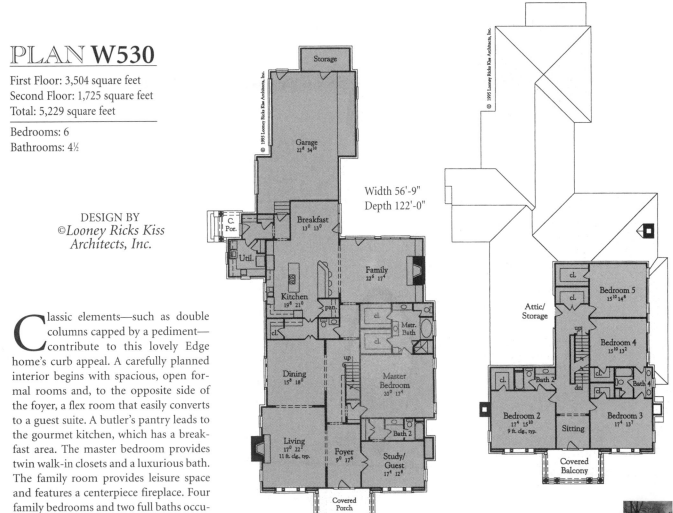

Classic elements—such as double columns capped by a pediment—contribute to this lovely Edge home's curb appeal. A carefully planned interior begins with spacious, open formal rooms and, to the opposite side of the foyer, a flex room that easily converts to a guest suite. A butler's pantry leads to the gourmet kitchen, which has a breakfast area. The master bedroom provides twin walk-in closets and a luxurious bath. The family room provides leisure space and features a centerpiece fireplace. Four family bedrooms and two full baths occupy the second floor.

EDGE

Edge of Town

Arcadian Groves, Country Estates and Woodlands

The perimeter of a community is a place of transition from urban to rural, from community to countryside.

Comfortable Homes for Spacious Lots

Altamont Way

Photo by Riley & Riley Photography, Inc.

This home, as shown in the photograph, may differ from the actual blueprints. For more detailed information, please check the floor plans carefully.

A neighborly porch as friendly as a handshake wraps around this charming country home, warmly greeting family and friends. Inside, cathedral ceilings promote a feeling of spaciousness. The foyer opens to the great room, enhanced by a fireplace and built-in bookshelves. The formal dining room offers wraparound views and a door to a private area of the porch. A private master suite features a walk-in closet and lavish bath. A basement or crawlspace foundation is available.

PLAN 7601

Square Footage: 1,787
Bonus Room: 326 square feet

Bedrooms: 3
Bathrooms: 2

Width 66'-2"
Depth 66'-8"

DESIGN BY
Donald A. Gardner
Architects, Inc.

Rear View

VILLAGE   EDGE

Beaufort Lane

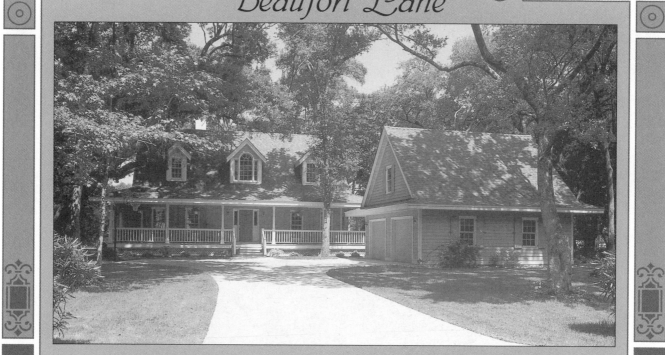

This home, as shown in the photograph, may differ from the actual blueprints. For more detailed information, please check the floor plans carefully.

Photo by Riley & Riley Photography, Inc.

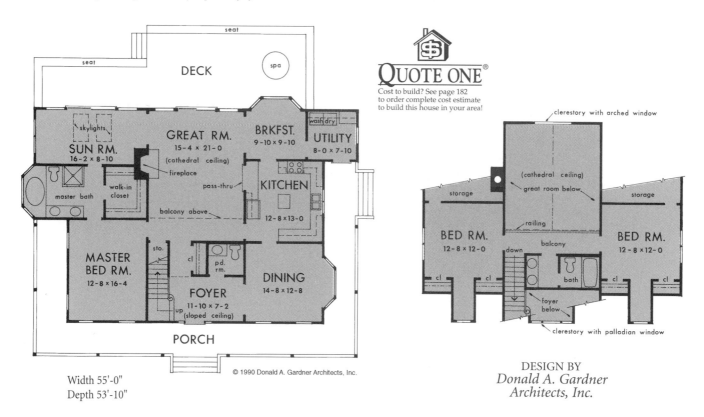

Width 55'-0"
Depth 53'-10"

© 1990 Donald A. Gardner Architects, Inc.

QUOTE ONE®

Cost to build? See page 182 to order complete cost estimate to build this house in your area!

DESIGN BY
Donald A. Gardner Architects, Inc.

PLAN 9623

First Floor: 1,651 square feet
Second Floor: 567 square feet
Total: 2,218 square feet

Bedrooms: 3
Bathrooms: 2½

The wraparound porch of this wonderful Edge home complements the deck and spa that extend the living area to the rear of the plan. A thoroughly up-to-date interior begins with a spacious great room, appointed with a fireplace, cathedral ceiling and arch-top clerestory. The central kitchen features a convenient food preparation island and wrapping counters. The master suite provides private access to a sun room. Two second-floor bedrooms share a balcony hall that provides an overlook to the great room. A basement or crawlspace foundation is available.

EDGE

Deer Isle Road

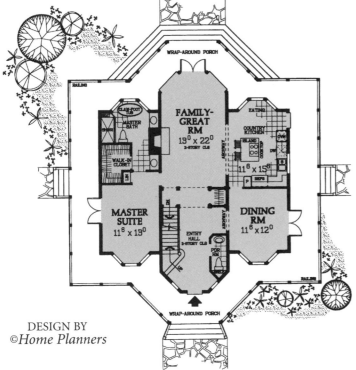

DESIGN BY
©*Home Planners*

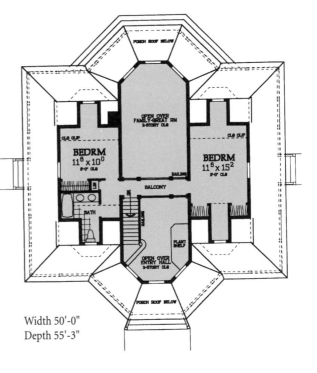

Width 50'-0"
Depth 55'-3"

PLAN 3620

First Floor: 1,295 square feet
Second Floor: 600 square feet
Total: 1,895 square feet

Bedrooms: 3
Bathrooms: 2½

This charming wraparound porch of this Southern-style farmhouse extends a hearty welcome to passersby. Guests may linger on the front porch but you'll want to invite them inside to see the two-story great room. Decorative columns and pilasters help define the open living area, which features a massive fireplace. An arched opening leads to the L-shaped country kitchen. Lovely French doors open from the spacious master suite to a private area of the porch.

Cost to build? See page 182
to order complete cost estimate
to build this house in your area!

Rocky Point Road

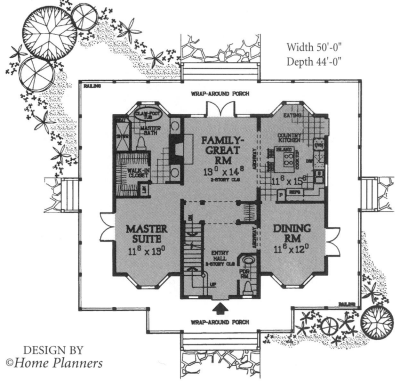

Width 50'-0"
Depth 44'-0"

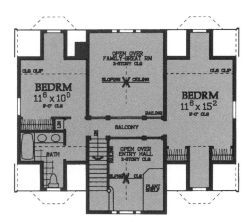

DESIGN BY
©Home Planners

QUOTE ONE®

Cost to build? See page 182
to order complete cost estimate
to build this house in your area!

PLAN 3619

First Floor: 1,171 square feet
Second Floor: 600 square feet
Total: 1,771 square feet

Bedrooms: 3
Bathrooms: 2½

There's nothing that tops gracious Southern hospitality—unless it's offered Southern farmhouse style! The efficient country kitchen shares space with a bay-windowed eating area. The two-story great room is warmed by a fireplace. The master suite offers room to curl up with a good book by the bay window. The second floor holds two family bedrooms and a full bath. Plans for an optional indoor swimming pool/spa and detached garage are included.

EDGE

Woodland Lane

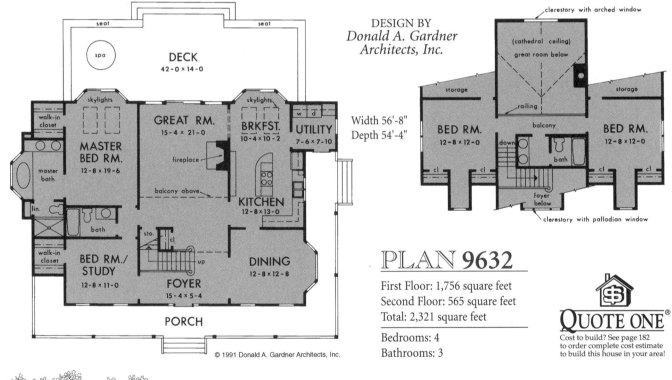

© 1991 Donald A. Gardner Architects, Inc.

DESIGN BY
Donald A. Gardner
Architects, Inc.

Width 56'-8"
Depth 54'-4"

DECK
42-0 × 14-0

seat   seat

spa

skylights   skylights

GREAT RM.   **BRKFST.**   **UTILITY**
15-4 × 21-0   10-4 × 10-2   7-6 × 7-10

walk-in closet

MASTER BED RM.
12-8 × 19-6

fireplace

master bath

balcony above

KITCHEN
12-8 × 13-0

lin.

bath

BED RM./ STUDY
12-8 × 11-0

sto.   cl

up

FOYER
15-4 × 5-4

DINING
12-8 × 12-8

walk-in closet

PORCH

© 1991 Donald A. Gardner Architects, Inc.

clerestory with arched window

(cathedral ceiling)
great room below

storage   storage

railing

BED RM.   balcony   **BED RM.**
12-8 × 12-0   12-8 × 12-0

down   bath

cl   cl   cl   cl

foyer below

clerestory with palladian window

PLAN 9632

First Floor: 1,756 square feet
Second Floor: 565 square feet
Total: 2,321 square feet

Bedrooms: 4
Bathrooms: 3

QUOTE ONE®
Cost to build? See page 182
to order complete cost estimate
to build this house in your area!

Rear View

A wraparound covered porch at the front and sides of this house and an open deck at the back provide plenty of outside living area. The spacious great room features a fireplace and cathedral ceiling. The island kitchen has a skylit breakfast room. The first-floor master bedroom includes a generous closet, garden tub, double-bowl vanity and shower. The second floor provides two bedrooms and a full bath with a double-bowl vanity. A basement or crawlspace foundation is available.

EDGE

Bailey Circle

© 1990 Donald A. Gardner Architects, Inc.

PLAN 9616

First Floor: 1,734 square feet
Second Floor: 958 square feet
Total: 2,692 square feet

Bedrooms: 4
Bathrooms: 3½

DESIGN BY
*Donald A. Gardner
Architects, Inc.*

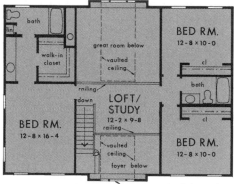

clerestory with palladian window

bath
lin
walk-in closet
great room below
vaulted ceiling

BED RM.
12-8 × 10-0
cl

LOFT/
STUDY
12-2 × 9-8
railing

BED RM.
12-8 × 16-4
railing
down

bath
cl

BED RM.
12-8 × 10-0

vaulted ceiling
foyer below

clerestory with palladian window

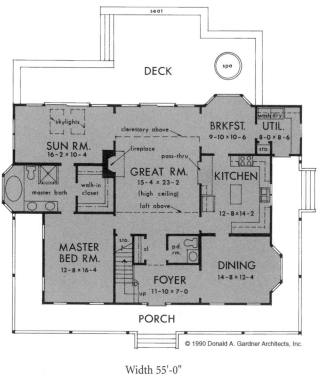

seat

DECK

spa

skylights

SUN RM.
16-2 × 10-4

fireplace

clerestory above

BRKFST.
9-10 × 10-6

wash dry

UTIL.
8-0 × 8-6

master bath

walk-in closet

pass-thru

GREAT RM.
15-4 × 23-2
(high ceiling)

loft above

KITCHEN
12-8 × 14-2

sto.

MASTER
BED RM.
12-8 × 16-4

sto.
cl

pd. rm.

DINING
14-8 × 12-4

FOYER
11-10 × 7-0
up

PORCH

© 1990 Donald A. Gardner Architects, Inc.

Width 55'-0"
Depth 59'-10"

A wraparound covered porch at the front and sides of this home and the open deck with spa and seating provide plenty of outside living area. A central great room features a vaulted ceiling, fireplace and clerestory windows above. The loft/study on the second floor overlooks this gathering area. Besides a formal dining room, kitchen, breakfast room and sun room on the first floor, there is also a generous master suite with garden tub. A basement or crawlspace foundation is available.

Rear View

Peachtree Corner

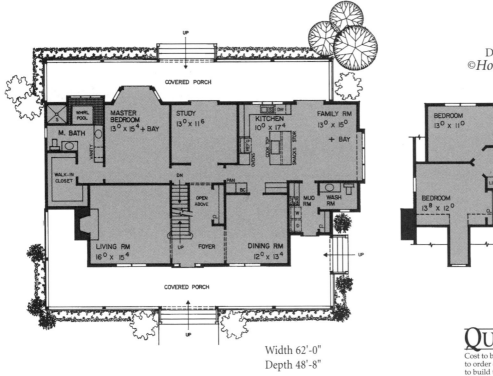

COVERED PORCH

UP

MASTER BEDROOM 13⁰ x 15⁴ + BAY

STUDY 13⁰ x 11⁶

KITCHEN 10⁰ x 17⁴

FAMILY RM 13⁰ x 15⁰ + BAY

WHIRL POOL

M. BATH

VANITY

REF'G

OVENS

COOK TOP

SNACKS STOR

WALK-IN CLOSET

DN

PAN

BC

OPEN ABOVE

CL

MUD RM

WASH RM

W D

LIVING RM 16⁰ x 15⁴

UP

FOYER

DINING RM 12⁰ x 13⁴

UP

COVERED PORCH

UP

Width 62'-0"
Depth 48'-8"

DESIGN BY
©Home Planners

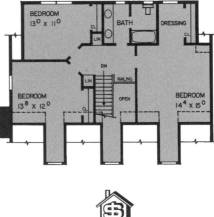

BEDROOM 13⁰ x 11⁰

BATH

DRESSING

CL

LIN

BEDROOM 13⁸ x 12⁰

LIN

DN

LIN

RAILING

OPEN

CL

BEDROOM 14⁴ x 15⁰

QUOTE ONE®

Cost to build? See page 182
to order complete cost estimate
to build this house in your area!

PLAN 3396

First Floor: 1,829 square feet
Second Floor: 947 square feet
Total: 2,776 square feet

Bedrooms: 4
Bathrooms: 2½

L D

Rustic charm abounds in this pleasant farmhouse rendi-
tion. Covered porches to the front and rear enclose living
potential for the whole family. Flanking the entrance foyer
are the living and dining rooms. To the rear is the L-shaped
kitchen with snack bar and an adjacent family room/breakfast
nook. A private study is tucked away next to the master suite. On
the second floor are three bedrooms and a full bath.

EDGE

Huxley Park Way

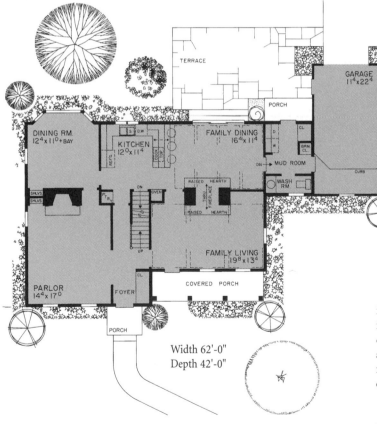

Width 62'-0"
Depth 42'-0"

DINING RM. 12⁴x11⁰+BAY
KITCHEN 12⁰x11⁴
FAMILY DINING 16⁴x11⁴
GARAGE 11⁴x22⁴
TERRACE
PORCH
MUD ROOM
WASH RM.
PARLOR 14⁴x17⁰
FOYER
COVERED PORCH
FAMILY LIVING 19⁸x13⁴
PORCH

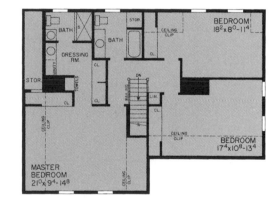

BATH
DRESSING RM.
STOR.
BATH
STOR.
BEDROOM 18²x8⁰-11⁴
BEDROOM 17⁴x10⁸-13⁴
MASTER BEDROOM 21⁰x9⁴-14⁸

This Early American farmhouse features the simple gable rooflines, shuttered multi-pane windows and stately entry pilaster of simpler times. A massive see-through fireplace is the focal point, providing warmth to the family living and dining rooms. Beam ceilings add to the country atmosphere. An efficient U-shaped kitchen easily serves both dining rooms and also provides a snack bar. Upstairs, sleeping quarters include two family bedrooms, which share a bath, and a master suite with its own glorious bath.

PLAN 2681

First Floor: 1,350 square feet
Second Floor: 1,224 square feet
Total: 2,574 square feet

Bedrooms: 3
Bathrooms: 2½

DESIGN BY
©Home Planners

VILLAGE | EDGE

Hanley Corner

C haracteristic of this pleasing Dutch Colonial style are elements such as the clapboard siding, the gambrel roofline, twin chimneys and two covered porches. The floor plans include a large family room with a raised-hearth fireplace and built-in desk. A convenient kitchen offers a pass-through to the family room. There is also a formal dining room, with a third fireplace and a butler's pantry with a wet bar. The master suite includes a pampering bath with a dressing area.

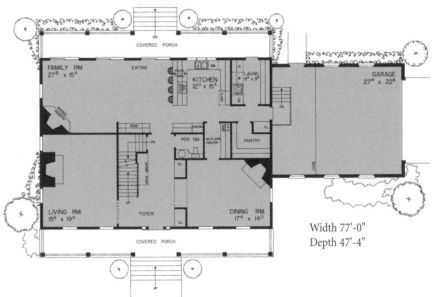

Width 77'-0"
Depth 47'-4"

PLAN 2697

First Floor: 1,752 square feet
Second Floor: 1,486 square feet
Total: 3,238 square feet

Bedrooms: 4
Bathrooms: 3½

DESIGN BY
© *Home Planners*

EDGE

Morenci Way

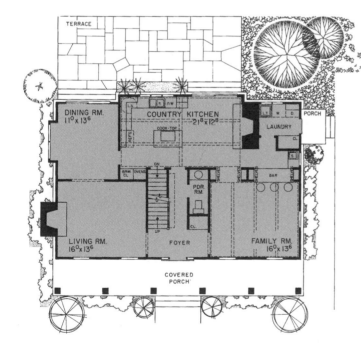

DESIGN BY
©*Home Planners*

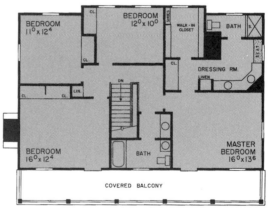

Width 44'-8"
Depth 36'-0"

PLAN 2664

First Floor: 1,308 square feet
Second Floor: 1,262 square feet
Total: 2,570 square feet

Bedrooms: 4
Bathrooms: 2½

D

A double porch highlights the Early American exterior of this Edge farmhouse. Much of its charm is in its symmetry—a centered entrance, well-spaced windows and a straightforward rectangular shape. Gathering areas dominate the front of the first floor: a living room with a fireplace and a family room with a wet bar. The country kitchen has a commanding fireplace, an island cooktop and plenty of space for informal dining. Upstairs, three family bedrooms cluster around a full bath.

EDGE

Matthew Place

This two-story Edge design faithfully recalls the 18th-Century homestead of Secretary of Foreign Affairs John Jay. The first-floor includes a grand living room, which has a fireplace and music alcove, and a library with a second fireplace and built-in bookshelves. The formal dining room leads to a country kitchen with a snack counter and a fireplace. Upstairs, three family bedrooms complement a spacious master suite with a walk-in closet, vanity seating and double lavatories.

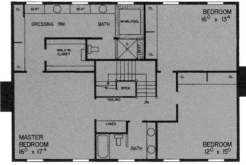

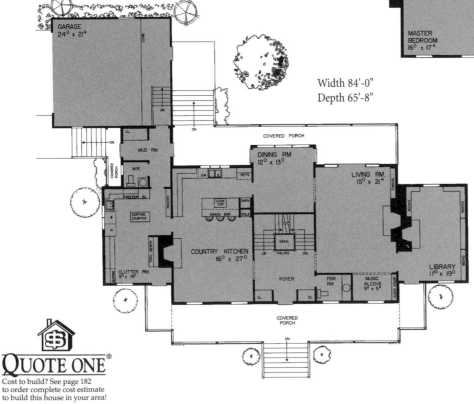

Width 84'-0"
Depth 65'-8"

PLAN 2694

First Floor: 2,026 square feet
Second Floor: 1,386 square feet
Total: 3,412 square feet

Bedrooms: 3
Bathrooms: 2½ + ½

L

DESIGN BY
©*Home Planners*

VILLAGE EDGE

Wadsworth Circle

Raised covered porches, finely detailed railings and four fireplaces lend a noble character to this Edge or Village farmhouse. Both the formal living and dining rooms have corner fireplaces—so does the family room. The tiled country kitchen provides wrapping counters, a planning desk and easy access to the utility room. On the second floor, the master retreat sports its own fireplace and a roomy dressing area.

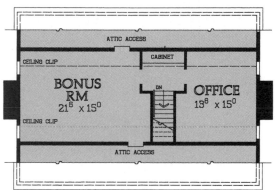

Third Floor

Width 40'-0"
Depth 40'-0"

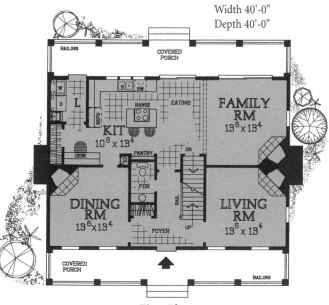

First Floor

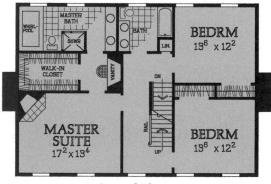

Second Floor

PLAN 3510

First Floor: 1,120 square feet
Second Floor: 1,083 square feet
Third Floor: 597 square feet
Total: 2,800 square feet

Bedrooms: 3
Bathrooms: 2½

DESIGN BY
©Home Planners

QUOTE ONE®
Cost to build? See page 182
to order complete cost estimate
to build this house in your area!

VILLAGE   EDGE

Schweitzer Lane

PLAN Y002

First Floor: 2,473 square feet
Second Floor: 1,233 square feet
Total: 3,706 square feet

Bedrooms: 3
Bathrooms: 2½

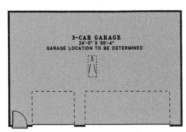

3-CAR GARAGE
24'-0" X 36'-4"
GARAGE LOCATION TO BE DETERMINED

This twin-gabled farmhouse is sure to please, with its covered front porch, large screened back porch and many other amenities. Inside, the foyer is flanked by a formal dining room and a cozy study. Double doors separate the foyer from the spacious great room. The master suite provides two walk-in closets, a separate exercise room and lavish bath. Upstairs, an absolutely luxurious bath will make family or guests feel like royalty. Please specify basement, crawlspace or slab foundation when ordering.

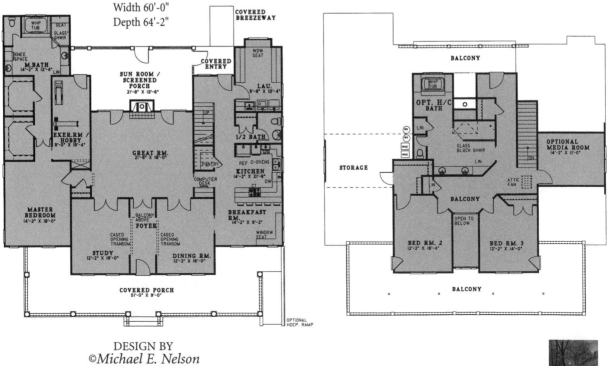

Width 60'-0"
Depth 64'-2"

DESIGN BY
©*Michael E. Nelson*
Nelson Design Group, LLC

EDGE

Graceful columns line the covered front porch of this fine country mansion. A spacious foyer extends a warm welcome to family and friends and leads to a formal dining room and a private study. To the rear of the plan, the gourmet kitchen boasts a hearth/breakfast room. Three bedrooms and two baths make up the second floor. Please specify crawlspace or slab foundation when ordering.

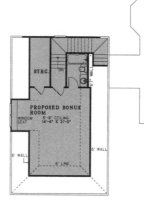

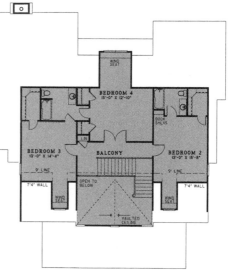

Width 92'-5"
Depth 64'-0"

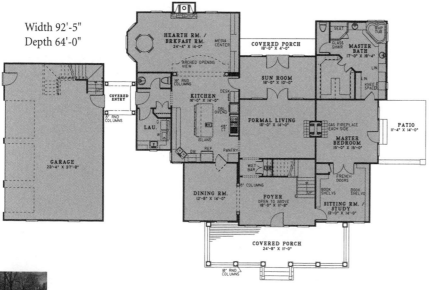

PLAN Y005

First Floor: 2,651 square feet
Second Floor: 1,089 square feet
Total: 3,740 square feet
Bonus Room: 497 square feet

Bedrooms: 4
Bathrooms: 4½

DESIGN BY
©*Michael E. Nelson*
Nelson Design Group, LLC

EDGE

Timberlyne Hollow

The kitchen is at the heart of this comfortable, sophisticated cottage, surrounded by the first-floor living areas. A spacious master suite dominates a private wing and provides a dressing area and whirlpool tub. Upstairs, a clustered arrangement of three family bedrooms leads to a balcony hall and additional storage space. There are porches both front and back and an optional porte cochere. This home is designed with a basement foundation.

Homeowner's Option: This garage may be customized to provide a rear entry.

PLAN T250

First Floor: 1,930 square feet
Second Floor: 1,238 square feet
Total: 3,168 square feet

Bedrooms: 4
Bathrooms: 3½

Width 72'-2"
Depth 74'-0"

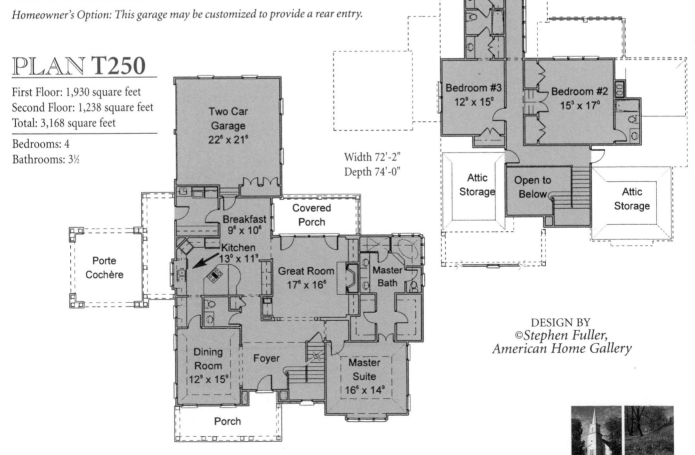

DESIGN BY
©*Stephen Fuller,*
American Home Gallery

VILLAGE EDGE

Spring Hollow

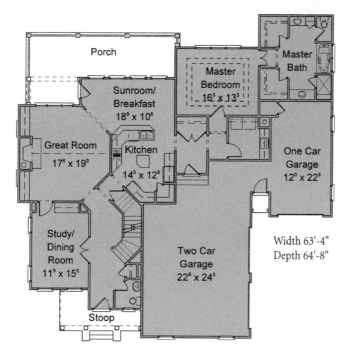

Porch

Sunroom/
Breakfast
18⁸ x 10⁶

Master
Bedroom
16³ x 13³

Master
Bath

Great Room
17⁶ x 19⁰

Kitchen
14³ x 12⁶

One Car
Garage
12⁰ x 22⁹

Study/
Dining
Room
11⁹ x 15⁰

Two Car
Garage
22⁶ x 24³

Stoop

Width 63'-4"
Depth 64'-8"

PLAN T251

First Floor: 1,865 square feet
Second Floor: 1,155 square feet
Total: 3,020 square feet

Bedrooms: 4
Bathrooms: 3½

DESIGN BY
©*Stephen Fuller,*
American Home Gallery

This enchanting Edge home calls up a sense of an upscale cabin in the woods. The board-and-batten exterior adds warmth, while the classic columns on the porch add style. The foyer features a dramatic curving staircase and leads to a room that can be used as a study, dining room or home office. The great room boasts a vaulted ceiling and opens to a bright sun room and spacious rear deck. The private master suite at the rear of the home features a large bath suite, walk-in closets and a garden view. This home is designed with a basement foundation.

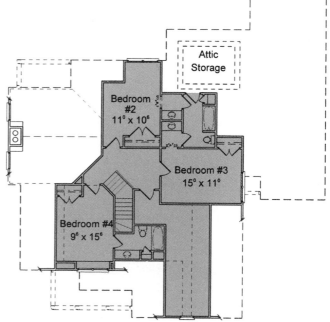

Attic
Storage

Bedroom
#2
11⁰ x 10⁶

Bedroom #3
15⁰ x 11⁰

Bedroom #4
9⁶ x 15⁶

EDGE

Mayfair Cottage

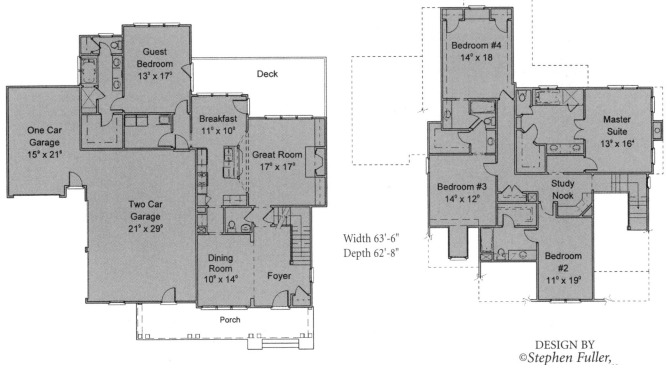

Width 63'-6"
Depth 62'-8"

DESIGN BY
©*Stephen Fuller,*
American Home Gallery

PLAN T253

First Floor: 1,512 square feet
Second Floor: 1,746 square feet
Total: 3,258 square feet

Bedrooms: 5
Bathrooms: 4½

Here's a sensational plan for the Edge or Village area of the neighborhood. A sophisticated shingle style mixes a very clean, cutting-edge look with the relaxed feel of a cottage, with details such as dovecote gables and flower boxes. Inside, the foyer leads to the lovely formal rooms. The great room, kitchen and breakfast room are combined into one generous open space that leads to a large back deck. The first-floor guest room is really a second master suite with ample backyard views. This home is designed with a basement foundation.

River Bend Way

This home, as shown in the photograph, may differ from the actual blueprints.
For more detailed information, please check the floor plans carefully.

Photo by Northlight Photography

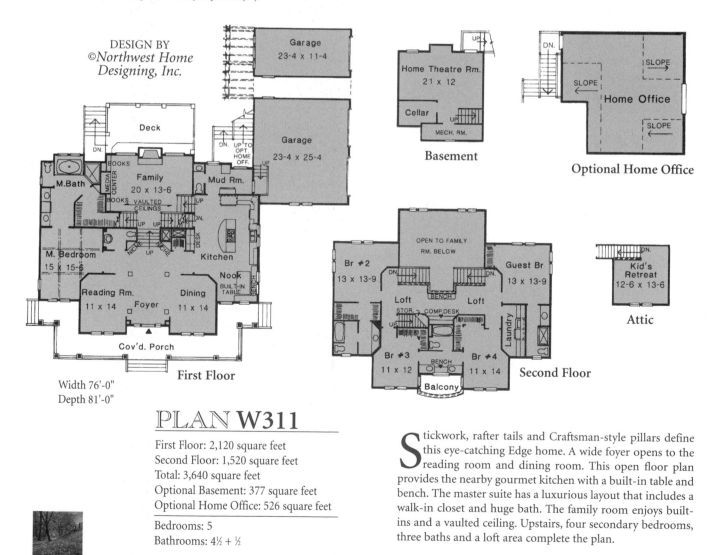

DESIGN BY
©*Northwest Home*
Designing, Inc.

Garage 23-4 x 11-4

Garage 23-4 x 25-4

Deck

M.Bath

Family 20 x 13-6 VAULTED CEILINGS

Mud Rm.

BOOKS / MEDIA CENTER / BOOKS

M. Bedroom 15 x 15-6

NICHE / NICHE / DESK

Kitchen

Nook BUILT-IN TABLE

Reading Rm. 11 x 14

Foyer

Dining 11 x 14

Cov'd. Porch

Width 76'-0"
Depth 81'-0"

First Floor

Home Theatre Rm. 21 x 12

Cellar

MECH. RM.

Basement

Home Office

SLOPE / SLOPE / SLOPE

Optional Home Office

OPEN TO FAMILY RM. BELOW

Br #2 13 x 13-9

Guest Br 13 x 13-9

Loft

STOR. / COMP. DESK

Loft

BENCH

Laundry

Br #3 11 x 12

BENCH

Br #4 11 x 14

Balcony

Second Floor

Kid's Retreat 12-6 x 13-6

Attic

PLAN W311

First Floor: 2,120 square feet
Second Floor: 1,520 square feet
Total: 3,640 square feet
Optional Basement: 377 square feet
Optional Home Office: 526 square feet

Bedrooms: 5
Bathrooms: 4½ + ½

Stickwork, rafter tails and Craftsman-style pillars define this eye-catching Edge home. A wide foyer opens to the reading room and dining room. This open floor plan provides the nearby gourmet kitchen with a built-in table and bench. The master suite has a luxurious layout that includes a walk-in closet and huge bath. The family room enjoys built-ins and a vaulted ceiling. Upstairs, four secondary bedrooms, three baths and a loft area complete the plan.

Foxborough Hill

PLAN T254

First Floor: 1,804 square feet
Second Floor: 1,041 square feet
Total: 2,845 square feet

Bedrooms: 4
Bathrooms: 3½

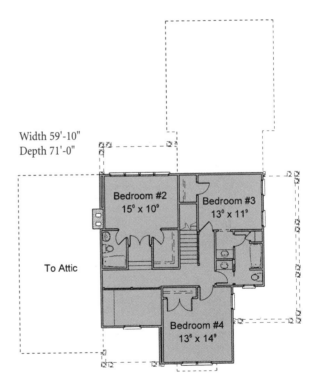

Width 59'-10"
Depth 71'-0"

There's a feeling of old Charleston in this stately home—particularly on the quiet side porch that wraps around the kitchen and breakfast room. The interior of this Village or Edge home revolves around a spacious great room with a welcoming fireplace. The left wing is dedicated to the master suite, which boasts wide views of the rear property. A corner kitchen easily serves planned events in the formal dining room as well as family meals in the breakfast area. A spacious front room easily converts to a parlor, study or den. This home is designed with a basement foundation.

Homeowner's Option: This garage may be customized to provide a rear entry.

DESIGN BY
©*Stephen Fuller,*
American Home Gallery

Roe Hampton Place

This beautiful home features an overhanging second floor with dramatic drop pendants. Inside this Village or Edge plan, the foyer offers great interior vistas past the staircase to the open great room. A gourmet kitchen overlooks the casual dining area, which leads outdoors for breakfasts on the rear porch. Upstairs, the master suite provides wide views to the backyard. Two additional bedrooms, a study alcove and a bonus room provide additional flexible space. This home is designed with a basement foundation.

PLAN T255

First Floor: 1,104 square feet
Second Floor: 1,144 square feet
Total: 2,248 square feet
Bonus Room: 220 square feet

Bedrooms: 3
Bathrooms: 2½

Bonus
22⁰ x 10⁰

Bedroom #2
14⁰ x 11⁰

Master Bedroom
15³ x 15⁹

WIC

Bedroom #3
11⁰ x 11⁶

Width 64'-0"
Depth 35'-0"

Porch

Kitchen

Breakfast
9⁰ x 14³

Great Room
19³ x 15⁰

Two Car Garage
22⁰ x 21⁰

9⁰ x 14³

Dining Room
12⁰ x 13⁰

Foyer

DESIGN BY
©Stephen Fuller,
American Home Gallery

VILLAGE | EDGE

Huntwick Place

With its simple, straightforward shapes—including shingles and shutters—this stunning Edge or Village home provides a touch of Colonial Nantucket. The entry leads to a spacious great room, the heart of this home. A centered fireplace and built-in shelves define this space, which provides a door to the rear deck. Upstairs, a gallery hall ends in a staircase that leads down to the breakfast area. Two large secondary bedrooms and a guest suite contribute to this home's spaciousness. This home is designed with a basement foundation.

Homeowner's Option: This garage may be customized to provide a rear entry.

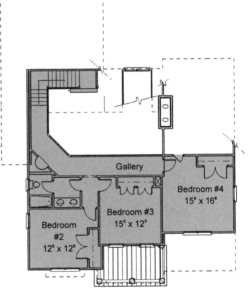

Width 72'-0"
Depth 72'-6"

Two Car Garage
24³ x 21⁸

Deck

Breakfast
14⁸ x 14³

Great Room
15⁸ x 18⁰

Master Bath

Porte Cochère

Kitchen
14³ x 12⁹

Master Suite
16⁰ x 16⁸

Dining Room
14⁰ x 12⁹

Porch

DESIGN BY
©*Stephen Fuller,*
American Home Gallery

Gallery

Bedroom #4
15⁶ x 16⁶

Bedroom #3
15⁰ x 12⁰

Bedroom #2
12⁶ x 12⁸

PLAN T258

First Floor: 1,840 square feet
Second Floor: 957 square feet
Total: 2,797 square feet

Bedrooms: 4
Bathrooms: 3½

VILLAGE | EDGE

Sawbranch Hill

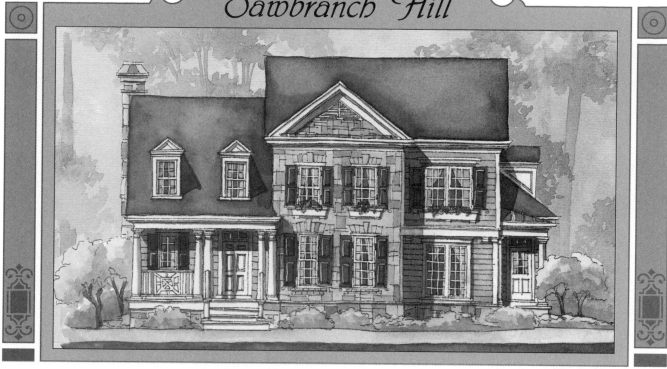

DESIGN BY
©*Stephen Fuller,*
American Home Gallery

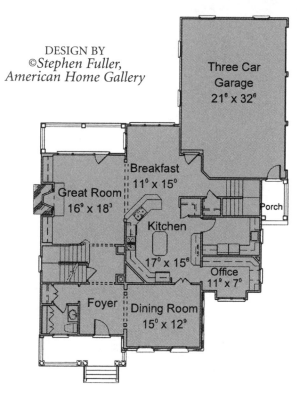

Three Car Garage
21⁶ x 32⁶

Breakfast
11⁰ x 15⁰

Great Room
16⁹ x 18³

Kitchen
17⁰ x 15⁶

Porch

Office
11⁹ x 7⁰

Foyer

Dining Room
15⁰ x 12⁹

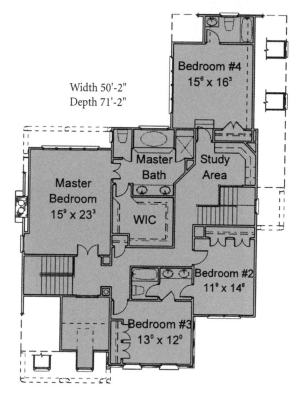

Width 50'-2"
Depth 71'-2"

Bedroom #4
15⁶ x 16³

Master Bedroom
15⁹ x 23³

Master Bath

Study Area

WIC

Bedroom #2
11⁹ x 14⁶

Bedroom #3
13⁰ x 12⁰

PLAN T259

First Floor: 1,619 square feet
Second Floor: 1,811 square feet
Total: 3,430 square feet

Bedrooms: 4
Bathrooms: 3½

A comfortable front porch provides the look of Country, while a "jetty" overhanging the front porch lends an element of Garrison style. The foyer, lit by a clerestory dormer, opens to the dining room and leads to the spacious great room with a porch in back. In the center of the plan, a dramatic kitchen provides space enough for more than one cook. A front staircase leads up to the master suite and provides definition between the formal and casual areas of the home. This home is designed with a basement foundation.

EDGE

Hedgewood Heights

PLAN T256

First Floor: 2,012 square feet
Second Floor: 1,254 square feet
Total: 3,266 square feet

Bedrooms: 4
Bathrooms: 3½

DESIGN BY
©*Stephen Fuller,*
American Home Gallery

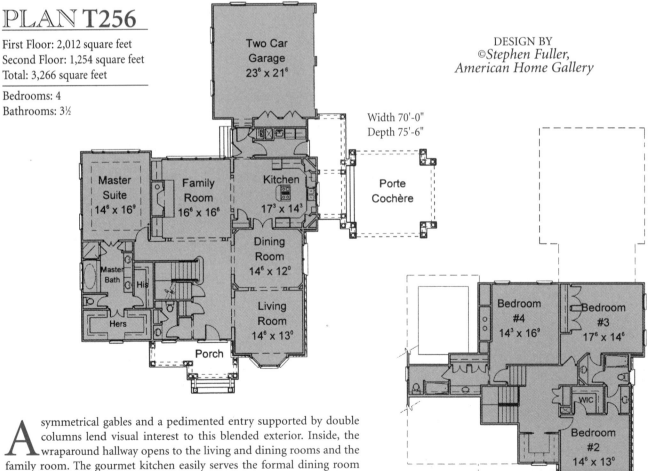

Width 70'-0"
Depth 75'-6"

Two Car Garage 23⁶ x 21⁶

Master Suite 14⁶ x 16⁹

Family Room 16⁶ x 16⁶

Kitchen 17³ x 14³

Porte Cochère

Master Bath

His

Hers

Dining Room 14⁶ x 12⁰

Living Room 14⁶ x 13⁰

Porch

Bedroom #4 14³ x 16⁹

Bedroom #3 17⁶ x 14⁶

WIC

Bedroom #2 14⁶ x 13⁰

A symmetrical gables and a pedimented entry supported by double columns lend visual interest to this blended exterior. Inside, the wraparound hallway opens to the living and dining rooms and the family room. The gourmet kitchen easily serves the formal dining room and conveniently opens to the family room. The master suite is tucked into a private corner of the plan. Spacious second-floor bedrooms share a full bath, while a nearby guest suite provides its own bath. This home is designed with a basement foundation.

Homeowner's Option: This garage may be customized to provide a rear entry.

EDGE

Lynmoor Square

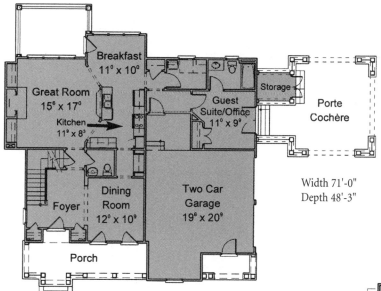

PLAN T257

First Floor: 1,726 square feet
Second Floor: 1,246 square feet
Total: 2,972 square feet

Bedrooms: 5
Bathrooms: 3½

Width 71'-0"
Depth 48'-3"

DESIGN BY
©*Stephen Fuller,*
American Home Gallery

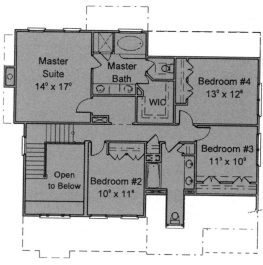

With an interior designed as one large open space, this Edge home combines elegance with convenience, for the utmost in comfortable living. The great room opens to the well-planned kitchen, which leads to the formal dining room through a butler's pantry. To the rear of the plan, the guest suite enjoys private access to a small side porch. Upstairs, the master bedroom is raised from the rest of the rooms, providing a private suite. Three additional bedrooms share the large central bath. This home is designed with a basement foundation.

Warrenton

© American Home Gallery, Ltd.

Deck

Keeping Room/Solarium
14⁰x10³

Breakfast
10³x13⁶

Kitchen
10⁰x15³

Two Car Garage
22⁰x23³

Great Room
14⁰x21⁶

Dn

Up

Foyer

Dining Room
13³x11⁹

Living Room
13³x14³

Porch

Width 65'-6"
Depth 49'-0"

Double-hung windows and shutters typify the Georgian Revival style, while an inset porch acknowledges more than a passing acquaintance with the Federal period in post-Revolutionary America. Columns create a charming entry to a well-cultivated and stylish interior design. The great room offers a focal-point fireplace and opens to a solarium with views of the rear property. Family and friends will gather in the bright breakfast area, open to the kitchen. The nearby deck poses an invitation to enjoy the outdoors. This home is designed with a basement foundation.

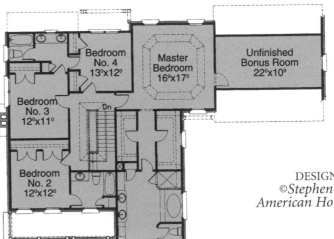

Bedroom No. 4
13⁰x12⁰

Master Bedroom
16⁰x17³

Unfinished Bonus Room
22⁰x10⁹

Bedroom No. 3
12⁰x11⁰

Dn

Bedroom No. 2
12⁰x12⁰

DESIGN BY
©Stephen Fuller,
American Home Gallery

PLAN T166

First Floor: 1,615 square feet
Second Floor: 1,510 square feet
Total: 3,125 square feet
Bonus Room: 255 square feet

Bedrooms: 4
Bathrooms: 3½

VILLAGE   EDGE

Brentwood

W elcoming and graceful, this home is perfect for those who entertain and enjoy the company of friends and guests. The front steps lead to a recessed entry, enhanced with pilasters and a classical cornice detail. The foyer opens to the formal dining room, which is served by a well-organized kitchen through a butler's pantry. A centered fireplace warms the spacious great room, which has a lovely triple window. The nearby breakfast area leads out to the rear deck, also accessed from the master suite. This home is designed with a basement foundation.

PLAN T229

First Floor: 1,355 square feet
Second Floor: 760 square feet
Total: 2,115 square feet

Bedrooms: 4
Bathrooms: 3½

Width 46'-0"
Depth 51'-8"

Bedroom No. 4
11⁰ x 10⁰

Bedroom No. 3
11⁰ x 12³

Future Study/Office
20⁹ x 15³

Bath

W.I.C.

Bedroom No. 2
10⁹ x 10⁹

Loft

Master Bedroom
11⁹ x 16⁰

Deck

Master Bath

Breakfast
11⁰ x 10⁰

Laundry

Great Room
14⁰ x 17⁰

Two Car Garage
20⁹ x 20⁹

Kitchen
9⁰ x 12⁰

Powder

Dining Room
10⁹ x 12⁰

Foyer
12⁶ x 11⁰

DESIGN BY
©Stephen Fuller,
American Home Gallery

VILLAGE EDGE

Briscoe Commons

This Village or Edge home reflects the Colonial architecture of the South, with a columned entry and paneled shutters. Inside, decorative columns open the foyer to the formal dining room, which opens through double doors to the gourmet kitchen. A cooktop counter overlooks the breakfast room, where a French door leads to a private porch. The central gallery hall connects with a secluded master suite, highlighted by a dressing area and a lavish bath. Upstairs, two bedrooms share a full bath. This home is designed with a basement foundation.

Homeowner's Option: This garage may be customized to provide a rear entry.

PLAN T143

First Floor: 2,025 square feet
Second Floor: 688 square feet
Total: 2,713 square feet

Bedrooms: 3
Bathrooms: 2½

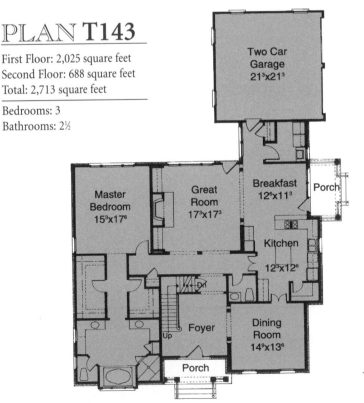

Two Car Garage
21³x21³

Great Room
17³x17³

Breakfast
12⁶x11³

Porch

Master Bedroom
15³x17⁶

Kitchen
12³x12⁶

Foyer

Up
Dn

Dining Room
14⁹x13⁶

Porch

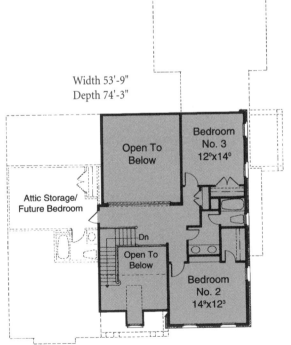

Width 53'-9"
Depth 74'-3"

Open To Below

Bedroom No. 3
12⁰x14⁰

Attic Storage/ Future Bedroom

Dn

Open To Below

Bedroom No. 2
14⁹x12³

DESIGN BY
©*Stephen Fuller,*
American Home Gallery

VILLAGE | EDGE

Ethridge Pointe

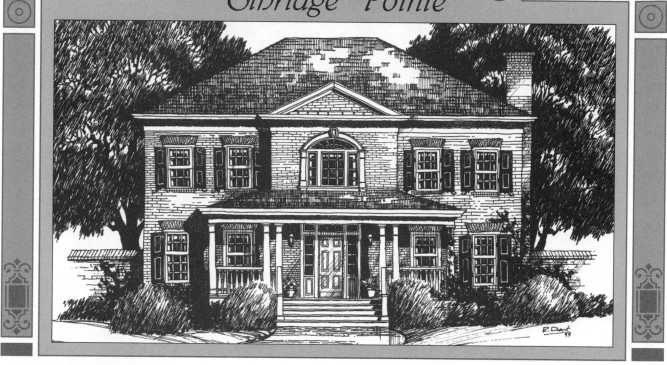

A graceful, arched transom sets off a clerestory window, complemented by a glass-paneled entry, rounded balusters and decorative columns on this traditional brick home. Inside, the foyer opens to the formal rooms as well as to casual living space. A fireplace warms the family room, enhanced by four lovely windows. To the rear of the plan, the gourmet kitchen has wrapping counters and a cooktop peninsula, which overlooks the bright breakfast room. Upstairs, a generous master suite has its own hearth. This home is designed with a basement foundation.

Homeowner's Option: This garage may be customized to provide a rear entry.

PLAN T145

First Floor: 1,501 square feet
Second Floor: 1,252 square feet
Total: 2,753 square feet

Bedrooms: 3
Bathrooms: 2½

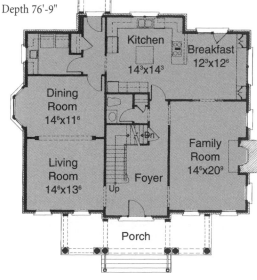

Two Car Garage 21³x21³

Width 46'-3"
Depth 76'-9"

Kitchen 14³x14³
Breakfast 12³x12⁶
Dining Room 14⁶x11⁶
Living Room 14⁶x13⁶
Foyer
Family Room 14⁶x20⁹
Up
Dn
Porch

Bedroom No. 2 14⁶x12³
Bedroom No. 3 12³x13⁶
Open To Below
Dn
Master Bedroom 14⁶x20⁹

DESIGN BY
©*Stephen Fuller,*
American Home Gallery

VILLAGE EDGE

Mauldin Place

PLAN T150

First Floor: 1,601 square feet
Second Floor: 1,520 square feet
Total: 3,121 square feet

Bedrooms: 4
Bathrooms: 3½

This captivating Georgian home features an amenity-filled interior that begins with a foyer that's open for the formal rooms, defined by lovely decorative columns, A central gallery hall leads to casual living space, which boasts a fireplace and built-ins, and to the kitchen, which has a cooktop island counter, a breakfast room and a planning office. The second floor includes three additional bedrooms, two full baths and a generous master suite with a walk-in closet and sumptuous bath. This home is designed with a basement foundation.

Homeowner's Option: This garage may be customized to provide a rear entry.

Width 49'-3"
Depth 74'-3"

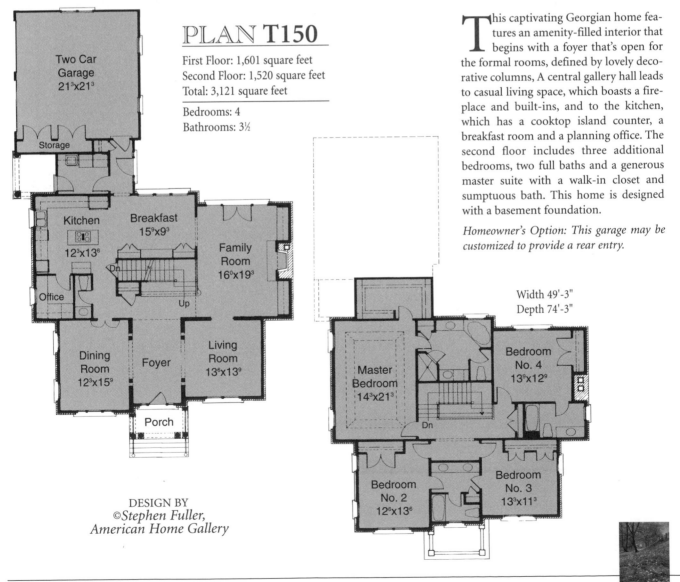

DESIGN BY
©*Stephen Fuller,*
American Home Gallery

EDGE

Liberty Way

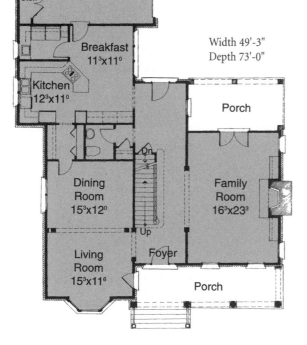

Stor.

Two Car Garage
21³x21³

Stor.

Breakfast
11³x11⁰

Kitchen
12³x11⁰

Dining Room
15³x12⁰

Dn

Up

Living Room
15³x11⁶

Foyer

Porch

Family Room
16³x23³

Porch

Width 49'-3"
Depth 73'-0"

DESIGN BY
*©Stephen Fuller,
American Home Gallery*

B eautiful bay windows and a copper-seam roof complement two balustrades on this Colonial-style home. A gallery foyer opens to a formal living room or parlor on the left and, to the right, a family room warmed by a fireplace. French doors open to the rear porch, which is decked with square columns. The well-planned kitchen overlooks a breakfast area and easily serves the formal dining room through a convenient butler's pantry. This home is designed with a basement foundation.

Homeowner's Option: This garage may be customized to provide a rear entry.

PLAN T146

First Floor: 1,609 square feet
Second Floor: 1,583 square feet
Total: 3,192 square feet

Bedrooms: 3
Bathrooms: 2½

Unfinished Bonus
9³x14⁰

Dn

Bedroom No. 2
16³x12³

Master Bedroom
15³x22⁰

Bedroom No. 3
16³x12⁰

EDGE

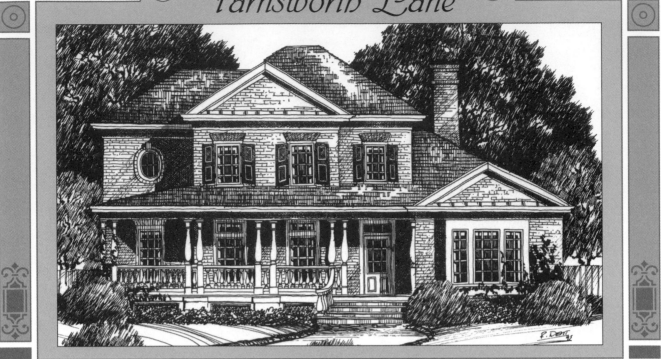

Farnsworth Lane

Gently curved balusters and transom windows introduce a well-planned interior within this sterling Georgian design. A stunning coffered ceiling sets off the great room. The gourmet kitchen is open to the breakfast room and boasts an island cooktop counter. In the master suite, a lavish bath includes a whirlpool tub, separate shower, twin vanities and a walk-in closet. Upstairs, two family bedrooms share a full bath. This home is designed with a basement foundation.

PLAN T144

First Floor: 1,787 square feet
Second Floor: 851 square feet
Total: 2,638 square feet

Bedrooms: 3
Bathrooms: 2½

Two Car Garage 21³x21³

Width 51'-3"
Depth 70'-6"

Deck

Great Room 16⁰x17⁰

Kitchen
Breakfast 12⁹x12⁹

13³x16⁶

Dn

Up

Dining Room 15⁰x12⁹

Foyer

Master Bedroom 15⁶x16³

Porch

Bedroom No. 2 13⁰x12⁶

Unfin. Storage 9⁰x21⁰

Dn

Bedroom No. 3 15⁰x12⁶

DESIGN BY
©*Stephen Fuller,*
American Home Gallery

VILLAGE | EDGE

Westbury

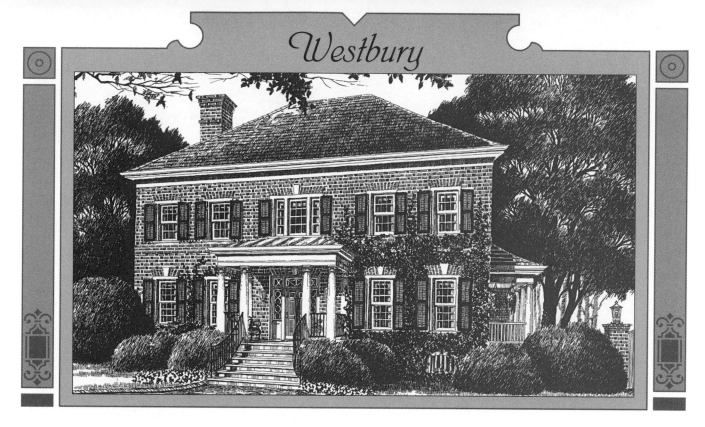

Elegant angles and an abundance of space make this a most appealing Village or Edge design. Columns decorate the formal dining room and define the great room. The spacious L-shaped kitchen features a desk, pantry, work island and the sunny breakfast room. The sumptuous master suite is replete with luxuries. Upstairs, two family bedrooms share a full hall bath and a large game room. This home is designed with a basement foundation.

PLAN T169

First Floor: 1,828 square feet
Second Floor: 1,552 square feet
Total: 3,380 square feet

Bedrooms: 4
Bathrooms: 3½

Width 54'-3"
Depth 70'-3"

DESIGN BY
©Stephen Fuller,
American Home Gallery

VILLAGE   EDGE

Franklin Post Road

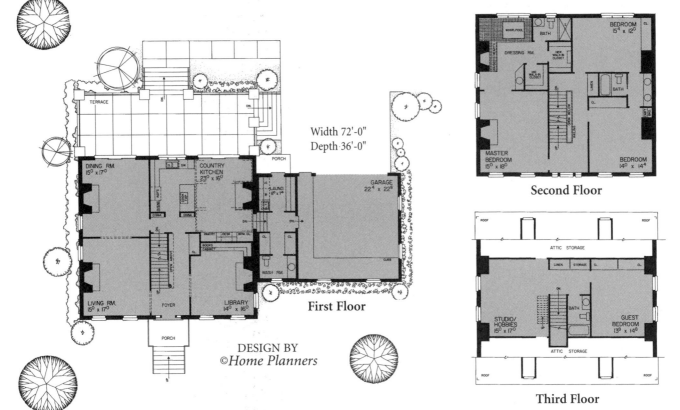

First Floor

DESIGN BY
©*Home Planners*

Width 72'-0"
Depth 36'-0"

Second Floor

Third Floor

PLAN 2975

First Floor: 1,656 square feet
Second Floor: 1,440 square feet
Third Floor: 715 square feet
Total: 3,811 square feet

Bedrooms: 4
Bathrooms: 3½

This Edge home's Georgian roots are evident in its symmetry, the Palladian window, keystone lintels, parapets and chimneys. Roof balustrades and arched transoms, however, speak a strictly Federal vernacular. The three massive chimneys support six fireplaces that warm the first-floor living areas. The country kitchen boasts an island cooktop counter, built-in desk and pantry. The second floor contains two family bedrooms in addition to the luxurious master suite, while the top floor adds a fourth bedroom and a hobby/studio area.

EDGE

Eleanor Circle

PLAN 2662

First Floor: 1,735 square feet
Second Floor: 1,075 square feet
Third Floor: 746 square feet
Total: 3,556 square feet

Bedrooms: 5
Bathrooms: 3½

L

The exterior of this stately brick home exhibits the symmetry and simplciity of Federal styling. The bow windows in the two wings are also hallmarks of that era. Two chimney stacks support fireplaces in the gathering room, study and breakfast room. The first floor also provides a formal entertaining zone—the parlor and dining room flanking the foyer. A handy mudroom with a powder room connects the kitchen to the laundry. Five dormers across the third floor provide natural light to two additional bedrooms and a reading niche.

QUOTE ONE®
Cost to build? See page 182
to order complete cost estimate
to build this house in your area!

DESIGN BY
©*Home Planners*

Width 64'-0"
Depth 64'-0"

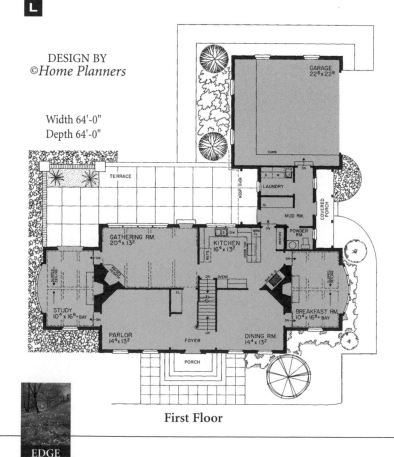

First Floor

Second Floor

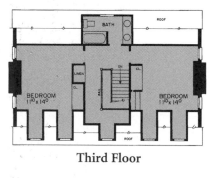

Third Floor

EDGE

The sophisticated facade of this Edge home is reminiscent of gentler times. Inside, a stunning arrangement of the formal rooms allows dinner guests to enjoy the fireplace. A butler's pantry leads to the gourmet kitchen, which provides a snack counter and a breakfast area with a mitered window. A flex room to the front of the plan can be used as a study or guest quarters. The master suite provides two walk-in closets and a private door to the side property. Upstairs, four bedrooms all have walk-in closets.

PLAN **W535**

First Floor: 3,500 square feet
Second Floor: 1,806 square feet
Total: 5,306 square feet

Bedrooms: 5 or 6
Bathrooms: 4½

DESIGN BY
©*Looney Ricks Kiss*
Architects, Inc.

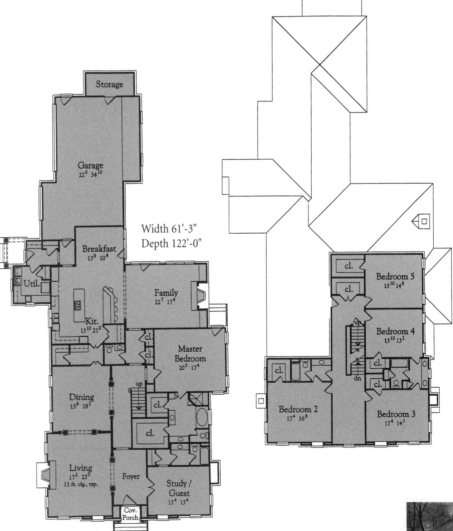

Width 61'-3"
Depth 122'-0"

Storage

Garage
22⁰ 34¹⁰

Breakfast
13⁰ 10⁸

Util.

Family
22⁷ 17⁴

Kit.
13¹⁰ 21⁰

Master
Bedroom
20⁰ 17⁴

Dining
15⁶ 18²

up

cl.

cl.

Living
17² 23⁰
11 ft. clg., typ.

Foyer

Study /
Guest
17⁴ 13⁴

Cov.
Porch

cl.

cl.

Bedroom 5
15¹⁰ 14⁸

up

Bedroom 4
15¹⁰ 13²

cl.

cl.

dn

Bedroom 2
17⁴ 16⁶

Bedroom 3
17⁴ 14³

EDGE

North James Place

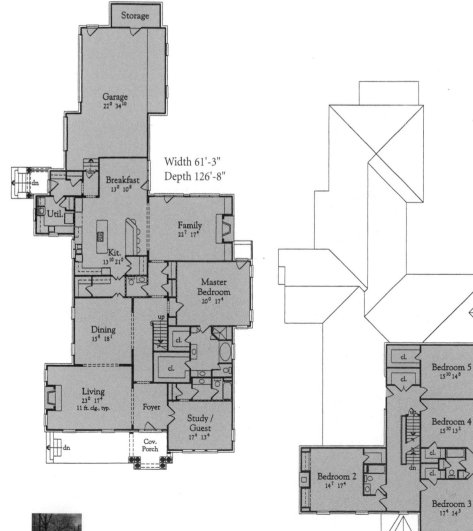

Storage

Garage
22⁰ 34¹⁰

Width 61'-3"
Depth 126'-8"

Breakfast
13⁰ 10⁸

dn

Util.

Kit.
13¹⁰ 21⁰

Family
22⁷ 17⁴

Master
Bedroom
20⁰ 17⁴

Dining
15⁸ 18¹

up

cl.

cl.

Living
23⁰ 17⁴
11 ft. clg., typ.

Foyer

Study /
Guest
17⁴ 13⁴

Cov.
Porch

dn

cl.

cl.

Bedroom 5
15¹⁰ 14⁸

up

Bedroom 4
15¹⁰ 13²

cl.

Bedroom 2
14⁷ 17⁴

dn

cl.

Bedroom 3
17⁴ 14³

Take a step back in time to the lighter, more attenuated architectural style of the Young Republic. This stately Edge home expresses the refined lines, distinctive gables and classic columns of that bygone era. Inside, a centered fireplace highlights the living room, which opens to the dining room through a graceful archway. A butler's pantry eases service from the gourmet kitchen—well-planned to handle crowd-size occasions. A flexible study/guest room offers a full bath. The master suite offers sensational amenities such as separate vanities and an angled oversized shower.

PLAN **W533**

First Floor: 3,471 square feet
Second Floor: 1,708 square feet
Total: 5,179 square feet

Bedrooms: 5 or 6
Bathrooms: 4½

DESIGN BY
©*Looney Ricks Kiss
Architects, Inc.*

Parker Ferris Way

DESIGN BY
©*Home Planners*

Width 50'-0"
Depth 80'-0"

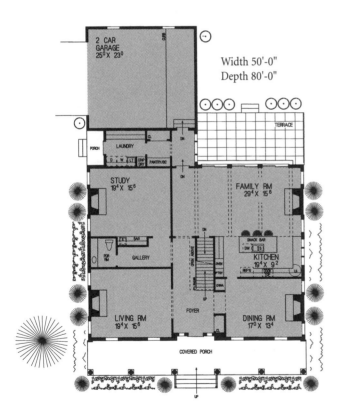

Quote One®

Cost to build? See page 182
to order complete cost estimate
to build this house in your area!

PLAN 2996

First Floor: 2,191 square feet
Second Floor: 1,928 square feet
Total: 4,119 square feet

Bedrooms: 4
Bathrooms: 2½

L **D**

With stunning 19th-Century style, this lovely Edge home looks ahead to a later trend of adding Greek Revival elements. Covered porches upstairs and down, round columns and the triangular pediment are faithfully reproduced in this adaptation. Four chimney stacks decorate the ends of the house and herald four hearths inside—in the living and dining rooms, family room and study. The second floor holds four bedrooms, including a master suite with its own fireplace, walk-in closet and relaxing master bath.

EDGE

Tatem Park Road

From the temple-style front to the angled balustrade on the roof, this home is a standout in any neighborhood. Tall columns support double porticos at the front and back of the house. A tiled foyer leads to the family area, which includes a U-shaped kitchen with a snack bar and a fireplace flanked by window seats. Fireplaces in the formal living and dining rooms add their welcoming glow for guests, while the fireplace in the master suite warms the homeowner's quiet time.

PLAN 3527

First Floor: 2,000 square feet
Second Floor: 2,000 square feet
Total: 4,000 square feet
Bonus Room: 264 square feet

Bedrooms: 4
Bathrooms: 3½

DESIGN BY
©Home Planners

Width 50'-8"
Depth 56'-8"

Quote One®
Cost to build? See page 182
to order complete cost estimate
to build this house in your area!

Tribeca Bridge Road

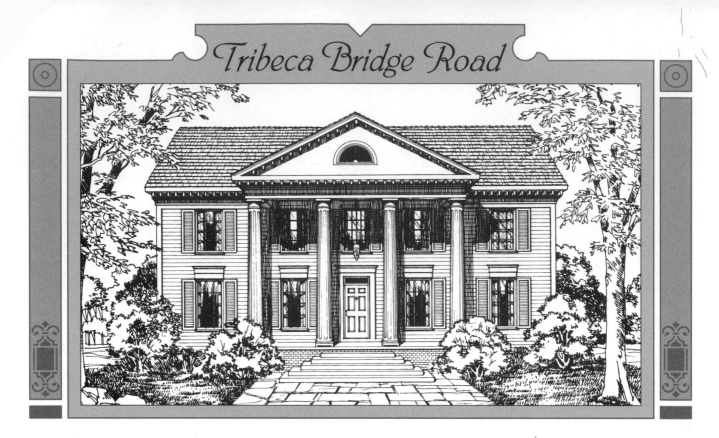

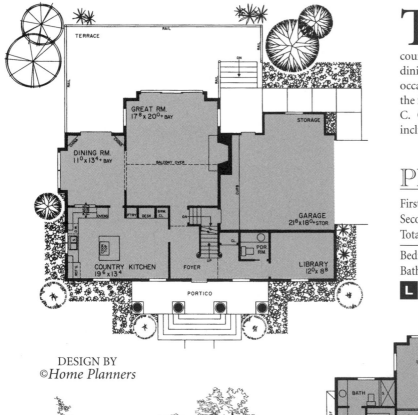

TERRACE

GREAT RM.
17⁸ x 20⁰ + BAY

DINING RM.
11⁰ x 13⁴ + BAY

BALCONY OVER

STORAGE

GARAGE
21⁸ x 18⁰ + STOR.

COOK
TOP

COUNTRY KITCHEN
19⁶ x 13⁴

FOYER

PDR.
RM.

LIBRARY
12⁰ x 8⁸

PORTICO

DESIGN BY
©*Home Planners*

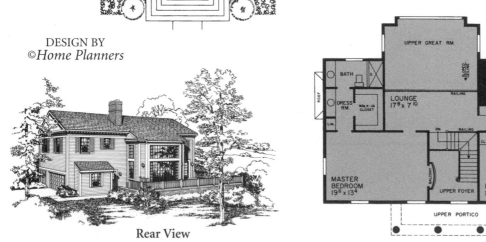

Rear View

This elegant exterior houses a very livable plan. Every bit of space has been put to good use. The well-planned country kitchen features an island cooktop counter, built-ins and a convenient pass-through to the dining room. The spacious great room is ready for any occasion, grand or cozy. A library thoughtfully placed to the front of the plan invites quiet conversation or an Arthur C. Clarke reading fest. Second-floor sleeping quarters include three family bedrooms and a grand master suite.

PLAN 2668

First Floor: 1,206 square feet
Second Floor: 1,254 square feet
Total: 2,460 square feet

Bedrooms: 4
Bathrooms: 2½

L

QUOTE ONE®
Cost to build? See page 182
to order complete cost estimate
to build this house in your area!

Width 52'-0"
Depth 42'-0"

UPPER GREAT RM.

ROOF

BATH

DRESS
RM.

WALK-IN
CLOSET

LOUNGE
17⁸ x 7¹⁰

RAILING

BATH

BEDROOM
11⁰ x 11⁰

LINEN

WASH.
& DRY.

MASTER
BEDROOM
19⁶ x 13⁴

UPPER FOYER

RAILING

BEDROOM
10⁸ x 11⁰

BEDROOM
10⁸ x 11⁰

UPPER PORTICO

EDGE

Lafayette Court

BACK PORCH

KIT
11⁰ x 11⁰

FAMILY RM
15⁰ x 12⁰

SNACK BAR

BREAKFAST NOOK

D.W.

D.

W.

PANTRY

UTILITY RM

RANGE

REF'G

SHLVS

NICHE

DINING RM
15⁶ x 13⁰

PDR

DOWN

MEDIA

2-WAY FIREPL

WD. BOX

LIVING RM
15⁰ x 12⁶

UP

FOYER

FRONT PORCH

Width 44'-0"
Depth 34'-0"

DESIGN BY
©*Home Planners*

MASTER BATH

WALK-IN CLOSET

BATH

LIN

BEDRM
15⁰ x 12⁰

SEAT

VANITY

SHLVS

DOWN

SHLVS

MASTER BEDRM
14⁶ x 14⁶

UP TO ATTIC

BEDRM
15⁰ x 12⁰

BALCONY

A double portico and Doric columns call up a sense of Early America with this Colonial design—a perfect fit for the edge of town. The grand pedimented entry leads to a tiled foyer, framed by formal rooms, each with its own hearth. The country kitchen provides a snack counter, breakfast nook and a lovely triple window. Upstairs, the luxurious master suite is clustered with two family bedrooms and a full hall bath. The third floor holds a large studio with a full bath.

PLAN 3520

First Floor: 1,232 square feet
Second Floor: 1,232 square feet
Third Floor: 421 square feet
Total: 2,885 square feet

Bedrooms: 4
Bathrooms: 3½

D

CLOSET

LIN

STUDIO
12⁹ x 18⁰

DOWN

RAILING

BATH

EDGE

Veneta Bay Drive

Photo by ©Jeffrey Jacobs/Architectural Photography

This home, as shown in the photograph, may differ from the actual blueprints.

This exquisite facade weds a distinctly modern look with traditional details such as a bay window, gabled roofline and Doric-style columns. Inside, the formal rooms flank a foyer that leads to a gallery hall. The living room's fireplace is positioned to allow dinner guests to enjoy its glow. A U-shaped kitchen also serves a casual eating area, which opens to the family room. Tall windows and a single door allow plenty of natural light to brighten the master suite. Upstairs, four family bedrooms share two full baths, a sitting area and gallery hall.

PLAN W506

First Floor: 1,915 square feet
Second Floor: 1,360 square feet
Total: 3,275 square feet

Bedrooms: 5
Bathrooms: 3½

DESIGN BY
©Looney Ricks Kiss
Architects, Inc.

Width 39'-2"
Depth 97'-2"

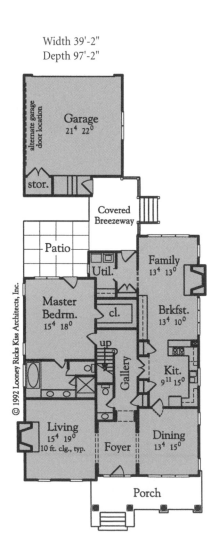

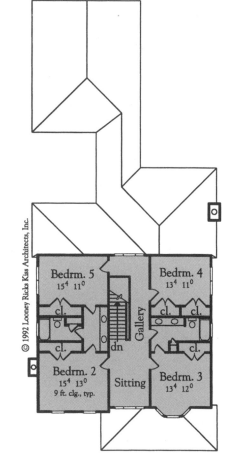

VILLAGE   EDGE

North Perry Bend

This home, as shown in the photograph, may differ from the actual blueprints.

Photo by ©*Jeffrey Jacobs/Architectural Photography*

Doric columns, a simple balustrade and an elliptical fanlight transom play in perfect harmony on this distinctive Village or Edge home. The foyer announces a gracious interior, starting with heart-stoppingly beautiful formal rooms. The dining room employs a butler's pantry to accommodate planned events. A relaxed but well-organized kitchen overlooks the casual living space, which has a fireplace. Lovely French doors lead outside to a covered porch and breezeway—a perfect beginning for a stroll around the neighborhood. The master suite provides a deluxe bath designed to please the homeowner.

DESIGN BY
©*Looney Ricks Kiss
Architects, Inc.*

PLAN W531

First Floor: 1,886 square feet
Second Floor: 1,016 square feet
Total: 2,902 square feet

Bedrooms: 3 or 4
Bathrooms: 3½

VILLAGE   EDGE

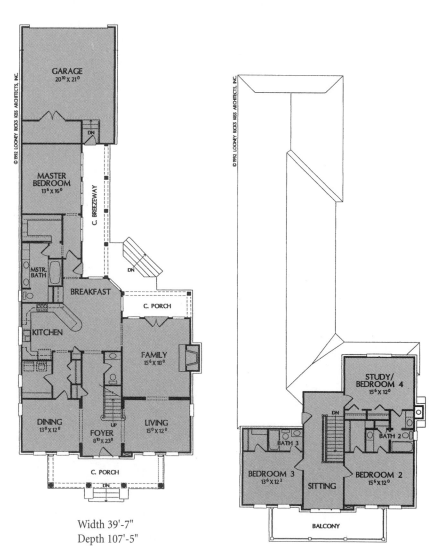

Width 39'-7"
Depth 107'-5"

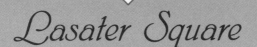

Lasater Square

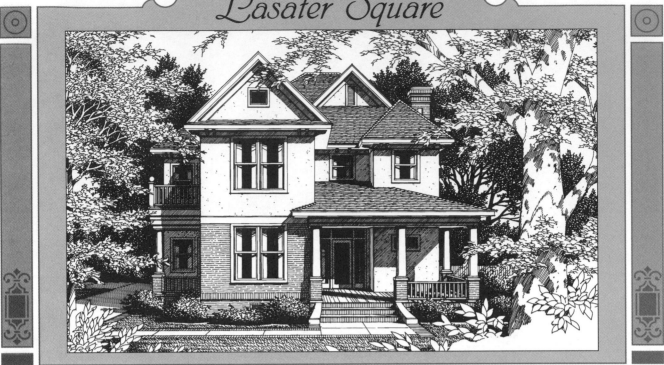

A simple four-square design, reminiscent of the 1940s, lends a landmark look to this Village or Edge home. Decorative columns and arches help define the spacious formal rooms. Three tall windows in the living room bathe the area with natural light. A secluded master suite includes twin walk-in closets, a whirlpool tub and separate shower. Two additional bedrooms and a full bath share the second floor. Please specify crawlspace or slab foundation when ordering.

DESIGN BY
©*Larry E. Belk Designs*

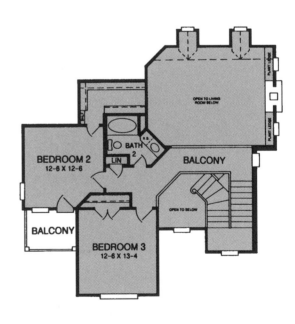

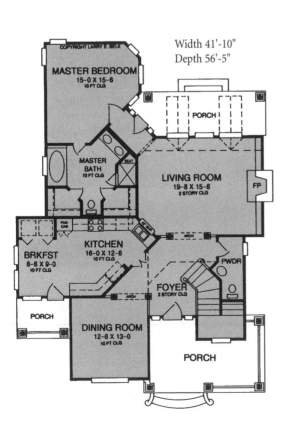

Width 41'-10"
Depth 56'-5"

COPYRIGHT LARRY E. BELK

MASTER BEDROOM
15-0 X 15-6
10 FT CLG

PORCH

MASTER BATH
10 FT CLG

LIVING ROOM
19-8 X 15-6
2 STORY CLG

FP

KITCHEN
16-0 X 12-6
10 FT CLG

BRKFST
8-6 X 9-0
10 FT CLG

PWDR

FOYER
2 STORY CLG

PORCH

DINING ROOM
12-6 X 13-0
10 FT CLG

PORCH

BEDROOM 2
12-6 X 12-6

BATH 2

LIN

BALCONY

OPEN TO LIVING ROOM BELOW

BALCONY

BEDROOM 3
12-6 X 13-4

OPEN TO BELOW

PLAN 8065

First Floor: 1,482 square feet
Second Floor: 631 square feet
Total: 2,113 square feet

Bedrooms: 3
Bathrooms: 2½

L

VILLAGE   EDGE

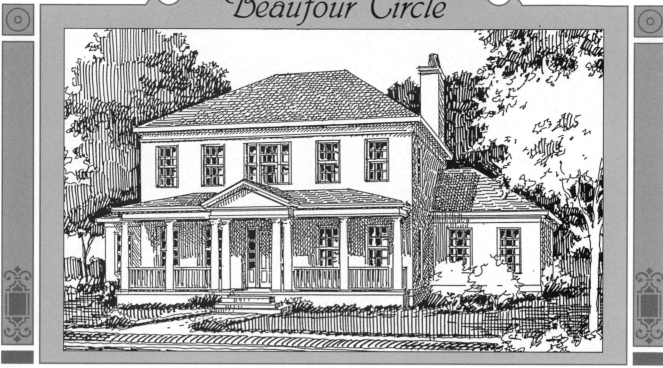

Beaufour Circle

PLAN W529

First Floor: 2,788 square feet
Second Floor: 1,240 square feet
Total: 4,028 square feet
Bonus Room: 481 square feet

Bedrooms: 6
Bathrooms: 5

DESIGN BY
©*Looney Ricks Kiss
Architects, Inc.*

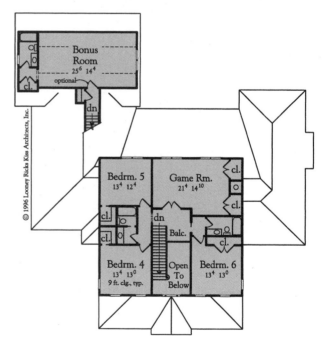

Width 77'-6"
Depth 82'-4"

© 1996 Looney Ricks Kiss Architects, Inc.

A beautiful hip roof with a protruding gable and double columns lend a touch of class and a sense of history to this lovely Edge or Village home. The formal dining room is placed opposite a quiet library—a perfect spot for dinner guests to gather or meet for quiet conversation. A grand gourmet kitchen provides a cooktop island and wrapping counters. The open arrangement of the kitchen and family room will allow the household cook to participate in conversation while preparing a meal. Split sleeping quarters maintain privacy for the master suite, which features a dressing area and lavish bath.

VILLAGE EDGE

Laureola Oaks Road

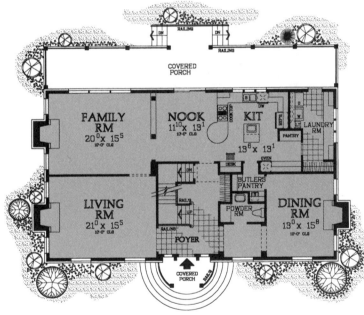

This grand entrance is based on the entry of a home built in 1827 for William Thomas Buckner near Paris, Kentucky. Curved steps lead to the raised front porch which has a rounded roof supported by stately columns. Inside, the central foyer features a two-story ceiling, Palladian window, an open staircase and high balconies. Three fireplaces contribute to the charm of the living, dining and family rooms. Upstairs, two secondary bedrooms share access to an extensive balcony.

QUOTE ONE®

Cost to build? See page 182 to order complete cost estimate to build this house in your area!

Width 56'-10"
Depth 53'-10"

PLAN 3513

First Floor: 1,855 square feet
Second Floor: 1,287 square feet
Total: 3,142 square feet

Bedrooms: 3
Bathrooms: 2½

DESIGN BY
©Home Planners

EDGE

Hemingway Court

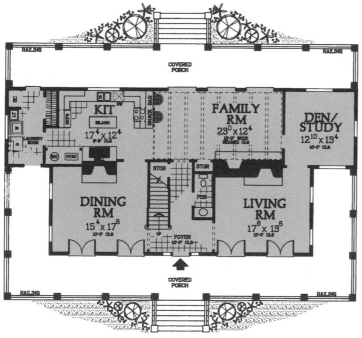

Two sets of dormers set off a signature hip roof and classic columns on this comfortable Southern-style home. An elegant tiled foyer opens to formal rooms on each side, and leads to a rustic family area that allows generous views. Lovely French doors create a striking ambience in the formal areas—and each of these rooms offers a warming fireplace. The second-floor sleeping zone offers three family bedrooms, a hall bath and a master suite with two walk-in closets, dual lavatories and a whirlpool tub.

DESIGN BY
©*Home Planners*

PLAN 3515

First Floor: 1,669 square feet
Second Floor: 1,627 square feet
Total: 3,296 square feet

Bedrooms: 3
Bathrooms: 3½

Cost to build? See page 182
to order complete cost estimate
to build this house in your area!

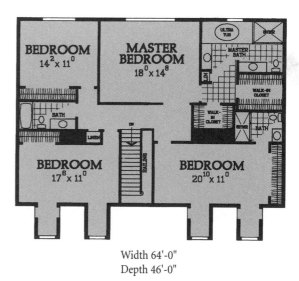

Width 64'-0"
Depth 46'-0"

Portsmouth Stream Road

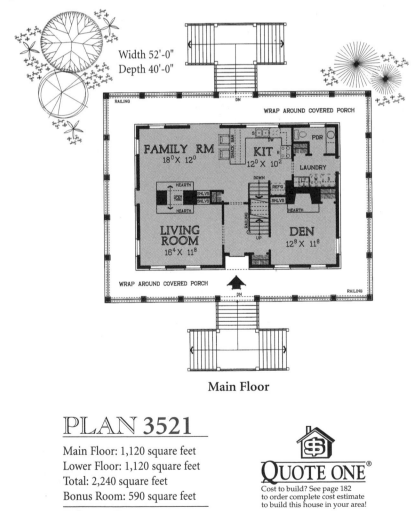

Width 52'-0"
Depth 40'-0"

FAMILY RM
18⁰ X 12⁰

KIT
12⁰ X 10²

PDR

LAUNDRY

HEARTH

OPEN THRU

HEARTH

SHLVS

SHLVS

SHLVS

HEARTH

LIVING ROOM
16⁴ X 11⁸

DEN
12⁸ X 11⁸

WRAP AROUND COVERED PORCH

WRAP AROUND COVERED PORCH

RAILING

Main Floor

This rural Colonial design calls up the charm of simpler times. Wraparound covered porches on both the lower and upper floors invite outdoor living. An entry and foyer lead up to a formal living room, as well as to casual areas designed with space to sprawl and relax. A through-hearth warms the living areas, while the den enjoys its own fireplace and built-in cabinetry. The lower floor offers a spacious master suite with a windowed bath and a private hearth. Two additional bedrooms share a full bath.

DESIGN BY
©*Home Planners*

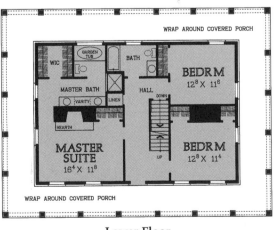

WIC

GARDEN TUB

BATH

BEDRM
12⁸ X 11⁶

MASTER BATH

VANITY

LINEN

HALL

DOWN

HEARTH

MASTER SUITE
16⁴ X 11⁸

BEDRM
12⁸ X 11⁴

UP

WRAP AROUND COVERED PORCH

WRAP AROUND COVERED PORCH

Lower Floor

PLAN 3521

Main Floor: 1,120 square feet
Lower Floor: 1,120 square feet
Total: 2,240 square feet
Bonus Room: 590 square feet

Bedrooms: 3
Bathrooms: 2½

L

QUOTE ONE®
Cost to build? See page 182
to order complete cost estimate
to build this house in your area!

EDGE

Eisler Park Way

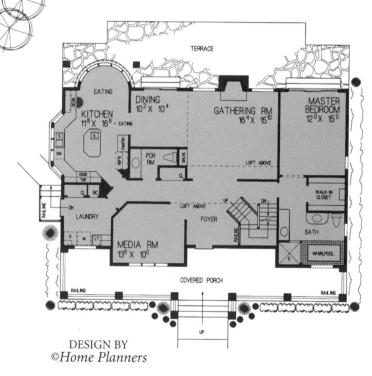

TERRACE

EATING

KITCHEN
11⁸ X 16⁸ · EATING

DINING
10² X 10⁴

GATHERING RM
16⁴ X 15¹⁰

MASTER
BEDROOM
12⁰ X 15⁰

PDR
RM

LOFT ABOVE

COOK
TOP

CL   BC

WALK-IN
CLOSET

DN

LAUNDRY

LOFT ABOVE

FOYER

UP   DN

BATH

MEDIA RM
13⁸ X 10⁰

RAILING

WHIRLPOOL

COVERED PORCH

RAILING

RAILING

UP

DESIGN BY
©Home Planners

PLAN 3321

First Floor: 1,636 square feet
Second Floor: 572 square feet
Total: 2,208 square feet

Bedrooms: 3
Bathrooms: 2½

L **D**

QUOTE ONE®
Cost to build? See page 182
to order complete cost estimate
to build this house in your area!

Width 52'-0"
Depth 46'-2"

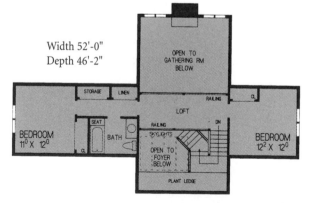

OPEN TO
GATHERING RM
BELOW

STORAGE   LINEN

RAILING

LOFT

BEDROOM
11⁰ X 12⁰

SEAT

BATH

RAILING

DN

SKYLIGHTS

OPEN TO
FOYER
BELOW

BEDROOM
12² X 12⁰

PLANT LEDGE

Cozy and functional, this bungalow has many amenities not often found in homes its size. To the left is a media room, to the rear the gathering room with fireplace. The gathering room is open to the formal dining room, which has rear-terrace access. The master suite also accesses the rear terrace and offers a luxurious bath. Upstairs, two secondary bedrooms connect with a loft area that overlooks the gathering room and foyer.

Rear View

EDGE

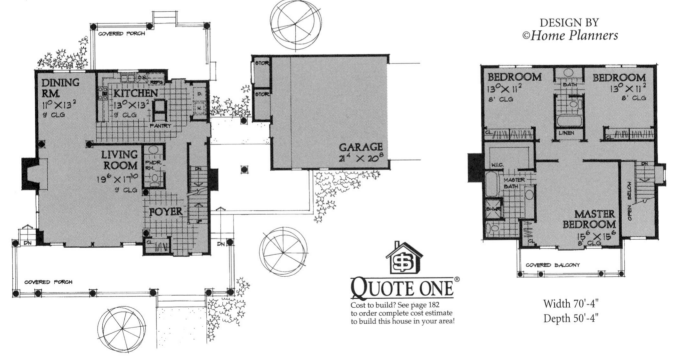

DESIGN BY
©*Home Planners*

COVERED PORCH

DINING
RM.
11⁰ × 13²
9' CLG

KITCHEN
13⁰ × 13²
9' CLG

PANTRY

LIVING
ROOM
19⁶ × 17¹⁰
9' CLG

PWDR.
RM.

FOYER

CL

DN

DN

COVERED PORCH

STOR
STOR

GARAGE
21⁴ × 20⁸

BEDROOM
13⁰ × 11²
8' CLG

BATH

BEDROOM
13⁰ × 11²
8' CLG

LINEN

W.I.C.

MASTER
BATH

OPEN BELOW

DN

MASTER
BEDROOM
15⁶ × 15⁶
8' CLG

COVERED BALCONY

Width 70'-4"
Depth 50'-4"

QUOTE ONE®
Cost to build? See page 182
to order complete cost estimate
to build this house in your area!

PLAN 3469

First Floor: 1,066 square feet
Second Floor: 1,006 square feet
Total: 2,072 square feet

Bedrooms: 3
Bathrooms: 2½

L

Our neo-classical farmhouse offers plenty of room for delightful diversions. A standing-seam roof adds a touch of history, while front and rear porches invite an enjoyment of the outdoors. A large living area with a fireplace can handle crowd-size entertaining as well as cozy gatherings. An amenity-packed kitchen, powder room and utility room round out the first floor. The second floor provides well-arranged sleeping quarters—with a large master bedroom—and two full baths.

EDGE

Shelter Island Drive

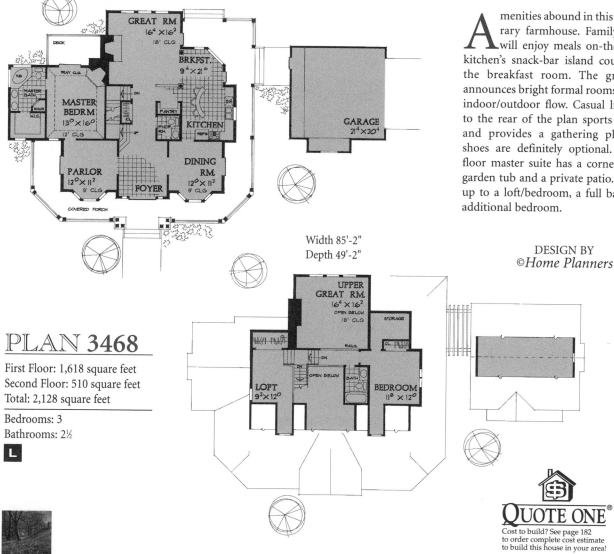

GREAT RM.
16⁴ × 16²
18' CLG

DECK

TRAY CLG.

TUB

MASTER
BATH

W.I.C.

MASTER
BEDRM
13⁰ × 16⁰
12' CLG

BRKFST.
9⁴ × 21⁶

DN

PANTRY

UP

KITCHEN

MUD
RM.

GARAGE
21⁴ × 20⁴

PARLOR
12⁰ × 11²
9' CLG

FOYER

DINING
RM.
12⁰ × 11²
9' CLG

COVERED PORCH

UPPER
GREAT RM.
16⁴ × 16²
OPEN BELOW
18' CLG

STORAGE

RAILG.

DN

DN

OPEN BELOW

BATH

LOFT
9² × 12⁰

BEDROOM
11⁸ × 12⁰

Width 85'-2"
Depth 49'-2"

PLAN 3468

First Floor: 1,618 square feet
Second Floor: 510 square feet
Total: 2,128 square feet

Bedrooms: 3
Bathrooms: 2½

L

Amenities abound in this contemporary farmhouse. Family members will enjoy meals on-the-go at the kitchen's snack-bar island counter or in the breakfast room. The grand foyer announces bright formal rooms with good indoor/outdoor flow. Casual living space to the rear of the plan sports a fireplace and provides a gathering place where shoes are definitely optional. The first-floor master suite has a corner hearth, a garden tub and a private patio. Stairs lead up to a loft/bedroom, a full bath and an additional bedroom.

DESIGN BY
©*Home Planners*

QUOTE ONE®
Cost to build? See page 182
to order complete cost estimate
to build this house in your area!

EDGE

Nassau Cove

True to its tropical roots, this island-style Village or Edge home features a raised living area announced by a symmetrical staircase and a charming balustrade. An unrestrained floor plan offers open, spacious living areas and well-defined sleeping rooms with outdoor views. An L-shaped kitchen with a prep island counter is open to the living areas. Two bedrooms on this floor share a full bath. The second floor is dedicated to a sumptuous master suite with a morning kitchen and an observation deck.

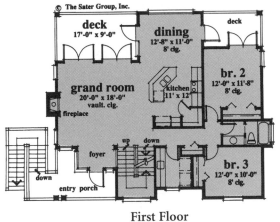

© The Sater Group, Inc.

deck
17'-0" x 9'-0"

dining
12'-8" x 11'-0"
8' clg.

deck

grand room
20'-0" x 18'-0"
vault. clg.

kitchen
11' x 12'

br. 2
12'-0" x 11'-8"
8' clg.

fireplace

foyer

up   down

br. 3
12'-0" x 10'-0"
8' clg.

down

entry porch

First Floor

DESIGN BY
©*The Sater Design Collection*

c The Sater Group, Inc.

garage
40'-0" x 20'-0" avg.

storage
13'-0" x 18'-0" avg.

stor./bonus
20'-0" x 20'-0"

up   stor.

up

lattice work
panel walls

Lower Floor

Width 44'-0"
Depth 40'-0"

observation deck

master
13'-0" x 14'-0"
vault. clg.

am kitchen

open to grand room below

down

© The Sater Group, Inc.

Second Floor

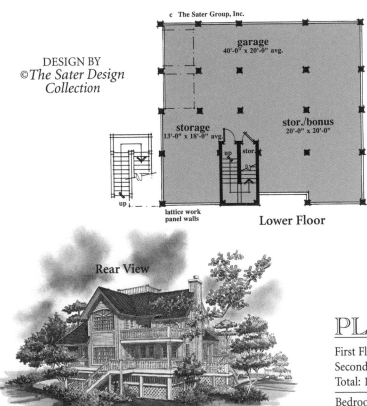

Rear View

PLAN 6654

First Floor: 1,342 square feet
Second Floor: 511 square feet
Total: 1,853 square feet

Bedrooms: 3
Bathrooms: 2

VILLAGE | EDGE

Guest Houses and Garages

Auxiliary Buildings to Enhance Property

The perfect complement to a home, outbuildings provide work or hobby space, quarters for guests and shelter for vehicles.

Cottages, Studios and Places for Parking

St. Martin Road

PLAN 6702

Square Footage: 484

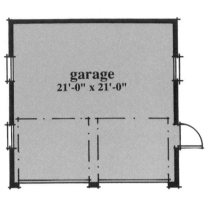

garage
21'-0" x 21'-0"

Width 22'-0"
Depth 22'-0"

Vented dormers and a high-pitched insulated metal roof dress up this two-car garage with quaint details that blend beautifully with any of the Traditional Neighborhood homes. With three windows and a side entry, this garage is convenient and well lit.

DESIGN BY
©*The Sater Design Collection*

Felix Circle

A roomy vestibule offers additional storage space with this stylish two-car garage. Flexible space above may be developed into a hobby/craft area, a home office or even guest quarters. Charming dormer windows allow views and cool breezes to enhance the bonus level.

PLAN 6703

Garage: 484 square feet
Vestibule/Stairs: 137 square feet
Upper Bonus Space: 264 square feet

DESIGN BY
©*The Sater Design Collection*

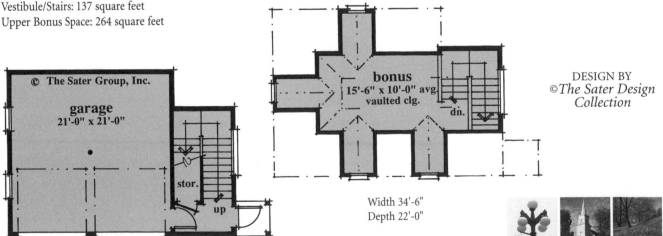

© **The Sater Group, Inc.**

garage
21'-0" x 21'-0"

stor.

up

bonus
15'-6" x 10'-0" avg.
vaulted clg.

dn.

Width 34'-6"
Depth 22'-0"

TOWN   VILLAGE   EDGE

Carmel Bay Drive

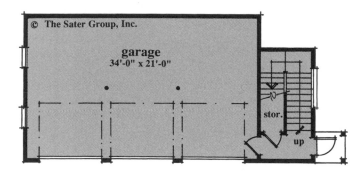

© The Sater Group, Inc.

garage
34'-0" x 21'-0"

stor.

up

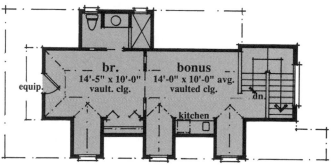

br.
14'-5" x 10'-0"
vault. clg.

bonus
14'-0" x 10'-0" avg.
vaulted clg.

equip.

kitchen

dn.

Option A

Width 47'-6"
Depth 22'-0"

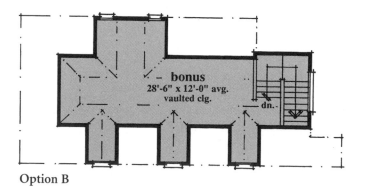

bonus
28'-6" x 12'-0" avg.
vaulted clg.

dn.

Option B

A portico-style entry is a warm welcome to this detached three-car garage, styled to complement many of the neighborhood designs. Bonus space above offers an additional living area or recreation room. With a morning kitchen, full bath, vaulted ceiling and three dormered windows, Option A may be developed as a comfortable guest suite or a private atelier. The entry vestibule provides ample storage space as well as a wrapping stair to the bonus level.

PLAN 6704

Garage: 770 square feet
Vestibule/Stairs: 137 square feet
Upper Bonus Space: 497 square feet

DESIGN BY
©*The Sater Design Collection*

EDGE

Miriam Circle

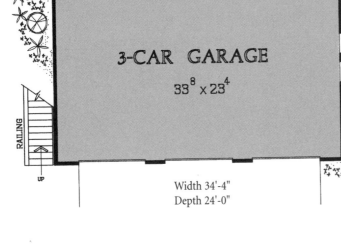

3-CAR GARAGE
33⁸ x 23⁴

RAILING

UP

Width 34'-4"
Depth 24'-0"

Attractive and functional, this impressive structure has room for three cars in the garage section and 670 square feet of living area—complete with kitchen, bathroom, bookshelves and closet—to use as an atelier or a private loft for guests. The angle of the steeply pitched gable roof is repeated in three gabled dormers, each with a tall narrow window framed with shutters. Access to the second-floor loft area is by a railed exterior stairway that ends in a small landing with its own covered roof.

DESIGN BY
©Home Planners

PLAN G206

Garage: 824 square feet
Studio/Loft: 670 square feet
Total: 1,494 square feet

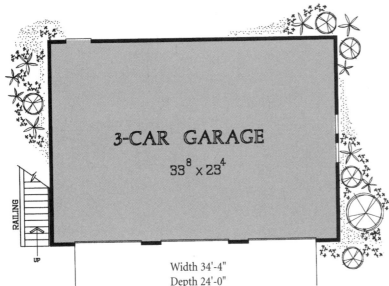

REFG RANGE   DW   SHWR   BATH
KITCHEN
BOOKSHELVES   CLOSET

DN

RAILING

CEILING CLIP

STUDIO/LOFT
33⁸ x 14²

EDGE

Magnolia Drive

PLAN G289

Garage: 900 square feet
Guest Cottage: 690 square feet
Total: 1,590 square feet

Bedroom: 1
Bathroom: 1

Width 36'-0"
Depth 25'-0"

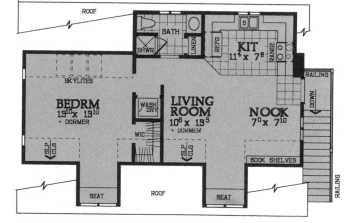

ROOF

BATH

SHWR · LINEN · REFG · KIT 11⁴ x 7⁸ · RANGE

SKYLITES · RAILING

BEDRM 13¹⁰ x 13¹⁰ + DORMER · WASH DRY · LIVING ROOM 10⁸ x 13⁵ + DORMER · NOOK 7⁰ x 7¹⁰ · DOWN

WIC

SLP CLG · SLP CLG · BOOK SHELVES

SEAT · ROOF · SEAT · RAILING

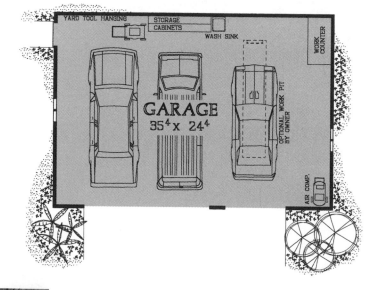

YARD TOOL HANGING · STORAGE CABINETS · WASH SINK · WORK COUNTER

GARAGE 35⁴ x 24⁴

OPTIONAL WORK PIT BY OWNER

AIR COMP.

An array of shingles, millwork and decorative touches sets off the exterior design of this Victorian-style garage and guest cottage. Charming dormers with circle-head windows highlight the facade, while an exterior staircase leads up to a well-planned apartment. An open nook with built-in shelves provides a window seat and serves as a complement to the living room and U-shaped kitchen. The bedrooms features a sloped ceiling, a walk-in closet, skylights and a window seat.

DESIGN BY
©Home Planners

EDGE

Portia Drive

PLAN G259

Garage: 594 square feet
Hobby/Game Room: 306 square feet
Total: 900 square feet

DESIGN BY
©Home Planners

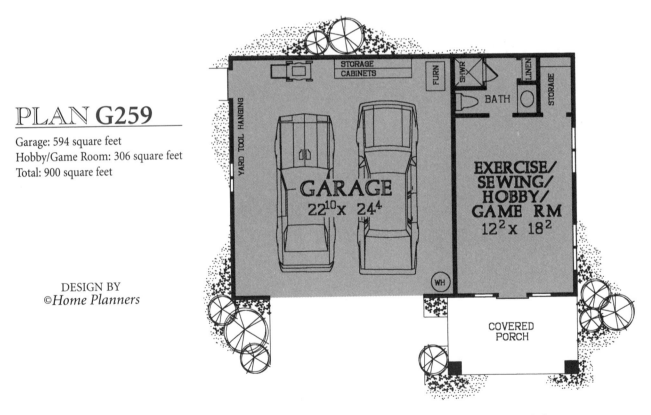

YARD TOOL HANGING

STORAGE CABINETS

FURN

SHWR

BATH

LINEN

STORAGE

GARAGE
22¹⁰ x 24⁴

EXERCISE/
SEWING/
HOBBY/
GAME RM
12² x 18²

WH

COVERED PORCH

Width 36'-0"
Depth 25'-0"

The two-car garage area of this plan provides essential space for parking, and the adjoining 300 square feet of optional-use area can be transformed into a game room, exercise room or hobby area. A convenient full bath is placed to the rear of this space, making it a perfect mudroom. An additional storage area provides plenty of room for yard and garden equipment and recycling bins.

VILLAGE EDGE

John's Bay Circle

A t the end of an arbor trellis is this stunning studio/garage. Like the carriage houses of old, this plan provides storage for vehicles on the ground floor and compact living quarters above. The arbor leads past the garage and up an exterior staircase to a studio apartment. The high, open living space is made cozy and warm by a wood stove. A breakfast counter helps define the kitchen and dining space, which complements the sitting area.

PLAN R128

Garage: 550 square feet
Living Quarters: 550 square feet
Total: 1,100 square feet

DESIGN BY
©*Home Planners*

Width 25'-0"
Depth 22'-0"

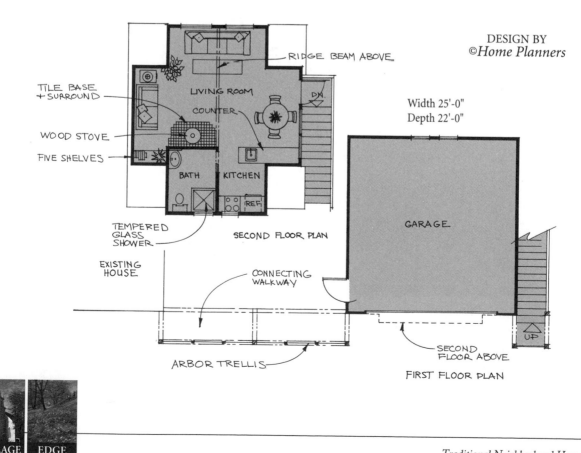

RIDGE BEAM ABOVE

TILE BASE + SURROUND

WOOD STOVE

FIVE SHELVES

LIVING ROOM

COUNTER

DN.

BATH   KITCHEN

REF.

TEMPERED GLASS SHOWER

SECOND FLOOR PLAN

GARAGE

EXISTING HOUSE.

CONNECTING WALKWAY

SECOND FLOOR ABOVE

UP

ARBOR TRELLIS

FIRST FLOOR PLAN

VILLAGE   EDGE

Jennifer Lane

Width 40'-0"
Depth 40'-0"

PLAN 3697

First Floor: 586 square feet
Second Floor: 486 square feet
Total: 1,072 square feet

Bedrooms: 2
Bathrooms: 2

QUOTE ONE®

Cost to build? See page 182
to order complete cost estimate
to build this house in your area!

The wraparound porch of this stunning cottage encourages an enjoyment of the outdoors and provides access to the primary living spaces. The great room opens from the porch and provides a fireplace and a powder room. The U-shaped kitchen and the morning nook lead outdoors to the rear porch—a perfect spot to enjoy pancakes. Upstairs, each of two bedrooms has a private bath and ample wardrobe space.

DESIGN BY
©*Home Planners*

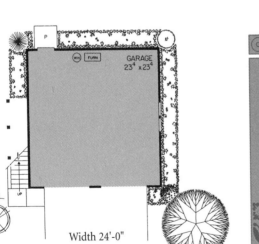

Width 24'-0"
Depth 24'-0"

Wild Sage Road

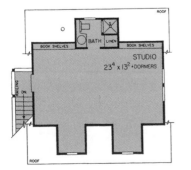

This design provides parking for two cars plus a second-floor studio with a bath and storage space. An exterior staircase leads up to the studio and ends in a sheltered landing. Two charming dormers set off the facade and provide plenty of natural light for arts and crafts. There's ample space for the college set to toss sleeping bags for a weekend visit.

PLAN G106

Square Footage: 428

DESIGN BY
©*Home Planners*

VILLAGE | EDGE

Samuel Circle

This versatile design features a unique siding pattern: a pinch of country with a dash of sophistication. Well-planned to take advantage of natural light from all sides, this design will make a perfect studio, game room or office. Add a shower in the lavatory and it becomes the perfect guest house. The kitchen is large enough for a stove and refrigerator, and a utility closet will permit a furnace and hot water tank. The front porch is a great place to kick off your shoes and relax.

PLAN G230

Square Footage: 320

DESIGN BY
©*Home Planners*

Width 20'-0"
Depth 16'-0"

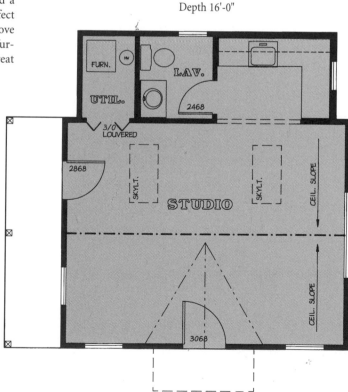

VILLAGE EDGE

When You're Ready To Order . . .

Let Us Show You Our Home Blueprint Package.

Building a home? Planning a home? Our Blueprint Package has nearly everything you need to get the job done right, whether you're working on your own or with help from an architect, designer, builder or subcontractors. Each Blueprint Package is the result of many hours of work by licensed architects or professional designers.

QUALITY

Hundreds of hours of painstaking effort have gone into the development of your blueprint set. Each home has been quality-checked by professionals to insure accuracy and buildability.

VALUE

Because we sell in volume, you can buy professional-quality blueprints at a fraction of their development cost. With our plans, your dream home design costs only a few hundred dollars, not the thousands of dollars that custom architects charge.

SERVICE

Once you've chosen your favorite home plan, you'll receive fast, efficient service whether you choose to mail or fax your order to us or call us toll free at 1-800-521-6797. For customer service, call toll free 1-888-690-1116.

SATISFACTION

Over 50 years of service to satisfied home plan buyers provide us unparalleled experience and knowledge in producing quality blueprints. What this means to you is satisfaction with our product and performance.

ORDER TOLL FREE 1-800-521-6797

After you've looked over our Blueprint Package and Important Extras on the following pages, simply mail the order form on page 189 or call toll free on our Blueprint Hotline: 1-800-521-6797. We're ready and eager to serve you. For customer service, call toll free 1-888-690-1116.

Each set of blueprints is an interrelated collection of detail sheets which includes components such as floor plans, interior and exterior elevations, dimensions, cross-sections, diagrams and notations. These sheets show exactly how your house is to be built.

Among the sheets included may be:

Frontal Sheet
This artist's sketch of the exterior of the house gives you an idea of how the house will look when built and landscaped. Large ink-line floor plans show all levels of the house and provide an overview of your new home's livability, as well as a handy reference for deciding on furniture placement.

Foundation Plan
This sheet shows the foundation layout

SAMPLE PACKAGE

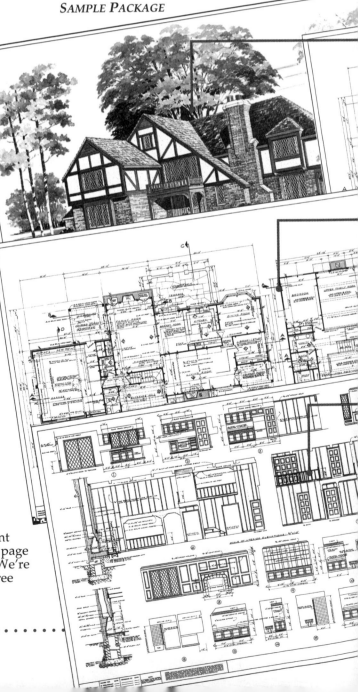

including support walls, excavated and unexcavated areas, if any, and foundation notes. If slab construction rather than basement, the plan shows footings and details for a monolithic slab. This page, or another in the set, may include a sample plot plan for locating your house on a building site.

Detailed Floor Plans
These plans show the layout of each floor of the house. Rooms and interior spaces are carefully dimensioned and keys are given for cross-section details provided later in the plans. The positions of electrical outlets and switches are shown.

House Cross-Sections
Large-scale views show sections or cut-aways of the foundation, interior walls, exterior walls, floors, stairways and roof details. Additional cross-sections may show important changes in

floor, ceiling or roof heights or the relationship of one level to another. Extremely valuable for construction, these sections show exactly how the various parts of the house fit together.

Interior Elevations
Many of our drawings show the design and placement of kitchen and bathroom cabinets, laundry areas, fireplaces, bookcases and other built-ins. Little "extras," such as mantelpiece and wainscoting drawings, plus moulding sections, provide details that give your home that custom touch.

Exterior Elevations
These drawings show the front, rear and sides of your house and give necessary notes on exterior materials and finishes. Particular attention is given to cornice detail, brick and stone accents or other finish items that make your home unique.

Note: Because of the diversity of local building codes, our blueprints may not include Electrical, Plumbing or Mechanical plans or layouts.

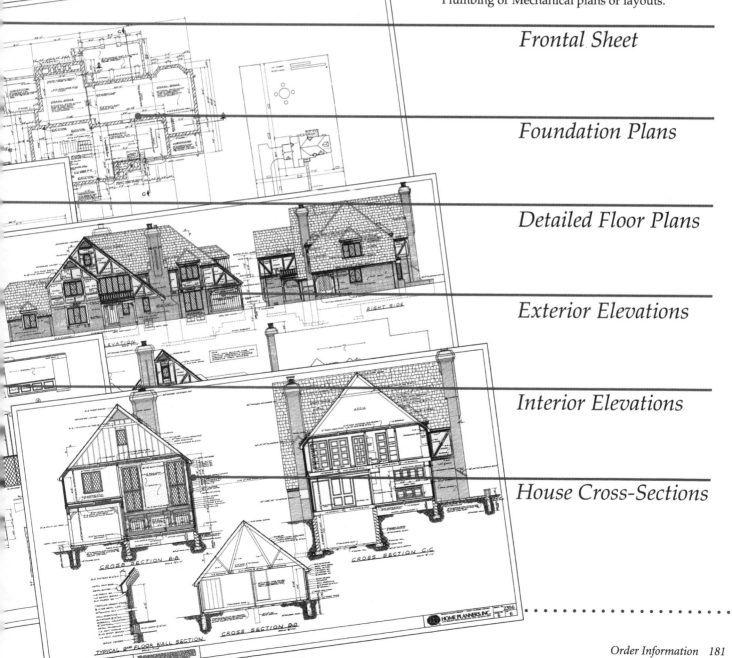

Frontal Sheet

Foundation Plans

Detailed Floor Plans

Exterior Elevations

Interior Elevations

House Cross-Sections

Important Extras To Do The Job Right!

Introducing eight important planning and construction aids developed by our professionals to help you succeed in your home-building project.

MATERIALS LIST

(Note: Because of the diversity of local building codes, our Materials List does not include mechanical materials.)

For many of the designs in our portfolio, we offer a customized materials take-off that is invaluable in planning and estimating the cost of your new home. This Materials List outlines the quantity, type and size of materials needed to build your house (with the exception of mechanical system items). Included are framing lumber, windows and doors, kitchen and bath cabinetry, rough and finish hardware, and much more. This handy list helps you or your builder cost out materials and serves as a reference sheet when you're compiling bids. A Materials List cannot be ordered before blueprints are ordered.

SPECIFICATION OUTLINE

This valuable 16-page document is critical to building your house correctly. Designed to be filled in by you or your builder, this book lists 166 stages or items crucial to the building process. It provides a comprehensive review of the construction process and helps in choosing materials. When combined with the blueprints, a signed contract, and a schedule, it becomes a legal document and record for the building of your home.

QUOTE ONE®

Summary Cost Report / Materials Cost Report

A new service for estimating the cost of building select designs, the Quote One® system is available in two separate stages: The Summary Cost Report and the Materials Cost Report.

The Summary Cost report is the first stage in the package and shows the total cost per square foot for your chosen home in your zip-code area and then breaks that cost down into various categories showing the costs for building materials, labor and installation. The total cost for the report (which includes three grades: Budget, Standard and Custom) is just $29.95 for one home, and additionals are only $14.95. These reports allow you to evaluate your building budget and compare the costs of building a variety of homes in your area.

Make even more informed decisions about your home-building project with the second phase of our package, our Materials Cost Report. This tool is invaluable in planning and estimating the cost of your new home. The material and installation (labor and equipment) cost is shown for each of over 1,000 line items provided in the Materials List (Standard grade), which is included when you purchase this estimating tool. It allows you to determine building costs for your specific zip-code area and for your chosen home design. Space is allowed for additional estimates from contractors and subcontractors. This invaluable tool is available for a price of $120 ($130 for Schedules C4–L4 plans), which includes a Materials List. A Materials Cost Report cannot be ordered before blueprints are ordered.

The Quote One® program is continually updated with new plans. If you are interested in a plan that is not indicated as Quote One®, please call and ask our sales reps. They will be happy to verify the status for you. To order these invaluable reports, use the order form on page 189 or call 1-800-521-6797.

Plan-A-Home®

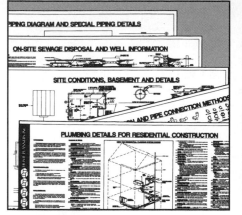

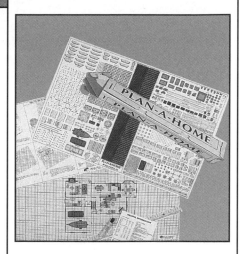

PLUMBING

The Blueprint Package includes locations for all the plumbing fixtures in your new house, including sinks, lavatories, tubs, showers, toilets, laundry trays and water heaters. However, if you want to know more about the complete plumbing system, these 24x36-inch detail sheets will prove very useful. Prepared to meet requirements of the National Plumbing Code, these six fact-filled sheets give general information on pipe schedules, fittings, sump-pump details, water-softener hookups, septic system details and much more. Color-coded sheets include a glossary of terms.

ELECTRICAL

The locations for every electrical switch, plug and outlet are shown in your Blueprint Package. However, these Electrical Details go further to take the mystery out of household electrical systems. Prepared to meet requirements of the National Electrical Code, these comprehensive 24x36-inch drawings come packed with helpful information, including wire sizing, switch-installation schematics, cable-routing details, appliance wattage, door-bell hookups, typical service panel circuitry and much more. Six sheets are bound together and color-coded for easy reference. A glossary of terms is also included.

Plan-A-Home® is an easy-to-use tool that helps you design a new home, arrange furniture in a new or existing home, or plan a remodeling project. Each package contains:

- **More than 700 reusable peel-off planning symbols** on a self-stick vinyl sheet including walls, windows, doors, all types of furniture, kitchen components, bath fixtures and many more.

- **A reusable, transparent, ¼-inch scale planning grid** that matches the scale of actual working drawings (¼-inch equals one foot). This grid provides the basis for house layouts of up to 140x92 feet.

- **Tracing paper** and a protective sheet for copying or transferring your completed plan.

- **A felt-tip pen,** with water-soluble ink that wipes away quickly.

Plan-A-Home® lets you lay out areas as large as a 7,500 square foot, six-bedroom, seven-bath house.

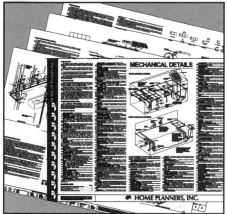

CONSTRUCTION

The Blueprint Package contains everything an experienced builder needs to construct a particular house. However, it doesn't show all the ways that houses can be built, nor does it explain alternate construction methods. To help you understand how your house will be built—and offer additional techniques—this set of drawings depicts the materials and methods used to build foundations, fireplaces, walls, floors and roofs. Where appropriate, the drawings show acceptable alternatives. These six sheets will answer questions for the advanced do-it-yourselfer or home planner.

MECHANICAL

This package contains fundamental principles and useful data that will help you make informed decisions and communicate with subcontractors about heating and cooling systems. The 24x36-inch drawings contain instructions and samples that allow you to make simple load calculations and preliminary sizing and costing analysis. Covered are today's most commonly used systems from heat pumps to solar fuel systems. The package is packed full of illustrations and diagrams to help you visualize components and how they relate to one another.

To Order, Call Toll Free 1-800-521-6797

To add these important extras to your Blueprint Package, simply indicate your choices on the order form on page 189 or call us toll free 1-800-521-6797 and we'll tell you more about these exciting products.
For customer service, call toll free 1-888-690-1116.

◨ *The Deck Blueprint Package*

Many of the homes in this book can be enhanced with a professionally designed Home Planners Deck Plan. Those home plans highlighted with a ◨ have a matching or corresponding deck plan available which includes a Deck Plan Frontal Sheet, Deck Framing and Floor Plans, Deck Elevations and a Deck Materials List. A Standard Deck Details Package, also available, provides all the how-to information necessary for building *any* deck. Our Complete Deck Building Package contains one set of Custom Deck Plans of your choice, plus one set of Standard Deck Building Details all for one low price. Our plans and details are carefully prepared in an easy-to-understand format that will guide you through every stage of your deck-building project. This page contains a sampling of 12 of the 25 different Deck layouts to match your favorite house. See page 186 for prices and ordering information.

SPLIT-LEVEL SUN DECK
Deck Plan D100

BI-LEVEL DECK WITH COVERED DINING
Deck Plan D101

WRAPAROUND FAMILY DECK
Deck Plan D104

DECK FOR DINING AND VIEWS
Deck Plan D107

TREND-SETTER DECK
Deck Plan D110

TURN-OF-THE-CENTURY DECK
Deck Plan D111

WEEKEND ENTERTAINER DECK
Deck Plan D112

CENTER-VIEW DECK
Deck Plan D114

KITCHEN-EXTENDER DECK
Deck Plan D115

SPLIT-LEVEL ACTIVITY DECK
Deck Plan D117

TRI-LEVEL DECK WITH GRILL
Deck Plan D119

CONTEMPORARY LEISURE DECK
Deck Plan D120

L *The Landscape Blueprint Package*

For the homes marked with an **L** in this book, Home Planners has created a front-yard landscape plan that matches or is complementary in design to the house plan. These comprehensive blueprint packages include a Frontal Sheet, Plan View, Regionalized Plant & Materials List, a sheet on Planting and Maintaining Your Landscape, Zone Maps and Plant Size and Description Guide. These plans will help you achieve professional results, adding value and enjoyment to your property for years to come. Each set of blueprints is a full 18" x 24" in size with clear, complete instructions and easy-to-read type. Six of the forty front-yard Landscape Plans to match your favorite house are shown below.

Regional Order Map

Most of the Landscape Plans shown on these pages are available with a Plant & Materials List adapted by horticultural experts to 8 different regions of the country. Please specify Geographic Region when ordering your plan. See pages 186–187 for prices, ordering information and regional availability.

Region	1	Northeast
Region	2	Mid-Atlantic
Region	3	Deep South
Region	4	Florida & Gulf Coast
Region	5	Midwest
Region	6	Rocky Mountains
Region	7	Southern California & Desert Southwest
Region	8	Northern California & Pacific Northwest

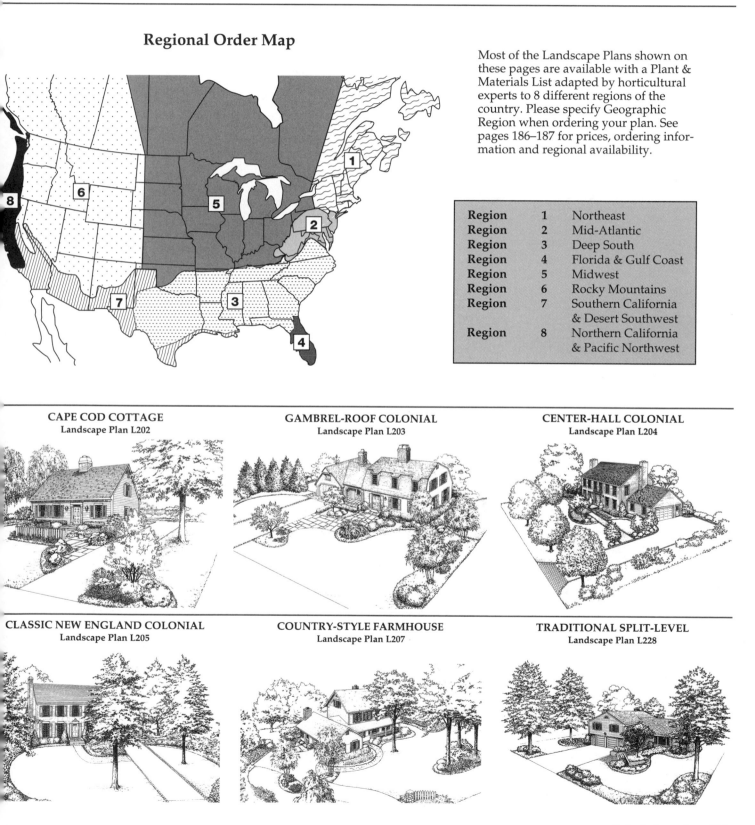

CAPE COD COTTAGE
Landscape Plan L202

GAMBREL-ROOF COLONIAL
Landscape Plan L203

CENTER-HALL COLONIAL
Landscape Plan L204

CLASSIC NEW ENGLAND COLONIAL
Landscape Plan L205

COUNTRY-STYLE FARMHOUSE
Landscape Plan L207

TRADITIONAL SPLIT-LEVEL
Landscape Plan L228

Price Schedule & Plans Index

Blueprint Price Schedule
(Prices guaranteed through December 31, 2000)

Tiers	1-set Study Package	4-set Building Package	8-set Building Package	1-set Reproducible Sepias	Home Customizer® Package
P1	$20	$50	$90	N/A	N/A
P2	$40	$70	$110	N/A	N/A
P3	$60	$90	$130	N/A	N/A
P4	$80	$110	$150	N/A	N/A
P5	$100	$130	$170	N/A	N/A
P6	$120	$150	$190	N/A	N/A
A1	$400	$440	$500	$600	$650
A2	$440	$480	$540	$660	$710
A3	$480	$520	$580	$720	$770
A4	$520	$560	$620	$780	$830
C1	$560	$600	$660	$840	$890
C2	$600	$640	$700	$900	$950
C3	$650	$690	$750	$950	$1000
C4	$700	$740	$800	$1000	$1050
L1	$750	$790	$850	$1050	$1100
L2	$800	$840	$900	$1100	$1150

Options for plans in Tiers A1–A4
Additional Identical Blueprints in same order for "A1–L4" price plans..$50 per set
Reverse Blueprints (mirror image) with 4- or 8-set order for "A1–L4" price plans............$50 fee per order
Specification Outlines...$10 each
Materials Lists for "A1–C3" price plans..........$60 each
Materials Lists for "C4–L4" price plans...........$70 each

Options for plans in Tiers P1–P6
Additional Identical Blueprints in same order for "P1–P6" price plans.......................................$10 per set
Reverse Blueprints (mirror image) for "P1–P6" price plans...$10 per set
1 Set of Deck Construction Details...............$14.95 each
Deck Construction Package............add $10 to Building Package price
(1 set of "P1–P6" price plans, plus 1 set Standard Deck Construction Details)
1 Set of Gazebo Construction Details..........$14.95 each
Gazebo Construction Package.......add $10 to Building Package price
(1 set of "P1–P6" price plans, plus 1 set Standard Gazebo Construction Details)

IMPORTANT NOTES
The 1-set study package is marked "not for construction."
Prices for 4- or 8-set Building Packages honored only at time of original order.

Index

To use the Index below, refer to the design number listed in numerical order (a helpful page reference is also given). Note the price index letter and refer to the House Blueprint Price Schedule above for the cost of one, four or eight sets of blueprints or the cost of a reproducible sepia. Additional prices are shown for identical and reverse blueprint sets, as well as other very useful products for many of the plans. Also note in the Index below those plans that have matching or complementary Deck Plans or Landscape Plans. Refer to the schedules above for prices of these plans. All plans in this publication are customizable. However, only Home Planners plans can be customized with Home Planners Home Customizer® Package. These plans are indicated below with this symbol: 🏠. See page 189 for information. Some plans are also part of our Quote One® estimating service and are indicated by this symbol: 🏠. Many plans offer Materials Lists and are indicated by this symbol: ✓. See page 182 for more information.

To Order: Fill in and send the order form on page 189—or call toll free 1-800-521-6797 or 520-297-8200. Fax: 1-800-224-6699 or 520-544-3086.

DESIGN	PRICE	PAGE	MATERIALS LIST	CUSTOMIZABLE	QUOTE ONE®	DECK	DECK PRICE	LANDSCAPE	LANDSCAPE PRICE	REGIONS
2660	C4	39	✓	🏠						
2662	C3	153	✓	🏠	🏠			L216	P3	1-3,5,6,8
2664	C1	129	✓	🏠		D113	P2			
2668	C1	158	✓	🏠	🏠			L214	P4	1-3,5,6,8
2681	C3	127	✓	🏠						
2694	C3	130	✓	🏠	🏠			L209	P3	1-6,8
2697	C2	128	✓	🏠						
2698	C1	56	✓	🏠						
2975	C3	152	✓	🏠						
2978	C2	99	✓	🏠						
2979	C1	96	✓	🏠						
2996	L2	156	✓	🏠	🏠	D111	P3	L235	P4	1-3,5,6,8
3313	C2	83	✓	🏠	🏠			L200	P3	1-3,5,6,8
3316	A3	60	✓	🏠	🏠			L202	P3	1-3,5,6,8
3318	A4	82	✓	🏠	🏠	D111	P3	L202	P3	1-3,5,6,8
3321	A4	167	✓	🏠	🏠	D116	P2	L209	P3	1-6,8
3382	C1	41	✓	🏠	🏠	D110	P2	L202	P3	1-3,5,6,8
3396	C1	126	✓	🏠	🏠	D111	P3	L207	P4	1-6,8
3468	A4	169	✓	🏠	🏠			L209	P3	1-6,8
3469	C2	168	✓	🏠	🏠			L204	P3	1-3,5,6,8
3496	C2	76	✓	🏠	🏠			L202	P3	1-3,5,6,8
3502	L2	29	✓	🏠	🏠	D111	P3	L224	P3	1-3,5,6,8
3503	L2	102	✓	🏠	🏠	D108	P2	L210	P3	1-3,5,6,8
3510	C2	131	✓	🏠	🏠					
3513	C4	164	✓	🏠	🏠	D111	P3	L214	P4	1-3,5,6,8
3515	C3	165	✓	🏠	🏠	D111	P3	L214	P4	1-3,5,6,8
3516	C2	103	✓	🏠	🏠			L202	P3	1-3,5,6,8
3517	C2	98	✓	🏠	🏠	D111	P3	L202	P3	1-3,5,6,8
3520	C3	159	✓	🏠	🏠	D115	P2			
3521	A4	166	✓		🏠			L282	P3	1-8
3523	C3	53	✓	🏠	🏠	D105	P2	L202	P3	1-3,5,6,8
3524	C1	52	✓	🏠	🏠			L202	P3	1-3,5,6,8
3526	C2	101	✓	🏠	🏠	D110	P2	L202	P3	1-3,5,6,8
3527	C4	157	✓		🏠			L202	P3	1-3,5,6,8
3619	A4	123	✓	🏠	🏠	D111	P3	L207	P4	1-6,8
3620	A4	122	✓	🏠	🏠					
3673	C1	81	✓	🏠	🏠	D110	P2	L292	P3	1-8
3674	A3	81	✓	🏠	🏠	D110	P2	L292	P3	1-8
3678	C1	79	✓	🏠	🏠			L282	P3	1-8
3697	A4	178	✓	🏠	🏠					
6616	A4	114						L223	P4	1-3,5,6,8
6617	A4	115						L223	P4	1-3,5,6,8

Before You Order . . .

Before filling out the coupon at right or calling us on our Toll-Free Blueprint Hotline, you may want to learn more about our services and products. Here's some information you will find helpful.

Quick Turnaround

We process and ship every blueprint order from our office within two business days. Because of this quick turnaround, we won't send a formal notice acknowledging receipt of your order.

Our Exchange Policy

Since blueprints are printed in response to your order, we cannot honor requests for refunds. However, we will exchange your entire first order for an equal number of blueprints at a price of $50 for the first set and $10 for each additional set; $70 total exchange fee for 4 sets; $100 total exchange fee for 8 sets . . . *plus* the difference in cost if exchanging for a design in a higher price bracket or *less* the difference in cost if exchanging for a design in lower price bracket. One exchange is allowed within a year of purchase date. **(Sepias and reproducibles are not refundable, returnable or exchangeable.)** All sets from the first order must be returned before the exchange can take place. Please add $18 for postage and handling via Regular Service; $30 via Priority Service; $40 via Express Service. Returns and cancellations are subject to a 20% restocking fee, and shipping and handling charges are not refundable.

About Reverse Blueprints

If you want to build in reverse of the plan as shown, we will include an extra set of reverse blueprints (mirror image) for an additional fee of $50. Although lettering and dimensions will appear backward, reverses will be a useful aid if you decide to flop the plan.

Revising, Modifying and Customizing Plans

The wide variety of designs available in this publication allows you to select ideas and concepts for a home to fit your building site and match your family's needs, wants and budget. Like many homeowners who buy these plans, you and your builder, architect or engineer may want to make changes to them. Some minor changes may be made by your builder, but we recommend that most changes be made by a licensed architect or engineer. If you need to make alterations to a design that is customizable, you need only order our Home Customizer® Package to get you started. As set forth below, we cannot assume any responsibility for blueprints which have been changed, whether by you, your builder or by professionals selected by you or referred to you by us, because such individuals are outside our supervision and control.

Architectural and Engineering Seals

Some cities and states are now requiring that a licensed architect or engineer review and "seal" a blueprint, or officially approve it, prior to construction due to concerns over energy costs, safety and other factors. Prior to application for a building permit or the start of actual construction, we strongly advise that you consult your local building official who can tell you if such a review is required.

About the Designers

The architects and designers whose work appears in this publication are among America's leading residential designers. Each plan was designed to meet the requirements of a nationally recognized model building code in effect at the time and place the plan was drawn. Because national building codes change from time to time, plans may not comply with any such code at the time they are sold to a customer. In addition, building officials may not accept these plans as final construction documents of record as the plans may need to be modified and additional drawings and details added to suit local conditions and requirements. We strongly advise that purchasers consult a licensed architect or engineer, and their local building official, before starting any construction related to these plans.

Local Building Codes and Zoning Requirements

At the time of creation, our plans are drawn to specifications published by the Building Officials and Code Administrators (BOCA) International, Inc.; the Southern Building Code Congress (SBCCI) International, Inc.; the International Conference of Building Officials; or the Council of American Building Officials (CABO). Our plans are designed to meet or exceed national building standards. Because of the great differences in geography and climate throughout the United States and Canada, each state, county and municipality has its own building codes, zone requirements, ordinances and building regulations. Your plan may need to be modified to comply with local requirements regarding snow loads, energy codes, soil and seismic conditions and a wide range of other matters. In addition, you may need to obtain permits or inspections from local governments before and in the course of construction. Prior to using blueprints ordered from us, we strongly advise that you consult a licensed architect or engineer—and speak with your local building official—before applying for any permit or beginning construction. We authorize the use of our blueprints on the express condition that you strictly comply with all local building codes, zoning requirements and other applicable laws, regulations, ordinances and requirements. **Notice: Plans for homes to be built in Nevada must be redrawn by a Nevada-registered professional. Consult your building official for more information on this subject.**

Foundation and Exterior Wall Changes

Most of our plans are drawn with either a full or partial basement foundation. Depending on your specific climate or regional building practices, you may wish to change this basement to a slab or crawlspace. Most professional contractors and builders can easily adapt your plans to alternate foundation types. Likewise, most can easily change 2x4 wall construction to 2x6, or vice versa.

Disclaimer

We and the designers we work with have put substantial care and effort into the creation of our blueprints. However, because we cannot provide on-site consultation, supervision and control over actual construction, and because of the great variance in local building requirements, building practices and soil, seismic, weather and other conditions, WE CANNOT MAKE ANY WARRANTY, EXPRESS OR IMPLIED, WITH RESPECT TO THE CONTENT OR USE OF OUR BLUEPRINTS, INCLUDING BUT NOT LIMITED TO ANY WARRANTY OF MERCHANTABILITY OR OF FITNESS FOR A PARTICULAR PURPOSE.

Terms and Conditions

These designs are protected under the terms of United States Copyright Law and may not be copied or reproduced in any way, by any means, unless you have purchased Sepias or Reproducibles which clearly indicate your right to copy or reproduce. We authorize the use of your chosen design as an aid in the construction of one single family home only. You may not use this design to build a second or multiple dwellings without purchasing another blueprint or blueprints or paying additional design fees.

How Many Blueprints Do You Need?

A single set of blueprints is sufficient to study a home in greater detail. However, if you are planning to obtain cost estimates from a contractor or subcontractors—or if you are planning to build immediately—you will need more sets. Because additional sets are cheaper when ordered in quantity with the original order, make sure you order enough blueprints to satisfy all requirements. The following checklist will help you determine how many you need:

____ Owner

____ Builder (generally requires at least three sets; one as a legal document, one to use during inspections, and at least one to give to subcontractors)

____ Local Building Department (often requires two sets)

____ Mortgage Lender (usually one set for a conventional loan; three sets for FHA or VA loans)

____ TOTAL NUMBER OF SETS

The Home Customizer®

"This house is perfect...if only the family room were two feet wider." Sound familiar? In response to the numerous requests for this type of modification, Home Planners has developed **The Home Customizer® Package**. This exclusive package offers our top-of-the-line materials to make it easy for anyone, anywhere to customize any Home Planners design to fit their needs. Check the index on pages 186-187 for those plans which are customizable.

Some of the changes you can make to any of our plans include:

- exterior elevation changes
- kitchen and bath modifications
- roof, wall and foundation changes
- room additions and more!

The Home Customizer® Package includes everything you'll need to make the necessary changes to your favorite Home Planners design. The package includes:

- instruction book with examples
- architectural scale and clear work film
- erasable red marker and removable correction tape
- 1/4"-scale furniture cutouts
- 1 set reproducible, erasable Sepias
- 1 set study blueprints for communicating changes to your design professional
- a copyright release letter so you can make copies as you need them
- referral letter with the name, address and telephone number of the professional in your region who is trained in modifying Home Planners designs efficiently and inexpensively.

The price of the **Home Customizer® Package** ranges from $650 to $1350, depending on the price schedule of the design you have chosen. **The Home Customizer® Package** will not only save you 25% to 75% of the cost of drawing the plans from scratch with a custom architect or engineer, it will also give you the flexibility to have your changes and modifications made by our referral network or by the professional of your choice. Now it's even easier and more affordable to have the custom home you've always wanted.

 ORDER TOLL FREE!
For information about any of our services or to order call
1-800-521-6797 or 520-297-8200
Browse our website:
www.homeplanners.com

BLUEPRINTS ARE NOT REFUNDABLE
EXCHANGES ONLY

For Customer Service,
call toll free 1-888-690-1116.

ORDER FORM

HOME PLANNERS, LLC
Wholly owned by Hanley-Wood, LLC
3275 WEST INA ROAD, SUITE 110
TUCSON, ARIZONA 85741

THE BASIC BLUEPRINT PACKAGE
Rush me the following (please refer to the Plans Index and Price Schedule in this section):

_____ Set(s) of blueprints for plan number(s) _____. $_____
_____ Set(s) of sepias for plan number(s) _____. $_____
_____ Home Customizer® Package for plan(s)_____. $_____
_____ Additional identical blueprints in same order @ $50 per set. $_____
_____ Reverse blueprints @ $50 per set. $_____

IMPORTANT EXTRAS
Rush me the following:

_____ Materials List: $60 (Must be purchased with Blueprint set.)
Add $10 for a Schedule C4–L4 plan. $_____
_____ **Quote One®** Summary Cost Report @ $29.95 for one, $14.95 for each additional, for plans _____ $_____
Building location: City _____ Zip Code _____
_____ **Quote One®** Materials Cost Report @ $120 Schedule P1–C3; $130 Schedules C4–L4, for plan_____ $_____
(Must be purchased with Blueprints set.)
Building location: City _____ Zip Code_____
_____ Specification Outlines @ $10 each. $_____
_____ Detail Sets @ $14.95 each; any two for $22.95; any three for $29.95; all four for $39.95 (save $19.85). $_____
❏ Plumbing ❏ Electrical ❏ Construction ❏ Mechanical
(These helpful details provide general construction advice and are not specific to any single plan.)
_____ Plan-A-Home® @ $29.95 each. $_____
DECK BLUEPRINTS
_____ Set(s) of Deck Plan _____. $_____
_____ Additional identical blueprints in same order @ $10 per set. $_____
_____ Reverse blueprints @ $10 per set. $_____
_____ Set of Standard Deck Details @ $14.95 per set. $_____
_____ Set of Complete Building Package (Best Buy!)
Includes Custom Deck Plan _____.
(See Index and Price Schedule)
Plus Standard Deck Details $_____
LANDSCAPE BLUEPRINTS
_____ Set(s) of Landscape Plan _____. $_____
_____ Additional identical blueprints in same order @ $10 per set. $_____
_____ Reverse blueprints @ $10 per set. $_____

Please indicate the appropriate region of the country for Plant & Material List. (See Map on page 185): Region _____

POSTAGE AND HANDLING	1–3 sets	4+ sets
Signature is required for all deliveries. **DELIVERY** (No CODs) (Requires street address—No P.O. Boxes)		
•Regular Service (Allow 7–10 business days delivery)	❏ $15.00	❏ $18.00
•Priority (Allow 4–5 business days delivery)	❏ $20.00	❏ $30.00
•Express (Allow 3 business days delivery)	❏ $30.00	❏ $40.00
CERTIFIED MAIL If no street address available. (Allow 7–10 days delivery)	❏ $20.00	❏ $30.00
OVERSEAS DELIVERY Note: All delivery times are from date Blueprint Package is shipped.	fax, phone or mail for quote	

POSTAGE (From box above) $_____
SUBTOTAL $_____
SALES TAX (AZ, MI, & WA residents, please add appropriate state and local sales tax.) $_____
TOTAL (Subtotal and tax) $_____

YOUR ADDRESS (please print)
Name _____
Street _____
City _____ State _____ Zip _____
Daytime telephone number (_____) _____

FOR CREDIT CARD ORDERS ONLY
Please fill in the information below:
Credit card number _____
Exp. Date: Month/Year _____
Check one ❏ Visa ❏ MasterCard ❏ Discover Card ❏ American Express
Signature _____

Please check appropriate box: ❏ Licensed Builder-Contractor
❏ Homeowner

ORDER TOLL FREE!
1-800-521-6797 or 520-297-8200

Order Form Key
TB77

Helpful Books & Software

Home Planners wants your building experience to be as pleasant and trouble-free as possible. That's why we've expanded our library of Do-It-Yourself titles to help you along. In addition to our beautiful plans books, we've added books to guide you through specific projects as well as the construction process. In fact, these are titles that will be as useful after your dream home is built as they are right now.

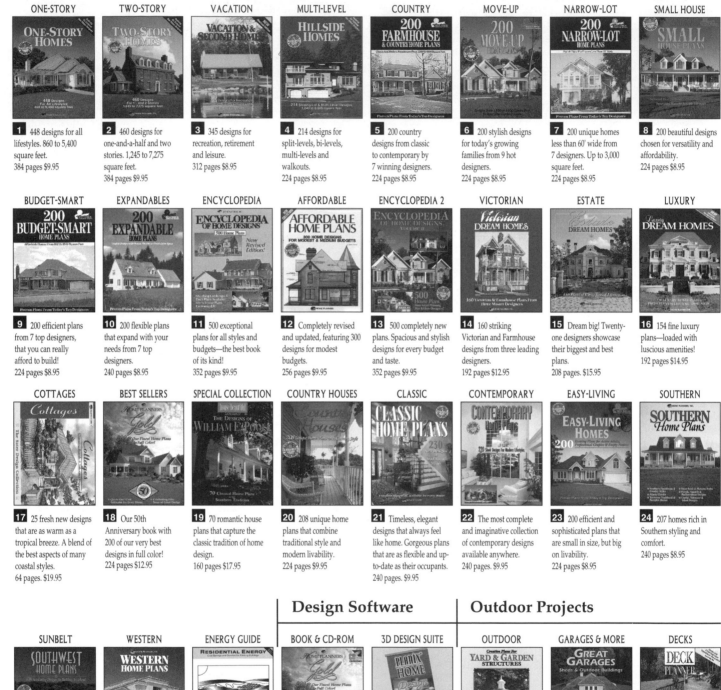

ONE-STORY	**TWO-STORY**	**VACATION**	**MULTI-LEVEL**
1 448 designs for all lifestyles. 860 to 5,400 square feet. 384 pages $9.95	**2** 460 designs for one-and-a-half and two stories. 1,245 to 7,275 square feet. 384 pages $9.95	**3** 345 designs for recreation, retirement and leisure. 312 pages $8.95	**4** 214 designs for split-levels, bi-levels, multi-levels and walkouts. 224 pages $8.95

COUNTRY	**MOVE-UP**	**NARROW-LOT**	**SMALL HOUSE**
5 200 country designs from classic to contemporary by 7 winning designers. 224 pages $8.95	**6** 200 stylish designs for today's growing families from 9 hot designers. 224 pages $8.95	**7** 200 unique homes less than 60' wide from 7 designers. Up to 3,000 square feet. 224 pages $8.95	**8** 200 beautiful designs chosen for versatility and affordability. 224 pages $8.95

BUDGET-SMART	**EXPANDABLES**	**ENCYCLOPEDIA**	**AFFORDABLE**
9 200 efficient plans from 7 top designers, that you can really afford to build! 224 pages $8.95	**10** 200 flexible plans that expand with your needs from 7 top designers. 240 pages $8.95	**11** 500 exceptional plans for all styles and budgets—the best book of its kind! 352 pages $9.95	**12** Completely revised and updated, featuring 300 designs for modest budgets. 256 pages $9.95

ENCYCLOPEDIA 2	**VICTORIAN**	**ESTATE**	**LUXURY**
13 500 completely new plans. Spacious and stylish designs for every budget and taste. 352 pages $9.95	**14** 160 striking Victorian and Farmhouse designs from three leading designers. 192 pages $12.95	**15** Dream big! Twenty-one designers showcase their biggest and best plans. 208 pages. $15.95	**16** 154 fine luxury plans—loaded with luscious amenities! 192 pages $14.95

COTTAGES	**BEST SELLERS**	**SPECIAL COLLECTION**	**COUNTRY HOUSES**
17 25 fresh new designs that are as warm as a tropical breeze. A blend of the best aspects of many coastal styles. 64 pages $19.95	**18** Our 50th Anniversary book with 200 of our very best designs in full color! 224 pages $12.95	**19** 70 romantic house plans that capture the classic tradition of home design. 160 pages $17.95	**20** 208 unique home plans that combine traditional style and modern livability. 224 pages $9.95

CLASSIC	**CONTEMPORARY**	**EASY-LIVING**	**SOUTHERN**
21 Timeless, elegant designs that always feel like home. Gorgeous plans that are as flexible and up-to-date as their occupants. 240 pages. $9.95	**22** The most complete and imaginative collection of contemporary designs available anywhere. 240 pages. $9.95	**23** 200 efficient and sophisticated plans that are small in size, but big on livability. 224 pages $8.95	**24** 207 homes rich in Southern styling and comfort. 240 pages $8.95

Design Software   Outdoor Projects

SUNBELT	**WESTERN**	**ENERGY GUIDE**	**BOOK & CD-ROM**	**3D DESIGN SUITE**	**OUTDOOR**	**GARAGES & MORE**	**DECKS**
25 215 designs that capture the spirit of the Southwest. 208 pages $10.95	**26** 215 designs that capture the spirit and diversity of the Western lifestyle. 208 pages $9.95	**27** The most comprehensive energy efficiency and conservation guide available. 280 pages $35.00	**28** Both the Home Planners Gold book and matching Windows™ CD-ROM with 3D floorplans. $24.95	**29** Home design made easy! View designs in 3D, take a virtual reality tour, add decorating details and more. $59.95	**30** 42 unique outdoor projects. Gazebos, strombellas, bridges, sheds, playsets and more! 96 pages $7.95	**31** 101 multi-use garages and outdoor structures to enhance any home. 96 pages $7.95	**32** 25 outstanding single-, double- and multi-level decks you can build. 112 pages $7.95

Landscape Designs

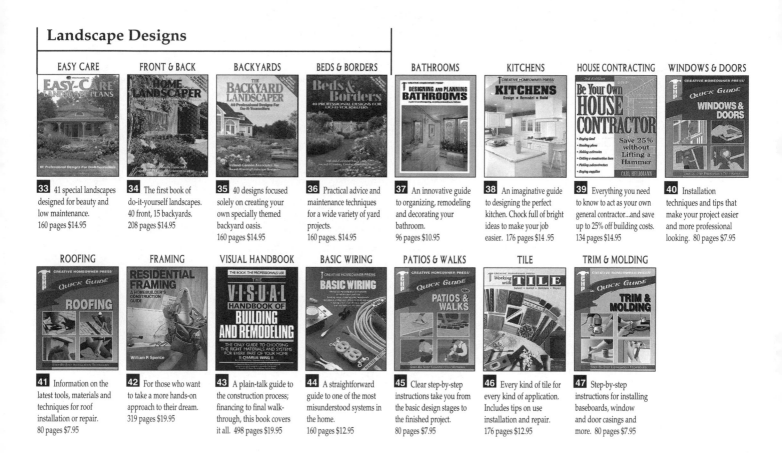

| EASY CARE | FRONT & BACK | BACKYARDS | BEDS & BORDERS | BATHROOMS | KITCHENS | HOUSE CONTRACTING | WINDOWS & DOORS |

33 41 special landscapes designed for beauty and low maintenance. 160 pages $14.95

34 The first book of do-it-yourself landscapes. 40 front, 15 backyards. 208 pages $14.95

35 40 designs focused solely on creating your own specially themed backyard oasis. 160 pages $14.95

36 Practical advice and maintenance techniques for a wide variety of yard projects. 160 pages. $14.95

37 An innovative guide to organizing, remodeling and decorating your bathroom. 96 pages $10.95

38 An imaginative guide to designing the perfect kitchen. Chock full of bright ideas to make your job easier. 176 pages $14 .95

39 Everything you need to know to act as your own general contractor...and save up to 25% off building costs. 134 pages $14.95

40 Installation techniques and tips that make your project easier and more professional looking. 80 pages $7.95

| ROOFING | FRAMING | VISUAL HANDBOOK | BASIC WIRING | PATIOS & WALKS | TILE | TRIM & MOLDING |

41 Information on the latest tools, materials and techniques for roof installation or repair. 80 pages $7.95

42 For those who want to take a more hands-on approach to their dream. 319 pages $19.95

43 A plain-talk guide to the construction process; financing to final walk-through, this book covers it all. 498 pages $19.95

44 A straightforward guide to one of the most misunderstood systems in the home. 160 pages $12.95

45 Clear step-by-step instructions take you from the basic design stages to the finished project. 80 pages $7.95

46 Every kind of tile for every kind of application. Includes tips on use installation and repair. 176 pages $12.95

47 Step-by-step instructions for installing baseboards, window and door casings and more. 80 pages $7.95

Additional Books Order Form

To order your books, just check the box of the book numbered below and complete the coupon. We will process your order and ship it from our office within two business days. Send coupon and check (in U.S. funds).

YES! Please send me the books I've indicated:

☐ 1:VO	$9.95	☐ 25:SW	$10.95
☐ 2:VT	$9.95	☐ 26:WH	$9.95
☐ 3:VH	$8.95	☐ 27:RES	$35.00
☐ 4:VS	$8.95	☐ 28:HPGC	$24.95
☐ 5:FH	$8.95	☐ 29:PLANSUITE	$59.95
☐ 6:MU	$8.95	☐ 30:YG	$7.95
☐ 7:NL	$8.95	☐ 31:GG	$7.95
☐ 8:SM	$8.95	☐ 32:DP	$7.95
☐ 9:BS	$8.95	☐ 33:ECL	$14.95
☐ 10:EX	$8.95	☐ 34:HL	$14.95
☐ 11:EN	$9.95	☐ 35:BYL	$14.95
☐ 12:AF	$9.95	☐ 36:BB	$14.95
☐ 13:E2	$9.95	☐ 37:CDB	$10.95
☐ 14:VDH	$12.95	☐ 38:CKI	$14.95
☐ 15:EDH	$15.95	☐ 39:SBC	$14.95
☐ 16:LD2	$14.95	☐ 40:CGD	$7.95
☐ 17:CTG	$19.95	☐ 41:CGR	$7.95
☐ 18:HPG	$12.95	☐ 42:SRF	$19.95
☐ 19:WEP	$17.95	☐ 43:RVH	$19.95
☐ 20:CN	$9.95	☐ 44:CBW	$12.95
☐ 21:CS	$9.95	☐ 45:CGW	$7.95
☐ 22:CM	$9.95	☐ 46:CWT	$12.95
☐ 23:EL	$8.95	☐ 47:CGT	$7.95
☐ 24:SH	$8.95		

Canadian Customers
Order Toll-Free 1-877-223-6389

Additional Books Subtotal $_____
ADD Postage and Handling $__4.00__
Sales Tax: (AZ, MI, & WA residents, please add appropriate state and local sales tax.) $_____
YOUR TOTAL (Subtotal, Postage/Handling, Tax) $_____

YOUR ADDRESS (Please print)

Name _____

Street _____

City _____ State_____ Zip _____

Phone (_____) _____—_____

YOUR PAYMENT
Check one: ☐ Check ☐ Visa ☐ MasterCard ☐ Discover Card ☐ American Express
Required credit card information:
Credit Card Number _____

Expiration Date (Month/Year) _____/_____

Signature Required _____

Home Planners, LLC
Wholly owned by Hanley-Wood, LLC
3275 W. Ina Road, Suite 110, Dept. BK, Tucson, AZ 85741

TB77

Contributors

Jim Constantine is the Director of Planning and Research with the Princeton office of Looney Ricks Kiss, specializing in understanding consumer and community preferences to help gauge the impact and acceptability of TND concepts. He has contributed to Better Homes and Gardens *Home Plan Ideas*, among other publications. J. Carson Looney, FAIA, a founding principal of the firm, is a skilled practitioner of neotraditional town planning. He was named one of five rising stars whose residential work forecasts the century ahead (*residential architect*, January-February 1999).

Andres Duany is an architect and town planner whose work has redefined the American community. He and his wife Elizabeth Plater-Zyberk are recognized as leaders of the urban design revolution known as the New Urbanism. Duany Plater-Zyberk & Company have completed over 140 new towns and community revitalization projects, including Seaside, Florida—the 1980 project that spawned an ongoing debate on the alternatives to suburban sprawl.

Larry E. Belk Designs

Through the years, Larry Belk has worked with individuals and builders alike to provide a quality product. Flowing, open spaces and interesting angles define his interiors. Great emphasis is placed on providing views that showcase the natural environment.

Stephen Fuller, American Home Gallery

Stephen Fuller, Inc., a full-service residential design firm specializing in community master planning, custom and pre-designed homes, modifications and interior design, was established with the tenets of innovation, quality, originality and uncompromising architectural artistry in Traditional, European and Americana designs. Especially popular in the Southeast, Stephen Fuller's plans are known for their extensive detail and custom touches.

Donald A. Gardner Architects, Inc.

The South Carolina firm of Donald A. Gardner was established in response to a growing demand for residential designs that reflect constantly changing lifestyles. The company's specialty is providing homes with refined, custom-style details and unique features such as passive-solar designs and open floor plans.

Home Planners

Headquartered in Tucson, Arizona, with additional offices in Detroit, Home Planners is one of the longest-running and most successful home design firms in the United States. With over 2,500 designs in its portfolio, the company provides a wide range of styles, sizes and types of homes for the residential builder.

Looney Ricks Kiss Architects, Inc.

Established in 1983, Looney Ricks Kiss is a full-service architectural, interior design, planning and research firm with offices in Memphis, Nashville and Princeton. Their design focus encompasses the full integration of market awareness, land planning and architecture. More than 190 regional and national awards attest to their design excellence.

Alan Mascord Design Associates, Inc.

Founded in 1983 as a local supplier to the building community, Mascord Design Associates of Portland, Oregon began to successfully publish plans nationally in 1985. The company's trademark is creating floor plans that work well and exhibit excellent traffic patterns.

Nelson Design Group

Since 1985, Nelson Design Group has maintained a focus on residential design that embraces traditional ideals and fosters interaction between neighbors. The NDG home blends yesterday's style with today's technology—and satisfies the firm's primary philosophy for residential design: "It's not just a home, it's a neighborhood."

Northwest Home Designing, Inc.

Northwest Home Designing is a family-owned and operated firm that was founded on a simple principle: create custom home designs that are unique to the needs and desires of its customers. Their detailed approach has earned the firm numerous awards for innovative design.

Park House Properties, LLC

Park House Properties specializes in efficient plans that provide rear-entry garages, a feature that fosters neighborhood interaction and helps create an unbroken and attractive streetscape. Their residential designs incorporate a high level of accessibility that makes them adaptable to the dynamic needs of today's homeowner.

The Sater Design Collection

The Sater Design Collection has a long-established tradition of providing South Florida's most diverse and extraordinary custom designed homes. This is exemplified by over 50 national design awards, numerous magazine features and, most importantly, satisfied clients.

To learn more about the New Urbanism and Traditional Neighborhood Development (TND), visit Duany Plater-Zyberk & Company at www.dpz.com